Intellectual Empathy

Critical Thinking for Social Justice

Maureen Linker

UNIVERSITY OF MICHIGAN PRESS | ANN ARBOR

Copyright © by the University of Michigan 2015

Published in the United States of America by the
University of Michigan Press
Manufactured in the United States of America
♾ Printed on acid-free paper

2018   2017   2016   2015   4   3   2   1

A CIP catalog record for this book is available from the British Library.

ISBN 978-0-472-07262-0 (hardcover : alk. paper)
ISBN 978-0-472-05262-2 (paper : alk. paper)
ISBN 978-0-472-12104-5 (e-book)

FOR JOHN, MAUREEN, AND KATHRYN: *My beloved first teachers at the great university that was our kitchen table.*

Contents

Acknowledgments

When my son was about six years old, he searched the house in frustration trying to locate a set of instructions for a new complicated Lego model he had received as a gift. After giving up on ever locating the booklet and sharing his dilemma with a friend, the suggestion was made that perhaps there was a video on YouTube demonstrating how to build that particular model. We searched online, and to my complete surprise there were a whole host of how-to videos made by different kids putting together various Lego sets.

What struck me as we learned about this genre was the number of children and adults who cared enough to patiently document the process for completing a project. These videos were not intended to make stars out of the instructors. In many cases only the narrator's hands were shown, and the focus was solely on the parts and the process. The objective of the videos was to share information in a clear, correct, and reliable way.

Throughout my life, I have always responded so deeply to people who act from this objective. Like the newly enlightened prisoner returning to the cave in Plato's *Republic,* there is something beautiful, generous, even optimistic in the effort to share what you know with others. To me it seems to stem from an obligation, a tacit duty that some people feel to continue meaningful conversations and projects by supporting fellow travelers.

There are many people who have shared with me what they know and have invited me into lifelong conversations, giving me a direction for my work. Some of them I do not know personally, but their work has had a profound influence on my thinking. Most prominently in this category are feminist philosophers and women's and gender studies scholars, among them Patricia Hill Collins, Marilyn Frye, bell hooks, Audre Lorde, Linda Martin Alcoff, Nancy Tuana, Sara Ruddick, Lorraine Code, Maria Lugones, Peggy McIntosh, Chandra Mohanty, and Genevieve Lloyd.

Among the philosophers and scholars I have been lucky enough to know personally, the following people have generously shared their time, knowledge, and most significantly their friendship, and I am truly grateful for their gifts. They are Suzanne Bergeron, Catherine Hundleby, Phyllis

Rooney, Ann Garry, Margaret Crouch, Ami Harbin, Lisa Schwartzman, and Jami Weinstein. Deborah Smith-Pollard suggested that I talk to an editor and consistently encouraged, challenged, supported, and cheered my efforts to get these ideas published. I have benefitted tremendously from her guidance and her friendship. Thank you all for setting the bar so high and keeping the work relevant and challenging. Thank you too for the times you actually sat at a bar (or the in-house nonalcoholic equivalent) with me while we discussed these challenges.

An earlier version of this manuscript benefitted from the careful and generous reading of outside reviewers. In the process of completing this book I have come to know three of them, and although any missteps are all my own, they provided incredible guidance. Thank you Catherine Hundleby, Alison Bailey, and Patrick Grzanka not only for the care you took with my work but also for the work that you do to address social injustices.

I have been fortunate to be part of an interdisciplinary academic women's writers group for more than twelve years with some of the sharpest, funniest, and most lovingly perceptive women I have ever known. They include Lora Lempert, Jackie Vansant, Georgina Hickey, Patricia Smith, and Carolyn Krauss. Thank you for all the time and attention you gave to several of these chapters—they and I are better for it.

At the University of Michigan–Dearborn I have had the benefit of some wonderful colleagues who were willing to read and/or think through some of the ideas that made their way into this book. Paul Hughes and Jonathan Smith both read early versions of the book proposal and provided helpful feedback as well as encouragement. Kathy Wider has been a mentor and a friend since I first arrived on campus, and her combination of theoretical precision and an ethical heart has served as an example for me my whole career. Gloria House hosted a series of faculty workshops on privilege and power, and some of the insights I gained from those meetings have made their way into these pages. Elias Baumgarten has led by example in his concern to address religious and cultural differences in the classroom. Marty Hershock has been a supportive colleague, friend, and Dean. Kate Davy is the uncommon provost who reminds you to protect your writing time when you are asked to serve on a committee. I am grateful for her reminders and her kindness. Christopher Burke, Francine Alexander, and Tiffany Marra have all provided helpful insights related to cognitive biases and world traveling.

University of Michigan–Ann Arbor's Office of Research along with University of Michigan–Dearborn's Office of the Provost both provided funding to further the publication of this book, and I am very grateful for their support. I would especially like to thank the students in my Fall 2014 Phil

390Q: Special Topics course at University of Michigan-Dearborn for contributions to this work.

My dearest friends Janet Farrell, Scott McCrossin, Mike Kelly, Melinda Bryce, Rachel Saputo, and Jonathan Lethem have each contributed something unique and especially meaningful to this project. I have benefitted so much from their humor and their unique genius.

My friends and family, including Nicole Stillman, Judy Laird, Jack Laird, Mike Laird, Jane Mineroff, Rosemary Colgan, Christine Dorta, Sheila Kostoff, Kevin Kostoff, Cathy Brown, and Marie Briganti, have all in a variety of different ways provided support and encouragement for this book. I want them to know how grateful I am for believing in this project.

I also want to thank the West Bloomfield Public Library for the many productive hours I spent in the Quiet Study Area overlooking the woods. I have never encountered a better-managed or more well-maintained public library than the one in my neighborhood.

Thank you to the staff at the University of Michigan Press, especially LeAnn Fields, Susan Cronin, and Renee Tambeau, and the team at Book-Comp, including Nicholle Lutz and M. Yvonne Ramsey, who provided much-needed help at various stages of this project.

To my editor and friend Melody ("Pace yourself, honey!") Herr at the University of Michigan Press, I am deeply grateful. From our first conversation in March 2012, Melody demonstrated great skill at virtuous listening and cooperative reasoning. She believed in this project and saw a bigger picture even while she encouraged me to develop the details. Melody consistently reminded me to look for greater dimensions and more depth in my analyses of conflict, and she cheered me on at every step. Her elegant aesthetic sense may not come through in my writing, but I hear her voice on every page.

Finally, I want to express my love and gratitude to Patrick Laird and our son Jackson. Thank you for all those days you understood that I had to work. Thank you too for all those days you did not and you dragged me away from the computer so that we could spend more time together. I love you both with all my heart and soul.

My greatest hope for you, Jackson, is that you will grow up to live in a world where empathy is seen as a sign of great intelligence and where the desire to exploit others for selfish gain is seen as a serious cognitive deficit.

Preface

Office Hours

I came to the Detroit metropolitan area in the late 1990s as a new assistant professor fresh from graduate school. Over time, I came to see the city and the region as a remarkable microcosm of the emerging challenges facing the United States in the twenty-first century. When I first arrived, racial disparities were on people's minds following the economic booms that seemed to have benefitted every corner of the American Midwest with the exception of inner-city Detroit. According to census data, between 1980 and 2000 the city of Detroit lost one-fifth of its population, including one hundred thousand white residents. The residents who remained were 80 percent African American, and half the households were made up of nonmarried families with children. While the poverty rate within the city had declined during those twenty years, residents were still among some of the poorest in the country and were certainly poorer than their white neighbors in the northern and western suburbs. The 2000 census also showed that the Detroit metropolitan area was the most racially segregated urban region in the United States. This fact drew national attention and put a spotlight on an issue that everyone in the region lived with daily. When the census data and subsequent news stories came out, I remember asking students in my critical thinking course, "How many of you think that racism is a significant factor facing the Detroit metropolitan area?" A majority of hands went up. I then asked, "How many people think that racism is a factor facing you and your neighbors living in and around Detroit?" Again, a majority of hands sprang into the air. Finally I asked, "How many of you here think that you are contributing to the racism that we are facing?" Not a single hand would rise.

After attempting some analysis with my students, I realized that although they were able to talk about race and racism in the abstract, they had a very hard time speaking out about their own attitudes and behaviors around race. One discussion I recall in particular involved the "riots" of the late 1960s. Several white students in the class shared how their own families, who had lived in the city for most of the early and mid-twentieth century, had fled practically overnight and left their homes without even putting them up for sale. After this discussion, an African American student in the class came to see me during office hours and explained that in his family they referred to the "riots" as "the uprising." He said that his parents had taught him about the history of racial discrimination in the city, particularly in the areas of policing, education, real estate, and housing. African Americans living in the city, as he was told by his parents and relatives, were regularly humiliated by store owners, discouraged from using the city's recreational facilities, and redlined to segregated neighborhoods with underfunded schools. The uprising was a violent reaction to years of discrimination and mistreatment.[1] When I asked this student why he had not made a point of challenging the notion of "riot" in class, he said, "I wasn't in the mood to defend myself against all those white students." And so, this young man did not see an opportunity to share his counternarrative, and the whole class missed the opportunity to critically assess our language choices and the prevailing narratives about the city's history. As the instructor, I began wrestling with text choices and teaching strategies so that my classroom would be the kind of place where this young man and all of my students could trust that their beliefs and experiences would be respectfully and critically heard.

Several years later and less than two years into the new millennium, the nation and the rest of the world were riveted by television coverage of the murder of nearly three thousand people in New York City's World Trade Center, at the Pentagon, and in a rural field in Pennsylvania. In addition to the tragic loss of life, September, 11, 2001, also transformed global politics, ushered in two new wars, introduced homeland security measures, and complicated public air travel. Many Americans also began to ask "Who are Muslims?" and "What do Muslims believe?" The racial and economic divisions that marked the Detroit metropolitan area of the mid to late 1990s were eclipsed by a new attention to the region's large Arab Muslim community. The University of Michigan's branch campus in the city of Dearborn, where I teach, was in the heart of this community, and so it was not long before national and international newspaper and television crews arrived to do stories on Muslims in America. In addition, agents from the Federal Bureau of Investigation were routinely in the area, and a significant number of our Muslim students reported that relatives and friends were being questioned and in some cases arrested despite their insistence that they had no ties to terrorist organizations. Some of our female students who wore the *hijab*, the head scarf traditionally worn by Muslim women, reported being harassed verbally or even spit on by people in passing cars or on the street. Non-Muslim students who make up the majority of our student body were also thrown into the national debate about Islam and often had to explain to their relatives and friends that they were not living under sharia law simply by attending school in Dearborn. For many of us who lived, worked, and attended school in Dearborn, it seemed that we were at the epicenter of a firestorm of controversy over Muslims, religious pluralism, and national security.

In 2003 just after the U.S. invasion of Iraq and before the capture of Baghdad, students in my Critical Thinking course were discussing the justification to go to war. A heated debate developed between two students regarding the existence or nonexistence of weapons of mass destruction and whether or not President George W. Bush had planned to invade Iraq from the time he came into office. After class and once again during office hours, a young woman in the course came to see me. She wore a *hijab* and was silent during the debate in class. She told me that she had some strong beliefs regarding the issue of going to war in Iraq and that she had relatives who lived in Iraq and feared for their lives. While she was no fan of Saddam Hussein, she did not believe that he had provided any support to al-Qaeda. I asked her why she hadn't contributed these beliefs to the argument that had gone on in class. She said, "The two students who were arguing that issue were not Muslim. Most of us here who are Muslim American would not dare express views in class that are critical of U.S. policy." Of course, I had a pretty good sense of why this was the case, but I asked her to be sure. "Because," she said, "even though I was born here and I am an American citizen, I am suspicious for most other Americans. I feel like as a Muslim that I lost the right to criticize American politics even though I mourned the loss of life on 9/11 and I see mistakes being made in the war with Iraq." Once again, the report I was getting during office hours could have provided nuance and complexity to the dialogue in class. I struggled once more to find texts and teaching materials that would help to create the kind of classroom where this young woman would not have to risk being perceived as a public enemy simply for developing her critical thinking abilities and where students could respectfully learn from each other.

Now into the second decade of the new millennium, racial divisions, Islam, and religious pluralism all continue to be significant issues facing the region and the nation. Yet among these challenges the issue that seems to be at the forefront of most of my students' thinking is the state of the economy. Once again, the Detroit metropolitan area serves as a paradigm case for the challenges facing the rest of the nation. The Motor City revolutionized industrial production in the United States and during the mid-twentieth century propelled thousands upon thousands of working-class men and women into unionized factory jobs and a middle-class life. The decline of manufacturing jobs, the dissolution of unions, and the housing crisis that were all at the heart of recent Occupy movements across the country have been issues facing the Detroit metropolitan region for more than a decade.

I was reminded of how long these problems have been going on after a discussion with a student, once again during office hours. The issues of white privilege and male privilege had come up in class because of some of the readings I now included in my courses concerning race and social differences. Students were considering examples of white male privilege, such as a majority of politicians in the United States are white males and a majority of chief executive officers are white males. An African American student criticized a seemingly popular cultural belief that we were living in a postracial society simply because Barack Obama had been elected president of the United States. After class, a nontraditional student (meaning a student who is older than the traditional freshman out of high school) came to see me. He was a man in his late forties, white, and generally very quiet in class. This student wanted to talk to me because he was troubled by the discussion of white male privilege that had come up in class. He said that he did not like admitting it, but his life was extremely difficult. He had been laid off from his job more than four years earlier. He lost his home in a foreclosure, and his wife and teenage daughter had recently left him. There did not seem to be any work available to him with just a high school diploma, so as a veteran he managed to secure some scholarship money and took a personal loan from a relative. He told me that he did not yet own a computer and did all of his college work using the library computers. He lived in a cheap rental in a high-crime neighborhood, and he said his financial situation was so precarious that if his car were to break down, he would not be able to afford the repairs necessary to get him back and forth to school. The discussion of white privilege eluded him. It was not that he necessarily disagreed that wealthy white men seemed to have particular advantages in American society; it was just that social class and a lack of education were also significant factors in his experience. When I asked him why he had not offered his perspective in class (without having to share the personal details), he said, "I don't want to come off sounding like a racist. If I start talking about how tough it is for some white men, I'll sound like a bigot to most of these kids." However, this student's experiences are an important part of the story of the stagnation in wages and the rising inequality in our country. His race and gender intersect in ways with his class and education to complicate the narrative of a monolithic white privilege. The loss of his perspective in the discussion means that we don't get the whole story, and collectively we lose the opportunity to critically analyze the multiple dimensions of prevailing social conditions.

Though some things have changed in the nearly fifteen years that I have been in the Detroit metropolitan area, some things have unfortunately remained the same. Racial divides continue to structure the metropolitan region, while the city of Detroit is under the authority of a nonelected emergency manager after filing the largest municipal bankruptcy in American history. The incredible inequality in education between inner-city Detroit schools, where the population is 88 percent African American and 85 percent of students are economically disadvantaged, still contrasts with the Detroit suburbs, where the population is 70 percent white and only 39 percent of students are economically disadvantaged.[2] The Michigan Civil Rights Commission observed that segregation was perpetuated not only by private discrimination but also by local, state, and federal agencies that continued to support and exacerbate the isolation of African Americans.[3] While African Americans in the city try to take advantage of the Schools of Choice program, implemented in 1995, and drive their children to first-ring white suburban schools hoping to give them better educational opportunities, white residents in the first-ring suburbs are driving their children to second-ring suburbs to escape integration. As the authors of a 2012 study commissioned by the Economic Policy Institute reported, "The highways of metropolitan Detroit are now filled in the morning and afternoon hours with the cars of parents taking their children to distant schools. There are low-income African American parents from Detroit taking their children to first ring suburbs where neighborhoods are changing. And middle class white parents from first ring suburbs are taking their children to the second ring."[4]

When the Learning Channel announced plans to air a reality television show in 2011 focusing on the lives of five Muslim American families in Dearborn, Michigan, the show was met with criticism and calls for boycotts. The Lowe's big-box chain pulled its sponsorship of the program, citing "concerns, complaints or issues from multiple sides of the viewer spectrum."[5] The identity of the suspects in the April 2013 Boston bombing raised fears within Muslim and Sikh communities, both targets of anti-Muslim violence after 9/11. Despite the fact that Sikhs practice a religion totally unrelated to Islam and that Muslims in the United States had nothing to do with either the 9/11 attacks or the Boston bombing, the perception exists that these groups are the same and thus are somehow implicated in the violence. Amardeep Singh, the program director for the Sikh Coalition, says that "What we're trying to do is let the public know that we're Americans, we share the concerns. We don't want this incident to allow us to turn on each other."[6] Yet the continued equivalence of "American" with "white European Christian" is reinforced with our country's history and heroes, media images of "typical" families in television and film, and the demographics of the most powerful and wealthy people in our nation. And just this morning while tuning in to the local television news, I watched a report with newscasters all wearing red Santa hats and sitting on a set framed with a Christmas tree and brightly wrapped gifts. The perception that you are somehow not American if you are not white and Christian is continually reinforced through social structures and institutions, which treat this perception as simply "normal" rather than continually constructed and commercially maintained.

Since the financial collapse of 2008, the economy in the Detroit metropolitan area has experienced a very slow and moderate recovery. The unemployment rate for May 2014 is currently at 9.0 percent, down from a peak of 16.7 percent in 2009.[7] The current rate of 9.0 percent is still higher than the state average of 7.5 percent and the national average of 6.1 percent.[8] The number of home foreclosures has started to stabilize (rather than rise), but social services continue to be reduced, and in 2013 nearly 1.8 million Michigan residents had their food stamps cut.[9] Meanwhile, student loan debt increases, so students face a hurdle even if they graduate. The federal government projected a 20 percent growth in student loan debt from the end of 2011 to the end of 2013. That growth rate is considerably higher than the growth in credit card debt over the same time, which is only about 2 percent.[10] The social and structural forces that worked together to limit opportunity for students in the Detroit metropolitan area are still there and are still having an impact on the hopes that my students have for the future and a decent standard of living.

Over the course of my nearly fifteen years teaching critical thinking, I have been frustrated by the disconnection between logic and the painful reality of institutional inequality and social divisions. While I have taught my students the skills of argument analysis, fallacy identification, and standards for credibility, I have struggled to find ways to effectively apply these skills to the daily challenges my students face in a polarized and adversarial society. After years of adding and deleting readings to my courses, developing and then abandoning assignments, and organizing and then reorganizing class examples, I decided to put together some of the best practices I have found for promoting critical thinking and, more important, *critical talking and listening* through an exploration of social differences. This book was inspired by the three students I described above and the countless others who came to my office to talk but did not feel comfortable, despite my best efforts at the time, speaking out in class. Their reluctance to publicly describe their experiences was the result of the structural limits and constraints that are put on our language and our lives. Their silence reveals the ways that social inequality and social pressures can shut down critical thinking and close off the chance for us to learn from each other. I hope that this book and the methods it provides will help to challenge the silence and reduce the pressure so that everyone involved in debates about social identity can give voice to their experiences. It has been my experience that when intellectually empathic dialogue about social identity and difference occurs, all of our thinking is enriched, and together we move in a direction toward critically solving the problems that we collectively face.

Introduction: Putting Up Walls

Sean and Zainab

Imagine the following scenario: two adults are meeting for the first time to collaborate on a project. The setting could be any place where people come together—such as a classroom, a boardroom, or a community center—to work on solving a problem. One member of this pair, let's call him Sean, is a white heterosexual Catholic male whose family's American roots began with his great-grandparents' emigration from Ireland in the late nineteenth century. Sean has grown up blue-collar and working-class. Imagine the other member of this pair, let's call her Zainab, who is an Arab Muslim heterosexual female; her family roots are in the Syrian middle class. Her parents emigrated from Syria thirty years ago, and Zainab and her siblings were all born in the United States. Zainab wears the *hijab,* or head scarf, traditionally worn by Muslim women. As they begin introducing themselves, Sean extends his hand to shake Zainab's and says, "Hi! Nice to meet you. I'm Sean." Zainab smiles politely and says, "I'm Zainab. Nice to meet you." But she does not extend her hand to shake his. Sean sitting there with his arm extended finally retracts it with an irritated look on his face. Zainab is now worrying if she has offended him. Sean is feeling embarrassed and has now decided that he does not particularly like Zainab. They begin their work, and at a point where she decides it is appropriate, Zainab takes a risk and says to Sean, "I apologize for not shaking your hand. In my faith, women do not touch men who are not family members. I just wanted to let you know." Sean takes in this information and appreciates Zainab letting him know that it was nothing personal. Zainab breathes a sigh of relief because she believes she cleared the air with Sean, and they can now get on with their work. However, after a few moments Sean says, "You know, not to be disrespectful, but you are in America now. Don't you think it is about time that you started using American customs instead of these ancient traditions?" Zainab is hurt by the comment and decides that Sean is a bigot. Rather than engaging him further, she concludes that it is not worth trying to educate him since she risks her own humiliation or his anger. She puts up a wall around her beliefs and decides to say nothing more about the issue. Sean, who took a risk asking the question, waits for Zainab's response, but she ignores the question and gets back to work on the project. Sean decides that Zainab is a brainwashed fundamentalist who lives in an archaic, backward world. He puts up a wall around his beliefs and decides to say nothing more about the issue. They continue on with their project work in frustration and discomfort. Sean and Zainab do a mediocre job, and once the project is finished, they can't wait to get away from each other.

This interaction between Zainab and Sean plays out in a hundred different ways in classrooms, offices, community gatherings, and virtual sites all over the United States. The social difference at play could be religion, race, ethnicity, sexual orientation, gender, disability, age, or socioeconomic class. Issues related to social identity often get in the way of open, respectful, and thoughtful dialogue between people.

Social Identity

Social identity refers to the ways that people define themselves and others in terms of their membership in social groups. Just as we have unique personalities—we can be introverted, extroverted, stubborn, optimistic—we also have social identities; we can be Latino, Jewish, bisexual, Republican, a woman. In most cases people self-identify with their social identity, but in some cases a social identity is attributed to a person or a group, and this attribution can be incorrect. For example, a person who identifies as bisexual might be mistakenly identified as straight if her or his romantic partner is of the opposite sex. In addition, our own understanding of our social identity might not match up with how others understand our social identity. For example, a person who identifies as Latino may be surprised to find that many non-Latinos assume that being Latino means being involved with gangs and criminals. So, while our social identity is something we often get to define for ourselves, it is important to remember that others ascribe social identities to us as well, and in some cases these can be incorrect, unfamiliar, and painful.

You may have had an experience like Sean and Zainab's yourself, and if so you may still recall the feelings of frustration, anger, or embarrassment you felt. If you have not had an experience like this, it does not mean that the problem isn't out there. You may have avoided the difficulty of social identity because, like many people, you tend to spend time with those who share many of your basic beliefs and values and tend to look like you or share your social traits.[1] If a majority of your social interactions are with people who share many of your beliefs and attributes, then the probability is low that you will have real clashes regarding worldviews. However, in our increasingly global world, the chance is high that you will at some point encounter an obstacle like the one faced by Sean and Zainab.

You may think that since you are a pretty reasonable person you will behave differently in Sean and Zainab's situation. As you read through the case of Sean and Zainab, you may have thought "I would never have said what Sean said!" or "I would never have reacted the way Zainab did!" Oftentimes when people consider cases of social conflict such as the one between Sean and Zainab, they don't identify with the awkward, angry, or frustrated respondent. Many of us believe that we are more reasonable, more polite, and perhaps more sensitive than either Sean or Zainab. In my own experience teaching social differences and critical thinking, most of my students begin with the belief that they are good people with fair and open minds. They attribute conflict to "those other people" who are always playing the "race card" or the "gender card" or the "gay card" or the "minority card" (whether "those other people" are claiming minority status based on religion, ethnicity, sexual orientation, disability, social class, or age). And most of my students who believe that they are basically good, reasonable people are good people.

However, the belief that we are good people does not prevent any of us from having a "Sean" or a "Zainab" moment when social differences arise and complicate our interpersonal encounters. By "we" here I mean all of us who welcome the opportunity to develop our critical thinking skills, particularly in the service of understanding social differences and social inequality. It is hard for most of us to manage social differences in a public context because we run the risk of offending someone or else being offended. Because of this, many of us may resort to erecting a wall around our beliefs so that we avoid sharing what we think about social difference and social inequality. We come to the conclusion that it is not worth the risk personally to engage with others who just don't get it and who most likely have a bias against what we believe or what we have experienced firsthand. If the encounter is in an academic or professional setting, we fear that if we engage further we will be labeled either a bigot or a whiner, thereby jeopardizing our credibility and maybe even our career. So the result is a stalled-out frustrating experience with no one really learning anything constructive from the conversation.

Systemic "Unseeing" and the Personal Nature of Identity

It is often in just these kinds of conversations that some of the most fruitful opportunities arise for developing our critical thinking skills. These kinds of dialogues are not easy for a variety of reasons. First and foremost is that there are a whole host of structural and institutionalized mechanisms that together make these kinds of dialogues so difficult. Media images, educational institutions, business and economic interests, and social and political systems all engage in what Sara Ahmed, a race and cultural studies professor at the University of London, calls an "unseeing" whereby the complexity and reality of social identity and inequality are flattened out into a narrative about individuals (not social systems) with good and bad attitudes (not systemic advantages and disadvantages).[2] Racism, sexism, heterosexism, religious bigotry, and other forms of bias and discrimination are often portrayed in American culture as the result of racist, sexist, and heterosexist individuals. If we see these forms of bias and discrimination as problems that individuals suffer from, then the solution is to treat (or punish) the individual.

The problem with focusing on changing the individual is that it fails to treat the surrounding media images, educational institutions, business and economic interests, and social and political systems within which individuals live. Gregory Mantsios, a sociologist at the City University of New York, points out that "A relatively small number of media outlets is producing and packaging a variety of our news and entertainment programs. The media plays a key role in defining our cultural tastes, helping us locate ourselves in history, establishing our national identity, and ascertaining the range of national and social possibilities."[3] Using the example of poor and working-class people, Mantsios explains that representations of their lives are relatively nonexistent in the media, and when they are referenced it is as either a faceless number, a subset of the population who are down on their luck, or people who only have themselves to blame. On the other hand, the interests of the wealthy are treated as the interests that "all of us" share. Stock and business reports that cater to a small subset of the overall population are given significant time and attention in news reports, and even weather and sports news, Mantsios argues, are slanted toward the interests of the wealthy. He cites a New York news radio program that keeps listeners up to date with ski conditions and reports. Even though the wealthy are not considered a social class but instead, as Mantsios explains, are an "aggregate of individuals" without special interests, interconnections, or common purposes, they do in fact have interests that, with the help of the media, become the interests of "us all." What becomes important then is that "we," those of us who are all encouraged to identify with the interests of the wealthy, can share a moral and intellectual superiority over the poor and disadvantaged.[4]

Critically Thinking about the Media

Here is an exercise: Watch an hour of a national morning television program such as *The Today Show* or *Good Morning America*. Keep track of the news and information, and then do a summary report of the topics covered during that hour. Based on this summary, what social groups are most directly targeted by this news and information? Think in detailed terms about social identity: age, economic class, gender, sexuality, race, ethnicity, religion, ability and disability. What picture do you get about what matters to America from these stories? Now using the same summary, describe who is left out in terms of social identity? Whose concerns are unseen and made invisible by this news and information? Choose another major media source such as television entertainment, film, popular music, advertising, or a major cable news and entertainment outlet, and do this exercise. Are the results similar? Why or why not?

If we are concerned with addressing social class biases and our focus is solely on changing individual attitudes, then we fail to address the enormous influence that the media has in perpetuating these divisions. Yet the media is only one of the large-scale systemic forces affecting our beliefs about social identity and social differences. Educational institutions, political systems, and economic and business interests all perpetuate biases by unseeing the unjust reality of social inequality and focusing almost exclusively on the interests of the most privileged and socially powerful.

One of the very significant factors that make social identity and social difference so difficult to discuss is that there are multiple and related systemic elements that work together to unsee and hence unspeak about the complexity of our experiences. What is left to be seen is an oversimplified set of either-or categories that is supposed to capture our experiences in oppositions, male or female, white or black, straight or gay, Christian or other religion (or none), able or disabled, middle class or poor, educated or uneducated, Republican or Democrat, American or other nationality. This set not only narrows the range of possibilities for describing our experiences but also positions one side of the duality against the other. This means that the very language we use to describe our experiences is already loaded with opposition.

The second factor that contributes to the difficulty of dialogues about social identity and social difference is that these conversations, while shaped by a history of inequality and influenced by the social systems surrounding us, are at the same time very personal. If there are multiple forces surrounding us and shaping our language into narrow, oppositional categories of experience, we still need to find ourselves within these categories. Our gender, our race and ethnicity, our sexual orientation, and our religion all play a role in the formation of some of our most personal beliefs and sense of who we are. It is already difficult for most of us to have an honest and authentic debate about controversial social issues such as gun control or abortion with someone who has views that are very different from our own. However, when the issue involves our social identity, the difficulty increases exponentially. This is because we believe that we are experts when it comes to our own experiences. If we describe what it is like to be our gender, our race, or our religion and our description is challenged by someone who does not share our gender, race, or religion, it can cut to the core of our sense of self. It is not surprising, then, that people often become defensive when their social experience is challenged. In ordinary contexts if you say you did something (e.g., you told someone that you had gone to the movies the day before), most everyone would believe you unless you had some kind of history of lying. How frustrating it would be if you casually shared with someone the fact of having seen a movie the day before and the person you were speaking to suddenly began challenging you to provide evidence that you had in fact been to the movies. You would understandably view the challenger as an arrogant jerk who was behaving like a prosecutor in some nonexistent trial.

In most circumstances in our daily lives we treat people as if they are credible. We ask a stranger for the time, and we assume that he is telling the truth. We ask a coworker or classmate if she knows when a meeting will be, and we take her at her word. In fact, credibility is the default for most of our conversations. It is only when we get to less mundane and more controversial issues that credibility is called into question—like in a trial. The difficulty of a context where social identity issues arise, as in Sean and Zainab's case, is that credibility is no longer the default, and yet neither participant understands why they have suddenly become suspicious. It feels personal to not be trusted. Moreover, if someone calls aspects of our identity into question or raises suspicions about how we express our identity, it can feel like the person is assuming a position of authority and control over us. So, it is not a surprise that Zainab became defensive and put a wall up around her beliefs. Of course her reaction, while understandable, did not make sense to Sean. Sean did not see that his question about Zainab's adherence to a particular religious practice carried with it an implied authority. Sean's question assumed that he knew what was appropriate religious behavior in contemporary American society, and a prohibition on shaking hands did not compute. Sean was unable to see that his standards for appropriate religious behavior were derived from his own experience and reinforced by the wider predominantly Christian culture surrounding him. That his personal experiences of religion match up in so many ways with the surrounding culture lends a "typical" or "normal" quality to his beliefs about religion. Therefore, his question, from his point of view, is not an assertion of power but rather a puzzlement about something that registers as "not normal." This sense of "normalcy" makes it extremely difficult for Sean to see that his question is an indication of his social privilege. When Zainab fails to answer him, he interprets it as rudeness rather than a reaction to his having called her faith and her citizenship into question.

Some of the most challenging debate contexts—and ones that are rife with faulty reasoning—are those where self-identity, social identity, and social relations come together as the primary focus. Racial identity and race relations, gender identity, dis/ability, sexual orientation, socioeconomic status, and ethnic and religious identity are all factors that can shut down reasonable dialogue. More often than not in these contexts, people are ready to point out the flaws or the lack of credibility in another person's claim before they have done the work of examining their own claims and methods of justification. In debates about social issues, most of us fail to see our common ground. We have little empathy or compassion for those whose conclusions are so different from our own, and we withdraw from real analysis because we fear that we will offend someone, that we will not be believed, or that we will never change the other person's mind.

These two factors—the social and structural systems that unsee social power and reduce our identity to either-or categories and the very personal way that we have come to form our identities within these categories—create obstacles to thinking critically about social identity and social difference. To get at these issues, it seems like we have to do two very different things at the same time. The first is opening up a wide lens for analysis so that we can examine the history of social inequality and its role in shaping contemporary systems of education, business, politics, and religion. The second is narrowing the scope of that lens significantly so that we can focus directly on our own individual beliefs, including the emotional content of those beliefs. This simultaneous wide and narrow focus means that we have to think broadly and specifically, intellectually and emotionally, and politically and personally all at the same time. It also means that we will have to combine some very different tools for analysis and also create some new ones of our own.

Know Thyself

Intellectual empathy is what we will call this combined effort to focus both widely and narrowly on social identity and social difference. More than two thousand years ago in Plato's dialogue *Phaedrus*, Socrates said, "I am not yet able, as the Delphic inscription has it, to *know myself*; so it seems to me ridiculous, when I do not yet know that, to investigate other things." The injunction to *know thyself* was carved into the stone above the Temple of Apollo and served as a theme for much of Socrates's teaching. While it may seem like a simple command, self-awareness and the matter of how our behavior affects other people are not easy to know. The requirement to *know thyself* is about more than just knowing the right facts and information or knowing the kinds of things we are good at doing. It requires self-awareness, self-understanding, and self-reflexivity. It also requires understanding the institutions and social systems that contribute to shaping our beliefs and our language. Critical thinking about social identity presents one of the best opportunities to develop these self-skills in relation to social issues, because it allows us to imagine different worldviews. Yet because of the embedded history of inequality in these identities as well as their very personal nature, it can feel so difficult to openly, respectfully, and sincerely share our beliefs and attitudes with others. We know that this is as hard in the classroom as it is in our communities, in the media, in politics, in online blog comments, and in global divisions and international affairs. Abortion, gay marriage, poverty, the 99 percent versus the 1 percent, social safety nets, affirmative action, belief in the one true God or not, and the justification to go to war are all examples of issues that arise from social differences, divide and often conquer relationships between people, and shut down constructive dialogue.[5]

To more effectively engage with social issues, we need to critically assess our own beliefs and attitudes about social identities and then develop the skills to listen responsibly to the beliefs and attitudes of those whose social experiences are different from our own. This is where it gets personal. It is one thing to debate an issue such as affirmative action in the abstract. It is quite another thing to debate the role that our race or our social class may be playing in our beliefs about affirmative action. The skills required for this latter debate are missing from most of our textbooks, and so the omission makes it seem as if our social identity is irrelevant to debates about social issues. Of course, we all know that it is not. If a black student is arguing for affirmative action and a white student is arguing against it, they and the students around them are silently drawing conclusions about how the debaters' race is playing a role in their positions. Interestingly, each debater is most likely thinking not about how race is affecting his or her own position but instead about how it must be affecting the other debater. This is because we have a much easier time believing that other people's beliefs are biased but a much harder time believing that about our own beliefs.[6] In addition, the social systems of inequality that surround and shape our beliefs about race will factor into how the debaters are perceived in terms of their credibility, reasonableness, and objectivity.

It is very difficult for most of us to account for these silent attitudes and perceptions. For one thing, they may not be operating at a conscious level. Negative and positive biases about race may register in our conscious thinking as judgments having to do with the individual person. Most of us (of all races) are more likely to think "He is a very aggressive person" or "He seems like a really reasonable person" rather than "He is black and therefore aggressive" or "He is white and therefore reasonable." Researchers have found that most Americans consciously subscribe to the idea that all people deserve equal treatment and opportunity and that racial integration is a desirable goal.[7] So, while it is true that we as a nation have evolved in terms of our beliefs about racial equality, there is still significant evidence that racial biases, rather than being eliminated, still linger in our unconscious beliefs and attitudes.[8]

Another reason these kinds of dialogues and debates are so hard is that many of us have had bad experiences talking publicly about our social identity and beliefs. We may not have been believed or may have been judged to be playing the race card or the gender card, leaving us feeling as if our beliefs and experiences are not legitimate. Others may have struggled with understanding their beliefs about social identity and in their efforts to express themselves may have been judged unfairly to be simply racist or sexist or homophobic. For those of us who have not had these bad experiences directly, we may nevertheless still feel anxiety because we know that the issues can get personal.

False Dichotomies

These difficulties emerge because of the combination of the unseeing of social systems and the oversimplified and polarized categories of social identity. As a result, the only options that seem to be available to us when talking about these issues publicly is a set of *false dichotomies*:

> Fight or flight
> Guilt or anger
> Shame or blame
> Culprit or victim
> Logic or emotion
> Winner or loser

Historical context

These false dichotomies limit our options and the roles we can take in dialogues and debates about social identity and social differences. If we choose to remain in the dialogue, then we have to fight and risk going to battle with someone who may accuse us of being a racist, a sexist, homophobic, right-wing, left-wing, a radical, a socialist, a tree hugger, etc., because of something we claim or something we experienced. Alternatively, if we take flight it means that we have to make a decision right from the start to disengage from conversations dealing with social controversies because it is not worth the trouble of angering someone or being misrepresented in public, and we won't change anyone's mind anyway.

Similarly, if we are so accused of harboring racist, sexist, biased beliefs, then it seems that the only options available to us are to become angry at the accusation or accept the charge and manage our guilt. If we identify racist, sexist, biased beliefs in others, we can either blame them if they fail to admit these beliefs or shame them by claiming that we see what they are unable to recognize. In this way, we position each other either as culprits and perpetrators of oppression or as innocent victims. Of course, the person who resists these limited roles can be charged with being too emotional and failing to be logical, another way to silence or shame a debater into withdrawing. With these dichotomies at work, someone will eventually emerge as the winner and the other as the loser, though the winner may win simply by intimidating, shaming, or chasing the loser away.

It is not surprising, then, that we see more of the fight option in online news comment sections where anonymous commenters make claims with no accountability to the people they target and no consequences for their own reputation. In public forums such as a classroom or a professional workshop, it is no wonder that many people choose the flight option and disengage. It is easier for us to believe that we are basically not racist, sexist, right-wing or left-wing radicals, etc.—that we are good people—and avoid the battle scars, saving the more controversial and honest conversation about these topics for those friends and family who share our views.

Of course, choosing to opt out may not present immediate risks, but there are longer-term consequences for failing to think beyond simply being a good person. Critical thinking is the process of exposing our beliefs to the standards of good reasoning, airing them out through examination and justification, and giving them the kind of attention that will make them more consistent and flexible. Because beliefs motivate our actions and decisions, examining our beliefs can promote actions and decisions that are more coherent and morally justifiable and are in our best interest. Beliefs that we withhold from critical thinking fail to benefit from this process and can lead us to decisions and actions that are inconsistent, morally irresponsible, and self-defeating.

Many people who avoid critically examining their beliefs about social identities wind up contributing to the very problems they hope to avoid. For instance, the person who says "I'm color-blind. I don't see race or ethnicity. I judge people solely on their character" is denying that race and ethnicity play any role in their thinking. However, it is absolutely unrealistic to imagine that people don't see race anymore than people don't see hair color or read facial expressions. Race and the related concept of ethnicity, whether it is a real biological category, a social construct, or a political tool, is nevertheless an organizing concept that we learn when we learn language as children. We commonly teach children about nations and cultures and holidays by relating these to different races and ethnicities. First graders would not understand the traditional American story of Thanksgiving if we did not identify one group of people as Native American and the other as British immigrants to the United States. Martin Luther King Jr. Day would not make much sense to elementary school students if King's story were not embedded in a discussion of civil rights and the history of discrimination against African Americans in our country. Chinese New Year would not make sense as a cultural event if it were not connected to Chinese history and Chinese people.

The point is that there is nothing inherently racist or biased about identifying groups as having a race or ethnicity. However, the person who says "I'm color-blind" is most likely making that claim in an attempt to avoid an open conversation about the related assumptions he or she has in connection with particular races and ethnicities. If, for instance, the person who claims to be color-blind was taught both that Native Americans participated in the first Thanksgiving and that Native Americans today basically get a free ride from the U.S. government (free college education, no taxes, financial reparations), then that person would be less likely on the basis of the latter belief to support policies that advocated for more public resources for Native Americans. However, if the person was taught that belief and never examined it critically or sought evidence to either support or disprove it, instead believing it because it simplified his or her belief system and corresponded with the beliefs of those people he or she associated with, then that person's belief would be a *stereotype*.

Rather than risk admitting stereotypes, many people hide them or only share them with others who hold the same stereotypical beliefs, thereby never subjecting them to the process of critical thinking. Many people worry that it is not politically correct to say negative things about social groups, so they withhold discussing their stereotypes in public and only share them with those who hold the same stereotypes and beliefs. The result is that many of us are walking around with stereotypes and unexamined beliefs that have a significant impact on our decisions and our actions. At the same time, many of us wish that stereotypes and all the associated problems of prejudice and bias would just go away because they cause so much social conflict. The social systems and institutions we described earlier that unsee the history and reality of social inequality wind up contributing to the perpetuation of the stereotypes. Implicit biases are operating within us and around us while everyone keeps saying explicitly that we are a nation that values justice and diversity. It should not be a surprise, then, that progress is so difficult and that social divisions are so hard to heal.

The very limited and extremely unappealing false dichotomies that we have inherited and incorporated into our own belief systems and that are reinforced through many powerful social institutions are not the end of the story. They do not have to be the only options and roles available to us. Intellectual empathy is a method for driving a wedge between these false dichotomies with the goal of creating new and more constructive possibilities for dialogue about social identity and social difference.

What Is Intellectual Empathy?

I use the term "intellectual empathy" for the work we will be doing in this book because it captures the *cognitive-affective* elements of thinking about identity and social difference. Traditional models of mental processing assumed that cognitive abilities such as thinking, remembering, and inferring were separated from emotional responses.[9] More recent research in cognitive psychology has shown that cognition and emotion can actually function interdependently so that things such as attention and memory can work more effectively when accompanied by feelings.[10]

Empathy is an emotion that seems to have significant cognitive dimensions. When we empathize, we imagine what it is like to feel what another person is feeling in a particular situation. Empathy is different in this way from sympathy, which is a feeling *for* a person without having to really understand what it is that person is actually experiencing. Empathy, according to cognitive psychologists Gordon Gallup and Steven Platek, is a byproduct of self-awareness, so the greater our capacity to know thyself, the greater our empathic abilities.[11] Empathy is not the same as actually walking in someone else's shoes or feeling another's pain, because we don't actually face the same circumstances a person faces when we empathize with her or him. Instead, we have to creatively imagine what it feels like by projecting ourselves into that person's situation. This is why a robust self-awareness helps us to empathize more effectively. We have to imagine being who we are in very different kinds of circumstances and then imagine how we would feel. When we empathize with someone, we are not necessarily trying to make that person feel more comfortable or take care of that person. Empathy, then, is not the same thing as morality, though there is a relationship between cruelty and a lack of empathy. Simon Baron-Cohen, a professor of developmental psychopathology at Cambridge University, uses the term "zero-negatives" to refer to people who lack empathy and who inflict harm on other people.[12] Other researchers have noted how racial empathy gaps lead whites to discount the pain felt by blacks and lead wealthy people to discount the hardships faced by the poor.[13] These empathy gaps mean that not only are some people just getting the facts wrong, but they are also compounding suffering by failing to acknowledge that others are suffering.

Intellectual empathy, then, assumes that reason and understanding must be supplemented with emotion and experience so that we can *know* in the fullest possible sense. This means knowing about ourselves and knowing as much as we can about other people's circumstances, particularly people whose circumstances are different from our own. In this way, intellectual empathy is not simply a psychological prescription for changing individual beliefs. It is a means for examining both the wide scope of social institutions and social inequality and the narrow scope of our own beliefs. When we employ intellectual empathy in our reasoning about social differences, we are not so much interested in gathering information about other people and their respective beliefs as we are in *looking at the situations people face through their eyes.*[14] This requires gathering reliable information, but it also requires critically and creatively imagining how that information is understood and processed by people whose experiences are different from our own and, perhaps most challenging, how we ourselves, with our own particular social identities, are seen and understood by people whose social identities are different from our own.

Intellectual empathy combines five skills that when used together make us more effective at understanding the social inequalities that other people face as well as the systems and structures that maintain these differences. These five skills include:

1. Understanding the invisibility of privilege (chapter 2),
2. Knowing that social identity is intersectional (chapter 2),
3. Using the model of cooperative reasoning (chapter 3),
4. Applying the principle of conditional trust (chapter 6), and
5. Recognizing our mutual vulnerability (chapter 6).

This book is a guide to developing these skills so that your ensuing discussions about social issues are less volatile, more productive, intellectually and critically engaging, and ultimately a real opportunity to know thyself by knowing the institutional constraints that limit our beliefs and our language. After teaching critical thinking and topics related to controversial social issues over the past fourteen years, I have come to recognize the kind of unproductive dialogue patterns that range from fight or flight to generating guilt or blame to simply shutting down. Each of these patterns follows a predictable and ultimately frustrating dead end. What I have learned is that with the right tools my students and I can successfully redirect the path of these discussions, opening up new possibilities with more engaging and intellectually beneficial outcomes.

Returning to Sean and Zainab, imagine if the conversation had gone more like this: Zainab, after not shaking Sean's hand, says, "I'm sorry. I don't mean to be rude, but given my faith, I am not comfortable touching a man other than the men in my family." Rather than reacting defensively, Sean could determine that Zainab took quite a risk sharing this with him and ease her potential discomfort by telling her so. "I appreciate you letting me know. I had no idea." Sean could see this as a real sign of Zainab's trust in him and an important opportunity to gain valuable cultural information. Meanwhile, Zainab would have confirmation that taking the risk of being honest and educating people about her faith was the right thing to do. Now, what if in the course of their conversation Sean says this: "You know not to be disrespectful, but you are in America now. Don't you think it is about time that you start using American customs and get past these ancient traditions?" Even though Zainab may initially feel defensive, she could forestall putting up a wall by remembering that she took an initial risk with Sean, and now he is taking one with her. Though she may not like his question, she could see it as Sean trusting her enough to engage her about her faith even while it is an indication of his social privilege. So, imagine Zainab responding with "Actually I was born in the U.S., so it is not like I came here from somewhere else. My parents emigrated from Syria, but I am an American. I'm not sure what you mean by American customs, but if you mean non-Muslim that does not seem to me like a very American way of thinking." Now, if we imagine that Sean remains respectfully engaged with this conversation—seeing it as an opportunity to learn more about Islam and his project partner—he might respond with "I guess you're right that American customs include lots of different things. It's just that shaking hands is so common. But, you know, I'm Catholic"—here Sean would be using analogical reasoning—"and I know my grandparents talked about how a lot of Protestants tried to discourage the Catholics in America from praying to saints or following the pope's authority. So yeah, I guess I'm glad that Catholics in the United States kept up their ancient traditions even when they were pressured not to." Here Sean has established common ground with Zainab, and he sees the initial inconsistencies in his own thinking and the way that his assumptions about what it was to be American or contemporary were limited.

If we imagined this conversation going further or Sean and Zainab becoming friends, they might discover that Sean's anxiety about Muslim traditions has something to do with his desire for the concept "American" to mean something that looks a lot like his family and friends. Sean might come to discover that Zainab has a similar desire for "American" to reflect her family and friends, even though they may look and behave differently from Sean's. However, there is a good chance that some of their important beliefs and experiences are shared. Both most likely see the value in the freedom to practice their religion in peace, both prioritize family and hard work, both enjoy holidays and celebratory meals with the family, and both are distressed by the downturn in the economy. Zainab may come to realize that Sean is not at all a bigot but instead is someone who has not had to really consider what it is like being a non-Christian and particularly a Muslim in post-9/11 America. After this conversation is over, Sean will take away with him important information about Islam, himself, and the concept of being American. He may hold back his hand in some future instance when meeting another woman wearing a *hijab* and instead respectfully nod and say, "I won't extend my hand but know that I am happy to meet you." We could imagine the woman in that case feeling exceedingly respected and Sean feeling that he himself is more knowledgeable and culturally aware. Similarly, Zainab will leave the conversation feeling glad that she took the risk and knowing more about how to address cultural differences and draw analogies between her experiences and the experiences of Americans of different faiths.

The story of Sean and Zainab is actually a summary of what happened over the course of a semester between two former students who worked together on a project in one of my courses. The conversation unfolded not in one sitting but instead over the course of several weeks. Unlike other scenarios where I watched people put up walls when the topic turned to social differences, in the case of these two students they remained open and engaged, maintaining mutual respect and continually seeing their differences as a learning opportunity. However, this didn't just happen because they were particularly nice people. They were opinionated, imperfect, practical people just like the rest of us. The difference, though, was that we had worked together on setting up some ground rules, and they had a method for how to proceed in their conversations. Most important, they established a basic level of mutual trust and respect, and both saw their time together as an opportunity to learn, not to win.

The purpose of this book is to provide you with those ground rules and methods so that you can think more critically and effectively about issues having to do with social identity. In chapter 1 we will see how our social beliefs are formed and why the distinction between logic and emotion has made it so difficult to assess and analyze our beliefs about identity. In chapter 2 we will look at social inequalities and the role they play in our social identity. In chapter 3 we will consider how the history of argument and debate has contributed to the false dichotomies that limit our social dialogues. In chapter 4 we will look at some common mistakes we make when taking in and processing social information, and in chapter 5 we will examine some common mistakes in expressing our beliefs and attitudes about social differences. In chapter 6 we move toward establishing some common ground so that we can more effectively talk about social identity and social difference, and finally in chapter 7 we will consider the ways that we can take intellectual empathy out into the world.

What This Book Is Not Going to Do

Now that I have told you some of the central objectives of this book, let me take a moment to say a few things about what this book is not intended to do. First, this book is not intended to necessarily change your beliefs. So, for instance, if you are a religious person who believes that certain claims are true in virtue of your religion, the goal of this book is not to argue you out of your beliefs. However, if one of your religious beliefs relates to social identities—for instance, you believe that homosexuality is sinful—then you may be asked to consider that belief in light of other beliefs you hold as well as the beliefs of those who may not share your view. Granted, this is not easy, but it is also not easy for a homosexual person who believes that he or she is entitled to the same rights as heterosexuals to be confident in his or her identity and belief in light of your belief. Both of you will have to take a risk to varying degrees, depending on who you are and in what context you express your beliefs. The point is that you may have to consider how consistent your belief is in relation to other beliefs you hold (such as the right to the free expression of religion, the belief that sexual orientation is or is not a choice, or the belief that discrimination on the basis of inherent characteristics is either fair or unfair) and the consequences that follow from your belief for those directly affected. Those who are directly affected might be sitting next to you in a class, at work, or at a PTA meeting or might be running for office. Whatever the case may be, you will be asked to think about how your beliefs have an impact on the lives of others. At the same time, you will be asked to consider how the beliefs held by others impact your life. And it is incumbent on you both to consider how you came to hold the beliefs you hold and why they persist. This process is not designed to argue you out of your beliefs but instead is designed to fine-tune your beliefs and give you the opportunity to understand how your beliefs about social identities exist not apart from social contexts but rather within them. We can only assess how well our beliefs are justified if we understand how they are formed and how they are confirmed through our experiences.

Second, this book is not intended to settle the score on some of the major controversial issues having to do with social identity in our society or around the globe. This book will not answer the question of whether or not immigration laws need to be reformed, whether or not a mosque should be built near Ground Zero in New York City, or whether or not gay marriage should be a federal legal right. Rather, this book will provide you with the groundwork for thinking critically about how our social beliefs develop through our interactions with social systems. The goal is for us to better identify the mistakes in reasoning and inconsistencies in logic and justification that limit our categories of identity and contribute to the volatility of social debate and the perpetuation of social injustice.

This book should give you a more empathic lens for viewing yourself and others in relation to the complexity of social identity controversies. The point is to challenge the false dichotomies and clear the air of some of the more noxious and irrational elements in controversial issues about social identity so that our dialogues can be richer and more productive. The goal of the book, then, is not to provide you with answers to all of the social problems we face but instead to embolden you with the skills to identify the relevant factors related to the issues of social injustice and evaluate the limits and constrictions of competing arguments.

Finally, this book is not intended to be a manual in political correctness, encouraging us all to join hands in a "Kumbaya" sing-along for peace and harmony. Now, let me say that I have no issue with correctness in all of its forms, including the political variety. However, the term "political correctness" has come to be equated with a restrictive use of language designed to not offend certain (seemingly hypersensitive) groups. In other words, political correctness, or being PC, has come to mean watching what you say around those "other people" who take great offense at jokes and stories. The negative connotations around being PC often stem from the fact that people don't like having to pay attention to their language or face the way that their humor or their anecdotes undermine the experiences of others. It would be easier all around if we could continue to use the language that we use unencumbered by social groups who object to our terminology. For instance, men who routinely referred to women as "dolls," "chicks," "babes," or "hags" in the workplace did not appreciate having their language criticized from the emerging women's movement of the late 1960s and early 1970s. Many of those men did not believe they were being sexist and described the objections from feminists as a bunch of whining from women who couldn't take a joke. But the more substantive issue was that men were being forced to consider their role in perpetuating injustices against women. Behavior and policies that were deemed simply "normal" for decades before were now being called into question, and men were asked to be accountable. The inevitable reaction for many men to the transition from being "normal" to suddenly being "sexist" was to become defensive and to hold tight to the existing power dynamics rather than move to an unknown. It was easier to blame the accuser than to call the whole social system into question along with your own personal system of beliefs.

Similarly, the civil rights movements and women's rights movements, and more recently the gay rights movement and the disability rights movement, have all, among other things, called attention to our language and the specific words and phrases that undermine the experiences of members of those groups. Having such significant historical movements develop during a relatively brief period of human history left many people feeling like too much was changing too fast. A variety of public figures fought back by defending their use of language and reducing those social movements to conspiracies designed to pressure the public into conforming to fashionable academic ideas.[15] Hence, "politically incorrect" became a badge of honor for those who believed they were brave enough to speak their mind and counteract the cultural pressure.

What all this amounts to is that the goal of this book is not to have you become more politically correct in the PC sense. Also, it is not a goal to have you become more politically incorrect. Rather, the whole divisive debate around political correctness is itself a symptom of a broader problem having to do with a lack of real critical thinking about social identity issues. Intellectual empathy will provide you with the groundwork for reasoning about these issues and hopefully move you past the politically correct–politically incorrect dichotomy. The direction we will take is toward self-knowledge and positive solutions to seemingly impossible conversations and enduring social injustices.

Questions for Review

1. Why is a focus on individual attitudes not enough if we want to transform our conversations about social identity and social differences?

2. What does it mean for an institution or an organization to unsee, in Sara Ahmed's sense? How is this different from not seeing?

3. Why is questioning someone about the accuracy of her or his experiences of bias or discrimination so different from how we treat most reports that people give about their experiences?

4. Describe at least three of the false dichotomies and explain how they are related.

5. Socrates is quoted as saying "know thyself." What does this mean, and why is it important for intellectual empathy?

6. Describe at least one thing this book is not intended to do and why.

Questions for Further Thinking and Writing

1. How do you see yourself when it comes to your social identity? Have you ever had the experience of someone mischaracterizing (or even insulting) some aspect of your social identity? How did you react? What factors do you think contributed to that person's ignorance of your social identity?

2. How would you support the point raised in this chapter that knowing thyself can actually increase the capacity for empathy? Respond to this by recounting a time when you mischaracterized (or even insulted) someone's social identity. What factors contributed to your ignorance of that social identity? Does reflecting on this experience help you to understand how other people can make mistakes about your social identity?

3. Read the following quote from philosopher Marilyn Frye's essay "Oppression." Think about how Frye's point about "barriers" illustrates structural racism as opposed to personal prejudices:

   > The boundaries of a racial ghetto in an American city serve to some extent to keep white people from going in, as well as to keep ghetto dwellers from going out. A particular white citizen may be frustrated or feel deprived because they cannot stroll around there and enjoy the "exotic" aura of a "foreign" culture, or shop for bargains in the ghetto swap shops. In fact, the existence of the ghetto, of racial segregation, does deprive the white person of knowledge and harm their character by nurturing unwarranted feelings of superiority. But this does not make the white person in this situation a member of an oppressed race or a person oppressed because of their race. One must look at the barrier. It limits the activities and the access of those on both sides of it (though to different degrees). But it is a product of the intention, planning and action of whites for the benefit of whites, to secure and maintain privileges that are available to whites generally, as members of the dominant and privileged group.[16]

Further Resources

Columbia University's Center for the Study of Social Difference (http://social difference.columbia.edu) has some excellent online resources related to social identity and social difference.

1 | The Web of Belief

How Beliefs Are Formed and Organized

In this book we will focus primarily on examining our beliefs about social identity and social differences. Before we begin that investigation, it will be helpful to think about the process of belief formation generally and the following kinds of questions: How do you form beliefs? How are your beliefs organized? When you give up or change a belief, how does that work? How are new beliefs added? We will begin this investigation by considering some basic perceptual beliefs and then move on to value judgments and moral beliefs. I will steer clear of social beliefs until we have an outline of the basic processes of belief formation and language acquisition. So, this is just a promise that we will get there by the end of the chapter. When I ask you to consider simple nouns such as "cup" and "furniture," remember that we are moving toward understanding more complex concepts such as social privilege and group distinctiveness.

For centuries, philosophers and more recently psychologists, neuro-scientists, and cognitive scientists (the term "cognition" refers to human thinking and reasoning processes) have been working together to investigate very fundamental questions about how we form beliefs and have been proposing theories and models to provide us with some answers. One important contributor to this work was the Harvard philosopher W. V. O. Quine, who has been described as "arguably the greatest American philosopher of the second half of the twentieth century and who revolutionized the study of knowledge, logic, language, and mathematics."[1]

In "Two Dogmas of Empiricism," now considered a classic paper, Quine introduced a model of belief structure that he went on to develop and refine in his later work.[2] He referred to this model as "the web of belief." The basic idea behind Quine's model is that our beliefs are interrelated in a systematic way, much like a spider web. If you pick a location at any one point on the web, you can trace a path to any other point on the web.

Figure 1.1: Web of Belief

If we think of our beliefs like points on the web, then every belief is interrelated and interconnected. Quine says that a change in the web, such as when we come to hold a new belief or give up a belief that we held previously, will produce effects through the entire system. He notes, however, that not all changes are equal. Beliefs that are at the outer edge of the web or are on the periphery have less impact and are easier to change than beliefs at the core. But Quine says that in principle, all of our beliefs can be revised. The beliefs at the core are the ones that we are least likely to revise, though, even in the face of counterevidence. The beliefs at the periphery are the ones that we have very little problem giving up or changing.

To understand the difference between peripheral beliefs and core beliefs, think of something that you believe but don't feel strongly about or for which you do not have lots of convincing evidence. For instance, you might think that President Barack Obama is six feet two inches tall because you remember reading it somewhere, though you can't remember where exactly. Now imagine a friend, who is obsessed with details about the American presidency, mentioning to you that President Obama is six foot one. You say, "Are you sure? I remember reading that he was six foot two." Your friend replies, "According to the medical exam released by the White House press secretary on February 28, 2010, the president is 185 centimeters, or six foot one." If your inclination is to respond "Oh, okay then, I guess I was wrong," your response is evidence that your belief in Obama being six feet two inches tall existed on the periphery of your web of belief, and for that reason it is easy for you to revise your belief. According to Quine, this means that there will still be some effect on your overall web even if the belief was peripheral. You may, for instance, believe more strongly now that your memory for measurements isn't that great, or your belief that your friend is a reliable source for presidential information might increase. The point is that even though it was easy to revise that belief, it still has some effect on your whole system of belief.

Now, imagine a belief that lies at the core of your web—something that was established in your belief system early in your life, has been extremely well confirmed, and is centrally connected to many of your other beliefs. This could be something like believing that you know your own first name. If a friend tried to convince you that your name was really something other than what you say it is, you would most likely find those attempts to be futile. You would insist that you have a copy of your birth certificate, you have firsthand direct experience of being called the name since early childhood, your parents continue to use the name to reference you, and so on. That is, you have a much higher and more stringent standard for evidence when it comes to beliefs that are at the core of your belief system. You will work hard to discount or deny any counterevidence, according to Quine, because a change in a core belief will have very significant and far-reaching effects on your overall web of belief. In this way, Quine says, we are conservative about revising our beliefs. The term "conservative" in this sense is not political conservatism but rather conservative in terms of not being inclined to change things, of wanting to maintain the status quo. Quine argues that once we have acquired and integrated core beliefs, we hold tight to them and resist revising them to avoid having to reconsider almost everything we believe. That is why when something happens that causes us to eventually revise a firmly held core belief, many of us feel that we are no longer sure what to believe. People who have had the unfortunate experience of being deceived by someone they loved and trusted will often report that they were no longer able to trust their own judgment or the behavior of others. It is often difficult for us to accept evidence that will undermine a core belief because the readjustment to our entire system of belief is so substantial and far reaching.

Quine concludes that our reluctance to change and revise core beliefs is actually a very successful evolutionary strategy that we inherited from our early ancestors. The idea is that early humans who held tightly to beliefs such as fire is hot or cutting skin is bad had much better survival rates than those who needed to continue testing and challenging those beliefs. In this way, a kind of "mattering map" emerged in our system of beliefs.[3] What matters most lies at the core of our web, and what matters less lies at the periphery. Over time such beliefs as fire is hot and others having to do with pain and pleasure or basic survival emerged at the core for most humans. However, given that humans have also migrated and traveled to different parts of the Earth and faced different conditions and utilized different resources, different groups of people prioritized different kinds of beliefs. For people who settled in desert regions, for instance, beliefs about sand and heat and snakes would take priority over beliefs about rain and cold. For people in mountainous regions, beliefs about heights and the dangers of winds and storms could take priority over beliefs about water or sand. It is not the capacity to form beliefs and organize them in a weblike system that makes us different as humans. Rather, what differs to a greater or lesser extent is how human groups have prioritized some beliefs at the core, others at the periphery, and still others as an intermediary that links the core and the periphery together.

Thought Experiment: Assessing Your Beliefs

Thought experiments. Philosophers and other theorists use the phrase "thought experiment" to refer to a method for clarifying ideas and testing the implications of our beliefs. Thought experiments help us to understand our beliefs and concepts and also provide evidence for our conclusions.

Your web of belief. Here is a thought experiment for you to consider: Think of a belief you hold that you could easily give up if you were presented with some relevant evidence. In other words, describe a case where it is easy to imagine giving up that belief. Now, imagine a belief you hold that seems nearly impossible to give up. What kind of evidence would even come close to leading you to question that belief? The answers to these questions reveal what kinds of beliefs are on the periphery of your web and what kinds of beliefs are at the core.

So far, we have been outlining briefly how beliefs are formed and how they might vary across people and regions even if the mechanism for forming and organizing beliefs is something we share as humans. In all the examples we have considered so far, from the height of the president to your name to the conditions of deserts or mountains, the beliefs were based on perceptions and memories of perceptions. These kinds of beliefs are *empirical*, meaning that we justify or verify them through observation and direct experience. But we have other beliefs within our web that are not simply the result of observation and sensory experience but instead are the result of *inference* and *evaluation*. For example, if you believe that it is wrong to steal something from a friend, this belief was not simply the result of you observing that stealing from a friend is wrong. You may have observed a theft or may have seen someone who was visibly upset after a theft, but your belief that it is wrong is a *moral* judgment based on a set of *values* that you hold.

Like empirical beliefs, values are another kind of belief within our web. Values come in two varieties. The first variety—such as stealing is wrong—is a moral belief. Moral beliefs often lie at the core, which means that they are generally very difficult for us to revise. The second type of value, aesthetic judgments or matters of taste, can be located in the core, in the intermediary, or even on the periphery of the web. For instance, if you think that a particular hat looks good on you and then a friend with a better sense of fashion objects, you might have a very easy time giving up or revising your belief that the hat looks good. On the other hand, if you believe that it is morally wrong to harm an innocent child, then it will be almost impossible for you to give up that belief no matter the circumstances or the reasons someone might use to persuade you. This is because strong moral convictions often occupy the center of our web of belief. Again, your moral and aesthetic values, like your empirical beliefs, will be uniquely organized within your web because you have your own mattering map. Someone who cares deeply about aesthetic judgments, such as an art critic or a designer, will likely have more aesthetic values located in and near the core of her or his web and will argue passionately to preserve her or his aesthetic ideals. Someone who has little to no moral sense, such as a sociopath, will not have moral beliefs at the core of her or his web but instead will have beliefs about effective ways to control and manipulate others. What matters to you arises from your personal history, including your genetic and health history, your family of origin, your social system, your culture, your environment, and your own ability to think and reason. Not everyone's web looks alike, but it is important to note that we all seem to have some overlap in terms of beliefs and their location within our web. Our web will likely have more in common with our family, friends, and social groups than with strangers, but even still, if we can communicate to some extent with a person or group, we must share some overlap in our webs of belief.

As evidence of this, consider that most of us are convinced by the things we see or witness. We find it very hard to be dissuaded of something when it is right in front of our eyes. In addition, many of us are relatively peaceful, nonviolent people who go about our day without physically or even verbally abusing others. We are generally law abiding and honest in the sense that we go to school, work, and family gatherings without stealing things, physically harming people, or committing crimes. Of course, these kinds of things unfortunately do happen, but they are not the norm. Most of us are living our lives day to day sharing many of the same basic values and peacefully pursuing our goals. We may face moral dilemmas, but the fact that they are dilemmas is evidence that we have moral standards and are troubled by some choices we have to make. If we did not have some common core of values, moral dilemmas wouldn't bother us—we would just do what was most convenient or most beneficial to us personally. So while it is true that our empirical beliefs and value judgments differ, there are some important overlaps and commonalities that connect us all so that we generally make sense of the world and each other. Think about how much we all coordinate with each other when we are driving in traffic. Certainly accidents happen, but for the most part people observe traffic patterns, stop at red lights, go at green lights, and make room for cars that are entering and leaving the highway. Consider too how much we coordinate basic moral expectations. When we are at school or work, we respect other people's property, don't steal things off their desks, and don't raise our voices or physically harm the people we have to work with just because we may disagree with them. These kinds of behaviors may seem so obvious to you that you wouldn't count them as moral. Yet a basic commitment to respecting other people and the things that matter to them is a foundation for moral thinking and action.

When we are not able to effectively coordinate with other people and we fail to make sense of the world and each other, the impasse or incongruence gets much more attention than our steady stream of successes. The inability to make sense to each other undermines our very humanity, since meaningful communication distinguishes us from other animals. So when we can't understand each other or we contradict each other, it gets our attention. To not be understood, to not make sense to others, evokes strong reactions, from frustration and anger to sadness and despair. It is not surprising then that these points of conflict are often what stand out when people think about different belief systems. But what I hope I have established is that these kinds of conflicts, while significant, should not eclipse the fact that in many less emotionally charged ways, we collaborate, communicate, and cooperate every day with a whole host of people whose beliefs systems are not identical to our own.

Now that we have described the web of belief, the different positions in the web (core, intermediary, and peripheral), and empirical beliefs and value judgments, we have the start of a picture of belief acquisition and belief formation. You come to this book with your own unique web of belief. This web began to form when you were in your infancy and you were able to associate causes with effects. When you cried and someone answered your cries with food or comfort, you formed beliefs about the efficacy of crying. Shortly before your first birthday you began to understand words, and around that birthday you started to produce them.[4] Around eighteen months of age, your language changed in two ways: vocabulary growth increased, and you began to learn words at a rate of one every two waking hours—and you kept on learning at that rate or faster through adolescence.[5] Between the last part of your second year and the middle part of your third year, your language bloomed into fluent grammatical conversation. This happens so rapidly that it overwhelms the researchers who study language acquisition, and no one has yet worked out the exact sequence. Sentence length increases steadily, and because grammar is a combinatorial system, the number of syntactic or grammatical types of sentences increases exponentially, doubling every month and reaching the thousands before your third birthday.[6] At the same time your web of belief, sensitive to new data and new experiences, is forming and organizing these words, sentences, and ideas into a belief system.

The picture I have painted thus far traces the formation of our web of belief with our experiences in the world and our capacity to understand and express ourselves using language. Language, then, is the expression of our beliefs. This makes sense, because when I make a claim like "Today is Thursday," you assume that I believe that today is Thursday. Most everything we claim we believe unless we are intentionally being dishonest or trying to fool someone. Even if I say "I'm not sure whether I liked the movie," I am still expressing the belief that I am not sure whether I liked the movie. Our claims are so much an expression of our beliefs that when someone actually says outright that he or does believe something like "I believe that today is Thursday," it sounds as if that person is not certain. When we converse with each other, we assume that what someone says is what he or she believes. That is why if you ask a friend "Do you know what time it is?" and he responds with "I believe it is 2 p.m." rather than "It is

2 p.m.," you interpret him in the first case as being unsure and in the second case as simply believing it is 2 p.m. Our assertions and claims are expressions of the beliefs within our web of belief.

However, there are other ways to express beliefs without using language. Behavior is often an expression of what someone believes. If I say "I need a pen" and I begin looking in the drawers of my desk, you can correctly infer that I believe there is a pen in the drawer of my desk. If you see me order a strawberry ice cream cone, you infer that I believe that strawberry ice cream is tasty. I don't have to express these beliefs linguistically for you to determine that I have these beliefs. Similarly, if you ask me whether you can borrow my pen and I hand it over willingly, you can infer that I believe that it is easy to share my pen. However, if you ask to borrow my laptop and I hesitate and change the subject, you can reasonably come to the conclusion that I believe that it is difficult to share my laptop. That the pen is my property would be a more peripheral belief within my web, but that the laptop is my property would be more central. Because of the centrality of the belief, it would be difficult for me to change or give up the idea that my laptop is my property and mine alone. What is worth noting here is that we can determine beliefs not simply from what people say but by how they behave and react. Behaviors and reactions can sometimes reveal beliefs that we did not even consciously know we had.

For instance, if you never thought about lending your laptop to someone and a friend asked to borrow yours and you felt very uncomfortable, your reaction is evidence of a certain set of beliefs. These could include the belief that your laptop is not the kind of thing to be shared, that if something happened to your laptop there would be terrible consequences for you academically or professionally, or that there is confidential information on your laptop that should not be easily accessible to your friend. You may not have even realized that you held these beliefs until your friend asked to borrow the laptop. The situation prompted a reaction that revealed your feelings and your beliefs on an issue you had never considered. Moreover, you find that your beliefs are strong, which means they are closer to the core of your web than they are to the periphery. It can be surprising to discover that we hold beliefs, particularly strong beliefs, that previously we were not aware we held.

Researchers who study belief refer to these as "the cognitive unconscious."[7] They are not referring to the unconscious in the more traditional Freudian sense having to do with beliefs that are repressed because they are too aggressive or sexually inappropriate. Rather, *cognitive unconscious* refers to the presumptions, perceptions, and beliefs that cause us to make instantaneous and automatic judgments. David Myers, a psychologist who researches cognitive unconscious, explains that "subliminal priming, implicit memory, implicit priming, emotional processing, [and] nonverbal communication" are all "active areas of research" in cognitive science.[8] What many of these researchers are finding is that unconscious thought processes powerfully determine many aspects of our lives, from how we perceive and react to other people to how we make moral decisions.

In 1995, two social psychologists named Anthony Greenwald and Mahzarin Banajin proposed the idea that in addition to unconscious judgments, social behavior too may not always be under a person's conscious control.[9] They argued that much of our behavior is driven by stereotypes that operate automatically and therefore unconsciously. Greenwald and Banaji's research corresponds with a wide variety of studies that have found implicit bias and unconscious stereotyping to be operative in people's thinking. For example,

- When rating the quality of verbal skills as indicated by vocabulary definitions, evaluators rated the skills lower if they were told that an African American provided the definitions than if a white person provided them.[10]
- By randomly assigning different names to resumes, researchers showed that job applicants with "white-sounding names" were more likely to be interviewed for open positions than were equally qualified applicants with "African American-sounding names."[11]
- When symphony orchestras adopted "blind" auditions by using a screen to conceal candidates' identities, the hiring of women musicians increased. Blind auditions fostered impartiality by preventing assumptions that women musicians have "smaller techniques" and produce "poorer sound" from influencing evaluation.[12]
- Opposing perceptions of female gender roles with perceptions of leadership roles cause evaluators to assume that women will be less competent leaders. When women leaders provide clear evidence of their competence, thus violating traditional gender norms, evaluators perceive them to be less likable and are less likely to recommend them for hiring or promotion.[13]

In 1997 Banaji and Greenwalt developed the Implicit Association Test (IAT), a computer-based test that measures people's unconscious attitudes. Since then more than two hundred studies have been published using the IAT. Overall, the IAT has been shown to be both reliable and valid in detecting an individual's level of implicit bias.[14]

Project Implicit and the Implicit Association Test

Project Implicit was founded in 1998 by three scientists—Tony Greenwald (University of Washington), Mahzarin Banaji (Harvard University), and Brian Nosek (University of Virginia). The goal of the organization is to educate the public about implicit social cognition and to provide a "virtual laboratory"—a novel way for researchers to collect data on the Internet. In addition, Project Implicit provides consulting, education, and training services in implicit bias, diversity and inclusion, leadership, the application of science to practice, and innovation.

You can take an Implicit Association Test on an array of social identities, including gender, race, disability, religion, ethnicity, and sexuality. The tests can be found at https://implicit.harvard.edu /implicit/selectatest.html.

We will say more in chapter 3 about cognitive biases, but for now the important point I want to establish is that beliefs can be both conscious and unconscious. Because beliefs can operate at multiple levels of awareness, it is important to pay attention to our reactions so that we can assess the unconscious beliefs operating at different levels within our web of belief. Doing so will give us clearer insight into what we believe, the strength or confidence of our beliefs, and whether or not we are justified in our beliefs. Attention to conscious and unconscious beliefs is the first step in Socrates's injunction to know thyself.

Concepts and Cognitive Schemata

Now that we have an understanding of the web of belief, the locations within the web, and the existence of conscious and unconscious beliefs, I want to consider the matter of how we form concepts. By "concept" I mean the general idea that we derive or infer from particular instances. The formation of concepts is essential for humans in learning language. When we are babies, we are faced with lots and lots of different stimuli. The adults around us point to some of these stimuli, making noises in repeated patterns. So, for instance, when you were a baby the adults around you pointed to the object you were drinking out of and said "Cup!" On another occasion you may have been drinking out of an object that looked different from the previous one they called "Cup!" but yet they called this one "Cup!" too. Imagine you were taken out to a restaurant. Another totally different-looking object is handed to you with milk inside, and you are told "Cup!" If your developing brain treated each of these three instances as totally different, you would not learn that the adults were trying to communicate to you that "Cup!" means the object you drink out of but varies in terms of size, shape, and color.

Of course, you are not consciously thinking about what the adults are doing (or even that there are a variety of sizes, shapes, and colors to this thing called "cup"), but your human capacity for language means that you are capable of unconsciously processing a variety of stimuli into a coherent concept.[15] As we said in the previous section, by the age of three you will be a fluent speaker of the language, creating sentences with the word "cup" and identifying new examples of cups without being instructed by adults. You will correctly identify a cup you have never seen before when you are at a friend's house, for example, and by age four you will make almost no mistakes in distinguishing noncups from cups. In short, you will have successfully constructed the concept "cup" without anyone formally outlining the features of cups, the variety of cups, or the essence of what it is to be a cup. You were able to construct this concept because you had the cognitive capacity to extrapolate from a variety of cup experiences to some general features that made up what it is to be a cup. We should note that this ability has captivated philosophers all the way back to Socrates and Plato and more recently has been captivating cognitive psychologists, neuroscientists, software engineers, and artificial intelligence researchers. What captivates these scholars is how it is that humans can take in a finite amount of limited data and from this form unified concepts that allow us to identify new examples of the concept, all the while being unable to articulate just how it is that we do it.

For instance, if I asked you to identify the furniture in a room, you would be very good at picking out furniture from nonfurniture. You would point to the tables, chairs, bookshelves, and sofa. You would most likely not point to clothing, books, appliances, and plants. Yet if I asked you to define the word "furniture" or to tell me exactly the criteria you used to distinguish furniture from nonfurniture, you would have a hard time coming up with a standard that included all furniture but excluded all nonfurniture. If, for example, you said "Objects that are in the house," that would be too broad and include too many instances of nonfurniture. It would also be too narrow, because it would exclude patio furniture and office furniture. If you said "The movable objects in a room that make it fit for living and working" (the definition in the Oxford English Dictionary), that would include coffee cups and photographs and sweaters and a whole host of other things that we wouldn't call "furniture." The dictionary actually offers us very little in the way of explaining the procedures we use when we distinguish instances of a concept from noninstances. So, the puzzle is how do we do it, and how do we do it so effectively? Even though we may not be able to come up with an adequate account of how we identify furniture, we nevertheless have no problem identifying new examples of furniture, and we know just the kinds of things we will find if we go to a furniture store. This means that we are not merely memorizing a list of the furniture we have already encountered, because then we would not be able to recognize new examples. There is some general set of characteristics that instances of furniture share and that we have internalized even though we can't exactly say what they are.

Scholars who have been interested in how we form concepts have come up with different theories to explain the process, but what I want to emphasize is that we do in fact form these concepts, which are essential to organizing the variety of stimuli we encounter in the process of learning language.[16] In addition, many of our most basic and fundamental concepts, formed at a very early age, enable us to effectively identify instances of the concepts despite the fact that it is difficult or nearly impossible to articulate exactly the criteria we use. The proof of the effectiveness of the concept is not in a justification we can provide but in our ability to successfully communicate with others. If you ask me "How do you know your concept of cup is correct?" my best answer would be to show you all the ways I successfully ask, answer, and use cup-talk in my daily life.

Now that we have a sense of what concepts are and how we form concepts, I want to move to a related and somewhat more complex idea from cognitive psychology. This is the notion of a *cognitive schema.* Jeffrey Young, director of the Cognitive Therapy Center of New York, defines schemata (sing. schema) in the following way: "Cognitive schemata are extremely stable and enduring themes that develop during childhood and are elaborated upon throughout an individual's lifetime. Schemata serve as templates for processing later experience."[17]

So, schemata are more than concepts, since they not only help us to pick out and categorize things in the world but also carry our associations, memories, and expectations related to the concept. Your schema for furniture, for instance, would not only allow you to identify furniture but would also entail your unique furniture template. If your grandmother was a furniture maker, for example, and you were fortunate enough to be surrounded by objects she made, you would have a different furniture schema than someone who may have grown up with shoddy secondhand furniture that was a source of embarrassment for the family. Or like many of us, you may have a furniture schema that is neither particularly positive nor particularly negative but simply a mix of some fairly positive and negative associations, memories, and expectations. Furniture then would be a fairly neutral schema within your system of beliefs.

Thus far I have outlined a view of concepts and cognitive schemata that I would like us to add to our understanding of the web of belief. Not only do we have conscious and unconscious beliefs that we express through language and behavior, but underlying these are the concepts and cognitive schemata that give our web depth along with a unique texture and pattern. The picture of your web of belief that should be emerging is one where concepts, cognitive schemata, and beliefs interconnect in complex ways to form a pattern of your experiences and your expectations. The web is flexible and in principle is revisable but has a tendency to resist radical changes, particularly to core beliefs and concepts. You bring this web with you into every situation. It is your system of belief, and while it uniquely reflects your personal history, it also shares features with others who hold beliefs similar to your own. Each day we are faced with the task of keeping our web consistent, coherent, and intact as we interact with the world. We add new beliefs, we revise old beliefs, and we work to preserve our core beliefs, making minor adjustments here and there as we move along in life. Given our cognitive schemata, we may approach some situations with excitement, others with dread, and still others with boredom or anger. Our underlying concepts and cognitive schemata carry associated emotions, memories, and expectations that will affect how we interpret new data. Some of this will happen in our conscious awareness, and some of it will not be accessible to us consciously. However, if we attend to our behavior, our reactions, our expectations, and our language, we can come closer to understanding all the dimensions to our web. To invoke Socrates's famous injunction once more, we will *know ourselves*. This is the foundation of becoming an effective critical thinker.

However, this book is about becoming an intellectually empathic critical thinker with a particular focus on issues of social justice. Everything I have said so far about the web of belief, the formation of concepts and cognitive schemata, and the importance of knowing one's self seems to have very little to do with either social identity or social justice. But as I promised at the start of this chapter, we are moving in that direction. We needed first to establish a model of how individuals form and maintain beliefs before we could consider how group interaction affects and is affected by individual belief. As we move along in the book we will get into more and more controversial territory, requiring you to consider your beliefs about race, gender, sexual orientation, socioeconomic class, politics, religion, and morality. For now we will progress carefully into that territory, making sure that we have established some sure footing before getting into that tougher terrain.

With that in mind, I want to add one final element to our understanding of concepts and cognitive schemata that will help us on our way. This is the emotional dimension that is involved when we learn concepts and schemata. Earlier I used the example of a child forming the concept "furniture" while surrounded by high-quality hand-crafted furniture made by the child's grandmother. I compared this with the child learning the same concept surrounded by furniture that was a source of embarrassment for the family. The point of the examples was to highlight how both children could effectively learn the concept "furniture" while each formed different cognitive schemata. That is, the child in the first case, let's imagine, has more positive associations with furniture such as family pride, comfort, prestige, and capability, while the child in the second case has more negative associations such as shame, discomfort, and deficiency. Of course, we are imagining children at the extremes of the furniture-experience spectrum. Most of us do not have strong associations one way or the other with furniture generally even if there was a certain chair we loved or a certain table we hated. The point again in the examples was to distinguish the basic concept from the cognitive schema. The cognitive schema includes the *affective* aspects of a concept, including the mood, feeling, and attitudes associated with the concept. As Frank Dattillio, a professor of psychiatry at Harvard Medical School, explains, "Recent research has proposed the idea that emotion and cognition strongly interact and are only minimally decomposable in the brain, and that the neural basis of emotion and cognition should be viewed as more strongly non-modular than once thought."[18] What Dattillio means is that when we learn a concept and form a cognitive schema, there is a strong interaction with the content of our associated emotions. Emotion and cognition are nonmodular, meaning they should not be thought of as separate and distinct entities but rather as a unit. Concepts and cognitive schemata contain the meaning, the standards for usage, and the emotional content that underlie our beliefs about the world. Remember that if we were unable to form concepts and schemata, we would never make sense of the world or develop language.

With that in mind, consider two different young children learning the same concept but with a different cognitive schema. In this case it is the concept "dog." The first child comes from a family of dog lovers, and from a very early age she has had experiences playing with the family dog, being taken in her stroller to say hello to neighborhood dogs, and meeting friendly dogs on her trips to the park with her parents and siblings. When she is read children's books that feature dogs, the adults in her life make positive connections to her dog and to dogs known to the family. She has stuffed dog toys, and as she gets older she accompanies the family to animal shelters taking care of sick and abandoned dogs. From a very early age this child has experienced a whole host of different creatures that are all called "dogs" by the people around her. Some are very small, some are big, some are brown, some are white, some are short-haired, and some are spotted. Overall, the child experiences an incredible variety of instances. Nevertheless, by the age of four she is very accurate at picking out dogs from nondogs, a clear indication that she has successfully learned the concept.

Imagine now a second child who grows up in a family with a tragic history of a dog attack. This child's father was the unfortunate victim of an attack to his face, which left physical and emotional scars. Imagine too that the child's mother never had positive experiences with dogs, and so given her husband's past she shares his fear and trepidation. In this house there is no family dog, and when the child is taken for a stroll in the neighborhood or through the park, her parents are certain to avoid any dogs and remind their child to stay away from dogs. When she is read books that include dogs in the story, she is reminded that dogs can be very dangerous. The story of what happened to her father and other cautionary tales that the family has collected are repeated often. This child, like the first child, has seen a wide variety of dogs out in the world, in books, and on television shows. And like the first child, by the age of four the second child is perfectly adept at distinguishing dogs from nondogs, thus revealing her mastery of the concept.

Clearly, both children understand the concept "dog," but each will likely have a very different cognitive schema. The difference would not be obvious on a spelling test or in the way the children used the word "dog" in a sentence. Rather, it would play out in the choice to approach a dog as opposed to avoiding one. It could be detected in the big smile and increased endorphins (feel-good hormones) for the first girl when she encounters a dog and the anxious expression and release of adrenaline (high-stress hormones) for the second girl.

The difference in their cognitive schema will affect the kinds of decisions each girl will make related to dogs as well as how they take in new information about dogs as they grow and mature. If the love for or fear of dogs is located close to the core of their webs of belief, then they will each have a strong inclination to preserve that belief in light of counterevidence. In other words, the girl who has come to believe that dogs are wonderful will seek out experiences to reconfirm that belief while discounting experiences that refute it, and the girl who has come to fear dogs will do the same. This tendency to emphasize experiences that confirm our strongly held beliefs while ignoring experiences that disconfirm them is known as *confirmation bias.* Confirmation bias is one of the most well-established *cognitive biases* documented in the psychological literature. Cognitive bias refers to a consistent pattern of thinking that results in poor reasoning. We will look closely at cognitive biases and the related notion of *logical fallacies* in chapters 4 and 5, but for now I simply want to make the connection between a resistance to revising core beliefs and the phenomenon of confirmation bias. Given that we are, as Quine noted, conservative with regard to radically revising our web of belief, it makes sense that confirmation bias is so pervasive. We tend to pay attention to information and experiences that make our web of belief stronger and more consistent, and we discount or ignore those that do the opposite. The problem is that in the process of maintaining our web and all of its connections, we may be missing out on important evidence. The challenge then is how to maintain a coherent web while still paying attention to information or experiences that may feel uncomfortable or unnecessary. I say "uncomfortable" and "unnecessary" rather than "false" because given the emotional content associated with our cognitive schemata, we may be overlooking important evidence. Our tendency toward confirmation bias is a tendency to hold on not only to the content of our beliefs but also the emotions and expectations associated with those beliefs. And when it comes to our beliefs about social identities such as race, gender, sexual orientation, class, religion, etc., the interaction between content and emotion is strong and sometimes volatile. For this reason, these are some of the most difficult beliefs for us to examine critically and empathetically.

Forming and Preserving Social Beliefs

So far the beliefs, concepts, and cognitive schemata that we have considered such as "cup," "furniture," and "dog" have had very little to do with social differences and social justice. These concepts are fairly neutral in the sense that they do not generally carry significant emotional content for most people. We started with these to get a sense of the process of concept and schemata formation. Now I want us to consider self-identity and group identity concepts. These carry far more emotional content because our sense of who we are as both individuals and members of various social groups relates directly to our self-esteem and self-understanding. One of the pioneers of social identity theory was the British psychologist Henri

Tajfel, who suggested that people identify with groups so as to *maximize positive distinctiveness*.[19] What this means is that our identification with particular social groups helps us to understand who we are while also making us feel good about who we are.

Social identity begins when we are very young as we are encouraged through language and behavior to identify with a specific gender, ethnicity, and religion. However, social identity is not fixed or absolute. Robin Cohen, a social scientist who has studied globalization and migration effects on identity, writes that "One can be Muslim in the Mosque, Asian in the street, Asian British at political hustlings and British when travelling abroad, all in a single day."[20] What Cohen is noting is that our identities can look and feel different within and outside of our home environments.

Many aspects of our social identity we did not choose, such as our gender, race, ethnicity, religion, and physical ability. These aspects of our identity are derived from a social history and are ascribed to us when we are very young. This does not mean that we cannot take great pride in these identities, only that they were shaped and attributed to us before we had a chance to shape them ourselves. In this way, social identity is relational. It does not come simply from within the individual. Social identity develops as a relationship between individuals, groups, and the wider world.

It is shocking sometimes for an individual to discover that her or his sense of self-identity does not match up with the way that the wider world perceives them. The young girl who hears a coach call a group of boys "ladies" as a put-down is learning that her sense of her own capability as a girl is not shared by the wider world. Along the same lines, the biracial child who discovers that he is only seen as one race by the wider world must find a way to navigate his sense of self with how others see him. So, we are not totally in control of our identities, given that the world will impose some aspects of our identities upon us. But we are also not locked into all of our identities, since we do have some control over what will become significant for us and how we will *maximize our positive distinctiveness*.

Adolescence is a time when many of us wrestle with our social identity and work to shape, transform, give up, and try on new identities. Language again is an important part of this process, as young people develop subcultures with specific words and phrases to identify with each other and apart from the adults in their lives.[21] This period of time is an opportunity to affirm some of the identities ascribed to us when we were children but also to create new ways of being. The process of maintaining and expressing our social identities continues throughout our lives as we move through different experiences. This is not to say, though, that our social identity is not stable. Social psychologists argue that even though we may present ourselves in different ways and highlight different aspects of our identity in different circumstances, we nevertheless view ourselves and others in pretty consistent terms and actively seek out situations that support our social identities.[22]

So, beliefs, concepts, and cognitive schemata related to our self-identity and group identity are also closely linked to our self-understanding and self-esteem. These are about the most personal kinds of beliefs we have, so when they become the topic for debate this can put us in a very vulnerable position. It is difficult to distinguish the content of our beliefs from the strong emotional associations that played a role in forming those beliefs. Furthermore, if our identification with groups is motivated by a need to maximize positive distinctiveness, then that process may have included minimizing the positive distinctiveness of groups other than our own.

For instance, consider that many adults teach values to children by comparing those who live by those values with those who do not. This is not in and of itself a bad thing, since comparisons and evaluations are part of teaching and learning. If I want my child to understand the value of honesty, I can tell him stories of people who have been dishonest along with the negative consequences they and others suffered. In so doing I am distinguishing honest people from dishonest people and strongly recommending that he identify with those who are honest. In fact, most moral education involves making comparisons between those who have been moral and those who have not. Families, communities, and even nations set goals for behavior and impart these goals to their members by drawing comparisons between right ways of behaving and wrong ways. So again, this in and of itself is not necessarily a bad thing. The problem arises when we shift from teaching right and wrong by comparing the actions that people may take to promoting positive group identity by putting down those groups other than our own. If I teach my son that honesty is better than dishonesty by positively evaluating those who are honest and negatively evaluating those who are dishonest, this is very different from taking the further step of saying that people "like us" are honest and people "not like us" are dishonest (however "like us" and "not like us" are defined). In this latter case I am attributing a negative characteristic to an entire group of people without providing any evidence that they in fact engage in that behavior. And that kind of evidence, that everyone in the group behaves a particular way, would be impossible for me to even obtain.

Yet in countless conscious and unconscious ways, adults impart values and maximize positive group identification for children by shifting their language from right and wrong action to good and bad people. "Those people" are categorized not by their actual behavior but rather by their membership within a group that is said to *typically* exhibit that behavior. This shift is an empirical cheat. The parent who says to a child "People like us are hardworking and those other people just want everything handed to them," for example, is not simply instilling the value of hard work but drawing a sharp distinction between themselves and "those other people." Rather than doing the work of providing evidence of actual people's actual behavior, adults can positively promote the characteristics and groups they want children to identify with by attributing negative characteristics to "those other people." In addition, social systems surrounding us, including the media, can reinforce these positive and negative group identifications by presenting images without any real evidence.

This, as you may have already figured out, is what is known as *social stereotyping*. Assuming that members of a group typically engage in a particular behavior just because they happen to belong to that group, rather than providing evidence of their behavior, is an unjustified assumption. Stereotypes can be positive or negative, and in some cases members of a group may even take pride in the stereotype attributed to them. However, even if it is positive or happily accepted, the stereotype is no more justified than if it was negative or denied.

Thought Experiment: Positive Group Distinctiveness in Your Own Life

List the social identities that you distinguish as your own. These can include gender, race, age, ethnicity, religion, socioeconomic class, ability, disability, sexual orientation, family status (e.g., married, parent, only child), or any other social identity that matters to you. Now consider how it is that your identity as a member of this group was and is positively reinforced by your family, your community, your schools, political leaders, media images, and businesses. Do any of these influential factors promote your positive group identification by comparing your group to the negative qualities of another group? Can you think of examples from childhood or from adolescence? Can you think of current examples?

If we return to our earlier discussion of concepts and cognitive schemata, we saw that it is a very natural and even necessary part of human language development for us to organize the complex array of inputs and stimuli into coherent categories. In addition, we noted that in so doing there are associated moods, feelings, and expectations that play a role in the construction of those categories. Finally, we recognized that this happens early in our development and involves processes and criteria that we cannot adequately articulate even while we are capable of effectively employing them. If we connect these points with what we have said so far about social stereotyping, we can begin to see how natural it is for children to take in explicit and implicit cues from the world around them to build concepts and schemata not simply about objects and events but also about social groups and social values. As noted earlier, families, communities, and even nations strive to impart values to children as well as adult citizens and in so doing sometimes take unjustified shortcuts that are emotionally loaded with positive and negative connotations. Given that our sense of self-identity and self-esteem is tied up with our social identity, it follows that social schemata will be close to the core of our web of belief, infused with a particular blend of complex and sensitive emotions and constrained by the set of examples and experiences that made up our formative years.

It is not surprising, then, that when a debate arises that puts these beliefs in the spotlight, our ability to reason calmly and effectively may be tested. We have a whole host of cognitive and emotional pressures working against revising these beliefs while simultaneously demanding that we protect our self-esteem. Under these conditions, it makes sense that we would lack the motivation to dispassionately assess whether our beliefs are in fact true, relevant to the issue at hand, and justified. Instead, many of us preserve our existing beliefs by going on the offensive and attacking challengers or alternatively withdrawing from the debate and thereby silently refusing to subject our beliefs to scrutiny. This is the fight-or-flight dichotomy described in the introduction and is so common in debates having to do with social identity.

To see how this process unfolds, think about a child growing up in a heterosexual household with adults who believe that same-sex relationships are morally wrong. Let's imagine that the adults do not overtly praise heterosexual behavior and go out of their way to explicitly put down same-sex couples. Rather, when encountering gay, lesbian, or bisexual couples either in the local community or in the media, the parents say things like "Well, that's sad. Such an attractive woman" or "I didn't realize he was one of those" or "That's sick." The child developing the concepts for "family," "normalcy," and "healthy" will strive to make her or his cognitive schema consistent with the values and the emotions conveyed in the family's comments and reactions. Moreover, every time a heterosexual relationship is treated as normal or explicitly positive in the family, as in the case of prom dates, engagement parties, wedding celebrations, and anniversaries, the child is presented with data that reaffirm the values and good feelings associated with heterosexuality. When, for example, a boy child hears "That is so cute!" in response to holding the hand of a young female friend but "Stop that!" in response to doing the same with a boy, he has to incorporate those responses into his web of belief in such a way that the seeming inconsistency works out to be consistent.

Framing all of these particular experiences for the child is a wider culture that reaffirms much of what he is picking up from the adults in his life. Heterosexuality is treated as the norm in the books, fairy tales, movies, and television shows he encounters. If we imagine that he is part of a religious community where heterosexuality is understood to be good and same-sex orientation is considered immoral, then he will be presented with even more data reaffirming his cognitive schema.

In presenting this case, I have tried to construct a scenario where the beliefs and attitudes affecting this child's conceptual development are clear but not necessarily extreme. Unlike the examples of the dog-loving and dog-fearing families, in this case the attitudes are not so overt. Yet they are clearly there, and in addition, unlike those more extreme cases, they are significantly reinforced by the wider culture at large. The reason I wanted to make this case less overt is to illustrate how much meaning families, communities, and the culture at large can convey to children without having to explicitly announce their intentions. Noam Chomsky, one of the most important linguists of the twentieth century, describes young children as "little linguists" making highly theoretical hypotheses about their language and then testing these hypotheses against the data provided by the language and behavior of those around them.[23] People sometimes refer to children as little sponges, absorbing everything around them. Chomsky's description of the little linguist provides a more accurate picture, since children do not simply absorb the words, moods, feelings, and actions surrounding them but instead construct and organize that data into a coherent weblike system of concepts and cognitive schemata. And as we have established, when this process involves social group identities, the interaction between belief and emotion is particularly strong.

Fast-forward to the future and imagine that this child is now a young heterosexual adult who has incorporated the beliefs and attitudes about sexuality derived from his family, his community, and his culture. Assuming that he has not had to face a challenge to these beliefs either personally or publicly, he will most likely maintain what he believes without much need for reflection. He will take these beliefs to be normal so much so that he will have a hard time seeing how they privilege one group of people over another. When he holds his girlfriend's hand in public, he will not see this as a social privilege but as simply normal behavior. When he considers the possibility of getting married, the thought that this is a right afforded to heterosexuals but not to same-sex couples will not occur to him. Yet the very same behaviors and considerations are fraught with anxiety and uncertainty for people who identify as gay, lesbian, or bisexual.

The inability to see how our social identities are also socially privileged is what Professor Peggy McIntosh, associate director of the Center for Research on Women at Wellesley College, calls the "ignorance of privilege." In her now famous essay "White Privilege and Male Privilege: A Personal Account of Coming to See Correspondence through Work in Women's Studies," published in 1988, McIntosh explains that social privilege is "like an invisible weightless knapsack of special provisions, maps, passports, codebooks, visas, clothes, tools and blank checks."[24] McIntosh emphasizes that these privileges are not distributed equally in American society, nor are they shared with those who do not have the same social identities. So, for example, a heterosexual identity is privileged in our society in ways that a same-sex sexual orientation is not. The privileges associated with heterosexuality are often invisible to those who have them because they take the support, freedoms, rights, and cultural approval of their sexuality to be simply normal, or just the way things are.

We will say quite a bit more about social privilege in the remainder of this book, but for now I want to emphasize that when we develop our social identities, some of what we identify with carries social privilege along with the emotional and cognitive elements that are part of forming our self-schema. The young boy we were imagining earlier who was shown approval for holding a girl's hand but not a boy's hand was taking in information and processing verbal and behavioral cues from his family, his friends, and the wider culture around him. In countless nonexplicit ways, he was receiving the message that heterosexuality is right and normal and same-sex relationships are not. If he eventually comes to identify as heterosexual and finds himself attracted to a specific girl, there are countless cultural mechanisms in place to foster that identity and positively explain the attraction. Of course, this doesn't mean that he will necessarily be happy or that his affection will be returned. Rather, any frustration or unhappiness he experiences related to romance will be limited to the very personal and particular facts having to do with him and the object of his affection. This is unlike the gay or bisexual adolescent, for instance, who will worry not just about whether he has a chance with a boy he likes but whether the expression of his affection will put him at risk of losing family support, friendships, and social acceptance.

For the heterosexual boy, the fact that he does not have the same worries is part of his *invisible knapsack of privilege*. He travels through family, school, and social circumstances with a greater ease not having to stop and present his credentials at various social checkpoints. Since social privilege lends ease to social movement, when it is operative it generally does not feel like anything special. When your car is in good working condition, for example, you think a lot less about the privilege of having a working car than you do when it is not working and your daily routine is disrupted.

Social Privilege

Understanding social privilege requires thinking about how some people have advantages in everyday ways that are not the result of hard work or merit. For example, if you are Christian in the United States, you have unearned benefits based simply on your religious identity. Because you are Christian, your holidays (i.e., Christmas, Easter) are nationally recognized, observed by most businesses and public institutions, and considered integral to the nation's history. If you ran for political office, your religion would not be held against you (assuming that your Christian denomination was considered mainstream). If you moved around the United States, it would not be difficult for you to find a religious community. Unlike atheists and adherents to non-Christian religions, you do not have to generally explain or defend your religious identity, you do not have to fear that you will be targeted because of your religious beliefs, and you can safely and openly observe your religion. While these benefits may simply feel normal to you and not particularly special, they are nevertheless not shared equally with non-Christians. These benefits accrue to you not because you earned them but because they have been systematically maintained and reinforced by our educational, political, and economic institutions. Is this an attack on your religious beliefs? Absolutely not. Rather, by identifying social privilege, we can begin to see how what is normal for some people is actually a systematic social benefit that disadvantages others. Being Christian should not be an assumed requirement for holding political office in the United States, just as being Hindu or atheist should not be a political liability.

The invisibility of social privilege combined with the strong cognitive and emotional elements within our web of belief can work together to reinforce confirmation biases. If we take our experiences as normal rather than unique to our personal history and culture while incorporating stereotypical messages about people who are not like us, we have little incentive to challenge our beliefs. Instead, we will most likely seek out others who share our experiences, thus reconfirming our beliefs and discounting data that might challenge beliefs close to our core. The problem with this is that while it might be a good strategy for basic beliefs about our own survival, such as "fire is hot," it is a very ineffective strategy for dealing with complex social issues. We have inherited a history of unjust social policies, stereotyping, privilege, and social disadvantage, despite the gains of the civil rights, women's rights, and gay and lesbian rights movements. While some of the most unjust social practices are now illegal, racism, sexism, homophobia, religious bigotry, and class conflict still poison our public debates and our social policies. When these issues come up in educational and professional settings, it can lead people to feeling anxious on one end of the spectrum and bored on the other: anxious because we fear we will be called upon to voice an opinion on one of these topics, upsetting someone in the room, or bored because the same old tired clichés of "can't we all just get along" will be trotted out without any real substantive discussion or analysis. The problem is that we don't really have adequate tools for *thinking critically* about these issues while also treating others and ourselves with compassion in the process.

We began this chapter with the model of the web of belief. We considered how beliefs as well as the cognitive and emotional content within our concepts and schemata are organized within the web. We recognized the human tendency toward confirmation bias, and we considered how together with the invisibility of social privilege these could make it hard for us to seek out evidence that might disconfirm our social stereotypes. With all of this in mind let's now move to chapter 2, where we will look much more closely at social beliefs in the context of real-world social circumstances. As the discussion progresses, the skills for being an intellectually empathic thinker will be outlined, giving us the tools we need for thinking critically and communicating effectively when the issue is social differences.

Questions for Review

1. Describe the web of belief in your own words. What qualities do beliefs at the center of the web have that make them different from beliefs at the periphery?

2. What does it mean to say that we are conservative with regard to changing our beliefs? How does this relate to confirmation bias?

3. How is behavior an indication of unconscious beliefs and attitudes? How do researchers test our implicit biases?

4. Describe the process of forming concepts from particular examples. Why is this not simply memorization?

5. What are cognitive schemata? How does the formation of cognitive schemata enrich our understanding and expectations about concepts?

6. What does it mean to maximize positive distinctiveness?

Questions for Further Thinking and Writing

1. After taking one of the IAT tests, consider the following questions. Did the IAT reveal something that surprises you? What reasons would you give to account for your results?

2. In what ways is your self-identity constructed from the inside out (by you) and the outside in (by the social and structural factors within which you live)? Describe this process, focusing on a particular aspect of your social identity. How much control do you feel you have when it comes to expressing and developing this aspect of your identity? In what ways do social and structural factors impede or interfere with your sense of this social identity?

Additional Resources

The Implicit Bias and Philosophy Research Project, http://www.biasproject.org, is an excellent online resource for scholars, researchers, publications, workshops, and news and information related to implicit bias and philosophy.

Peggy McIntosh, the author of "White Privilege: Unpacking the Invisible Backpack" and a pioneer in the field of social privilege and justice, has a web page at http://www.wcwonline.org/Active-Researchers/peggy-mcintosh-phd on the Wellesley Center for Women's website. There you can find her bio, links to the SEED (Seeking Educational Equity & Diversity) project, and news and information as well as her recent and past articles.

In addition, McIntosh has a TED-x talk available online titled "How Studying Systems of Privilege Can Strengthen Compassion," at http://tedxtalks.ted.com /video/How-Studying-Privilege-Systems;search%3Atag%3A%22tedxtimber laneschools%22, that provides a very thought-provoking overview of some of her central ideas.

2 | The Usual Suspects: Keeping People Engaged

Wouldn't a Color-Blind World Be Ideal?

When you hear the words "diversity" and "inclusion," what do you think? Do they strike you as important ideas worth promoting? Or do they instead seem like simple-minded buzzwords used by naive do-gooders? If you are like some people, they may remind you of mandatory work policies designed to increase race and gender quotas. For still others there is an even stronger reaction, like the one that Michael S. Berliner, a former director of the Ayn Rand Institute, and Gary Hull, a professor at Duke University and an expert on Rand's philosophy, share: "Advocates of 'diversity' are true racists in the basic meaning of that term: they see the world through colored lenses, colored by race and gender. To the multiculturalist, race is what counts—for values, for thinking, for human identity in general. No wonder racism is increasing: colorblindness is now considered evil, if not impossible. No wonder people don't treat each other as individuals: to the multiculturalist, they aren't."[1]

Berliner and Hull's response to diversity is that it promotes racism, since diversity advocates insist on seeing the world through race-colored lenses. Their objective is to encourage us to see each other as unique individuals whereby color blindness is a virtue. This *ultimate* goal is one that I would endorse. However, where I would strongly disagree with Berliner and Hull is in their construal of diversity as being concerned solely or most significantly with race and their assumption that we can become color-blind just by willing ourselves so.

Diversity, for the purposes of developing intellectual empathy, will refer to the value of incorporating a range of varied standpoints and perspectives in the pursuit of knowledge and social justice. This range certainly includes race as well as gender, but it should also include socioeconomic class, religion, physical disability, ability, sexual orientation, education level, and age. We will understand diversity in a more complex sense than simply racial diversity. We will also work under the assumption that human beings form cognitive schemata relative to their social experiences and surrounding stereotypes. Race identity, gender identity, and religious identity—in fact all social identities—have clear markers, or indicators, that play a part in how we learn about particular identities. As a child learning about people, there are clear indicators as to what constitutes "female" and what constitutes "male," from physical appearance, clothing options, and styles to family roles and job types. All of these are indicators of social identity. If a child did not see the world through a gendered lens, he or she would have a hard time communicating effectively about the people who make up his or her world. From using restrooms to following instructions about lining up boys on one side and girls on the other, the child would be conceptually and linguistically deficient (in our culture) if he or she were unable to form gender categories.

Now, I agree that it would be ideal if the world were not so clearly divided along gender lines. Imagine a world where the first question people asked when they hear about the birth of a new baby was not "Is it a boy or a girl?" but rather "How are you all feeling?" or "Tell us all about the baby's eyes." No doubt it would be a different world if each person were considered to be a unique individual known solely by her or his own particular characteristics. However, while that world might be different and even ideal, it is nevertheless far removed from the one we live in. Gender, race, religion, ethnicity, etc., are all categories of identity not simply because categorizing is natural and even essential for language learning but because these categories also have a moral and political history. Let me make very clear here that I am not saying the categories of social identity that make up our world and our beliefs are logically necessary or inevitable. Rather, what I want to make clear is that while categorizing is natural to language learning, the categories that we have learned are variable and subject to social, political, religious, and cultural influences.

For example, though our brains may organize stimuli into conceptual schemata, it is not necessary that "male" or "female" had to emerge as the only and most primary identifiers for an infant. The limited binary notions of male and female are not essential for understanding and communicating identities and relationships between people. In some Native American communities, for example, two-spirit people are those who are identified not as either male or female but instead as people who uniquely integrate aspects of both masculinity and femininity. Harlan Pruden and Melissa Hoskins, cochairs of the NorthEast Two-Spirit Society, write that

On the land we know as North America, there were approximately 400 distinct indigenous Nations. Of that number, 155 have documented multiple gender traditions. Two Spirit is a contemporary term that refers to those traditions where some individuals are a blending of male and female spirit. The existence of Two Spirit people challenges the rigid binary view of the world of the North American colonizers and missionaries, not just of a binary gender system, but a binary of this or that, all together.[2]

What we can all learn from the challenge that two-spirit people raise for the gender binary is that the way we organize the world through our language and our experience is particular to our history and inherited values. And this system of organization could still be changed and revised. The particular conceptual constructions of gender, race, class, etc., that we use are not the only ones ever used by humans, but they are the ones that we have inherited, and we cannot just pretend that they don't play a role in our system of belief. These categories are necessary for us to understand our history, our economic policies, our politics, and even our art. They are both a source of pride and a source of oppression and injustice. And it is often those people in the most socially privileged positions who, as we established in chapter 1, fail to see their own social identity. When your identity conforms to established social values, you may not even notice that you have a social identity. As we said, it just feels normal. Yet when your identity does not conform to social norms, you can suffer the indignities and injustices of undeserved social disadvantage.

It is not surprising, then, that many of the calls for a color-blind society often come from those who benefit from social privilege.[3] For example, being white and being male have a long history in the United States of being associated with intelligence, competence, leadership, authority, and moral goodness. (We can complicate this history by including social class, religion, and ethnicity, but for now we will think in broad social categories.) White men have had the opportunity to earn more financially than women and nonwhites, have held more positions of leadership, were the majority of students at the best schools, were held up as ideals of civility, and controlled most of the resources. None of these benefits afforded to white men required regular public announcements declaring that "white men are the best" (though clearly throughout our history women and nonwhite men were regularly declared incompetent or less than human). Rather, white men shown effectively managing education, economics, politics, art, and religion filled every history book, political election, business model, and, in more recent history, media and television. Women and nonwhite men were historically either absent or if portrayed at all were shown in a negative or oversimplified way. Any women or nonwhite men who succeeded were considered exceptional and a credit to their kind. All the while, the success of white men was attributed to their individual merit and ability, not to society being set up in such a way so as to provide benefits and opportunities to white men and obstacles to men of color as well as to women.

If you, as a white man, began to hear men of color and women raising objections about how a person's race or gender should not be a factor in whether or not the person received rights and benefits, it would be in your interest as a white man to downplay the benefits afforded to white men and agree that race and gender are irrelevant. You could insist that the advantages white men have has nothing to do with special privileges but rather individual hard work and merit. The fact that white men earn more, live in better areas, are arrested less, and have access to better education, resources, etc., is coincidental to being white and male. The fact that African Americans, for example, generally live in poorer areas, earn less, get arrested more, and have less access to education and resources has nothing to do with their being black. You sincerely believe that this difference is the result of the bad choices and lack of hard work of these particular individuals.

Under these conditions, it is not hard to see why you, as a white man, would want to shift the focus to who a person "really is" and not her or his "race or gender," since you are gaining unfair advantages just on the basis of your skin color and sex. It is also not hard to imagine that you do not actually see that you have these advantages, since you think of yourself as an individual and not a member of a social group. In fact, if men of color and women still insisted that race and gender were factors pushing you forward and holding them back, you could go on to accuse them of being obsessed with skin color and genitalia and argue that they are polarizing the society with their gender and race labels. In so doing you shift the charge of bias onto them, thereby allowing yourself to go on reaping the unfair advantages. In this way, downplaying social properties that have nothing to do with merit but nevertheless factor into the society's distribution of rights and goods lets you maintain your advantages while disparaging the disadvantaged group further by portraying its members as irrational and consumed with an arbitrary social factor.

Given this, it is important to ask who benefits and who loses when we insist that we don't see color or that we only judge people on the basis of their personality and not their social properties. Such thinking can make it more difficult to identify when social biases actually are operative, thus making the issue more volatile because it remains hidden and poorly understood. Moreover, it might be that our insistence on race or gender or religion being not such a big deal means that we silence those who are disadvantaged on the basis of those very same social properties. If we sincerely want to eliminate unfair practices, we should at least be committed to hearing from those who say they are being treated unfairly so that we can evaluate their claims. This doesn't mean that every charge of bias or discrimination is legitimate, only that we have to begin with a presumption in favor of those who claim bias rather than turning their reports against them as examples *of* bias. Such a move not only hides potentially relevant data but also harms those who put their credibility on the line for the sake of righting a social wrong. Those who are willing to take that risk should have our respectful attention, and their claims should be carefully considered both for the evidence they may provide and the credibility they deserve.

Presumption in Favor and Burden of Proof

In logic and critical thinking, we begin by assuming that claims are true unless we have reason to believe otherwise. So, if you missed a class or a meeting and you ask someone who was there what you missed, you assume that the information he or she gives you is true unless (1) you have evidence that this person has a history of lying or reporting unreliably, (2) the person's report conflicts with common knowledge and your personal experience, or (3) you receive a conflicting report from someone who was there and is equally reliable. If none of these three conditions are met, you should believe the report. This is known as *presumption in favor* of the report. And this is in fact how most of us operate. If you question the report without any of these conditions having arisen, then the *burden of proof* is on you to show why the report could be potentially questionable. You saying "Well, I just don't believe it" is not sufficient.

The desire for a color-blind world, then, is not in and of itself a bad thing. Nor is it bad to want people to be judged solely on the basis of their character and merit. However, it is either naive or arrogant to think that we can eliminate racial and gender bias by just wishing our belief system and our history away. We have to deconstruct the concepts and schemata we have inherited, including their emotional aspects, before we can reconstruct them and our society into something that is truer to the evidence and more socially just. To do this effectively, we have to hear the perspectives of a wide variety of people, especially people who have different experiences, so as to gain relevant evidence about their experiences as well as our own. Given the human tendency toward confirmation bias (see chapter 1), we have most likely not put ourselves in a position to challenge our social concepts and schemata. Diversity initiatives are one effort at doing this. Yet even people who would not equate diversity with racism might still be tired of hearing about diversity initiatives. To see why this might be so, consider the following scenario.

Diversity Fatigue: Eric and Cassandra

It is the evening of a new parent orientation at a local public middle school in a metropolitan region of the United States. As people help themselves to coffee and doughnuts, the principal politely asks for everyone's attention so that she can go over expectations and daily schedules. After some discussion about bus routes and lockers, the principal shifts gears to talk about the issue of diversity and inclusion in the district and in the school. She mentions that the school has a Multicultural Day event and emphasizes the value of difference among the students and in the larger community. The principal is looking for volunteers who would be interested in contributing to Multicultural Day events and asks if anyone would be willing to serve on a diversity and inclusion committee.

Eric, a white, Christian, working-class man and parent of two children, sips his coffee and thinks, "Here we go again. Not only do I have to hear about 'diversity' at work, but I have to hear about it at my kid's school." Eric is tired of discussions about diversity, because in his experience they are either about how hard other people have it or how good he supposedly has it. He has heard that as a white heterosexual male, he is socially privileged and has advantages unavailable to most every other social group. Eric, a divorced father who is struggling to maintain strong connections with his children both emotionally and financially, is also contending with caring for his aging parents. He also works in manufacturing, and his company has downsized as a result of the recession. Eric has already faced salary cuts, and he worries daily about holding on to his job. In addition, he is also in an alcohol recovery program and has dedicated himself to remaining sober despite the various stresses in his life. When Eric hears about the advantages that he apparently has as a white heterosexual male, he doesn't see it. His life feels hard, and his struggles are real.

Sitting in the same room is Cassandra. When she hears the principal mention diversity and inclusion, she too thinks "Here we go again." Cassandra is a middle-class biracial woman in a committed relationship with another woman and is also a mother. She had her son while she was still in high school and is no longer in contact with her child's father. Through the years Cassandra has had a lot of help from her own mother, which made it possible for Cassandra to finish college and earn a nursing degree. In Cassandra's experience, when community events highlighting diversity and inclusion are being planned, she is sought after as if she were the voice for all people of color or for the lesbian, gay, bisexual, and transgendered (LGBT) community. These kinds of events frustrate Cassandra, because she feels that her social identity should not be reduced to a simple set of categories. Also, the same people who seem to seek her out at work or in her son's school when diversity is the focus are nowhere to be found when it comes to inviting her and her current partner or her son to social events and birthday parties. Cassandra does not expect to become friends with the people at her son's school. Some families may politely acknowledge her and her partner at school functions, others will ignore them, and a few others might even be outright hostile. But Cassandra is used to this and does her best to protect her son from any negative consequences. Meanwhile, she is glad to have a good job and a close-knit community of friends outside of school and work who are like family to her and her partner and her son, particularly because she faced a variety of obstacles growing up, including racism, sexism, and discrimination based on her sexuality. Over the years Cassandra built up a supportive network mostly through her membership in a local Unitarian church. In addition, Cassandra's mother continues to play an important role in her daughter's and grandson's lives. Aside from stresses about money and how to keep her son happy and healthy, Cassandra has a lot in her life for which she is thankful. While she recognizes that her life is complicated, and though she often faces social injustices, she would prefer that less lip service was paid to diversity and inclusion and that more time was spent on addressing wage inequities, the prison-industrial complex, and climate change.

Though Cassandra and Eric are both parents sitting in the same room with some of the same concerns, it is reasonable to imagine that they might not ever take the chance in this forum to openly share their concerns about diversity. In fact, it is not unreasonable to imagine that most of the other people in the room, including the principal and the organizers of the Diversity Day event, will ever get the chance to hear what Eric and Cassandra are thinking. This is because Eric and Cassandra are suffering from what we will call *diversity fatigue*. Though it has set in for each of them for very different reasons, the outcome is the same. Eric and Cassandra are tired of hearing about diversity and inclusion because they don't identify with the social roles that seem to frame the discussion. Eric, a white heterosexual working-class male, does not feel particularly privileged because his life is filled with multiple stresses and anxieties. Cassandra, a biracial middle-class single mother who is currently dating a woman, does not feel a strong sense of identity as a person of color or a member of the LGBT community as a whole. With an African American mother and a white father whom she saw little of growing up, Cassandra has not come to identify strongly as either black or white. Her robust Christian faith and her past relationships with men have made her feel like an outsider with some in the LGBT community. Because of these experiences, Cassandra has worked hard to find the resources and the people who support her sense of self-identity and who will work with her to try to address social injustice.

Though Eric is facing a particularly tough time in his life and Cassandra is generally doing well, both have in common that their experiences feel oversimplified and misunderstood in conversations about diversity and inclusion. The diversity fatigue they are each feeling may be due in large part to the reductive categories of social identity that serve as the foundation for most conversations and initiatives geared toward diversity. Eric and Cassandra may also be equating personal happiness or unhappiness with social privilege and disadvantage. Since Eric feels stressed and anxious, it is even more difficult for him to see how he may be socially privileged in virtue of his race, gender, or sexual orientation. Similarly, because Cassandra is at a particularly good point in her life, it may be harder for her to focus on the social systems of disadvantage that can get in the way of her continued happiness and success. Neither Eric nor Cassandra wants to be the "usual suspect"—the case study for the privileged white male or the disadvantaged woman of color, respectively—in events and discussions about diversity and inclusion. Eric does not feel that he represents the privileged white male perspective, and Cassandra does not want to reopen old wounds so that she can teach people about the disadvantaged lesbian of color. As a result, Eric and Cassandra withdraw from the Diversity Day event and related committee work because they believe that they have very little to contribute and nothing to gain.

Eric and Cassandra represent two outliers in public discourse about diversity and inclusion. Unlike others who feel empowered and awakened by efforts to create inclusive and diverse communities, Eric and Cassandra feel drained and misunderstood. This is not because they equate diversity with racism or because they are hostile to justice and equity. Rather, their frustration comes from interpreting social debates as presenting them with only two options: *victim* or *culprit*. The feelings associated with these options are either *blame* or *guilt*. Since Cassandra does not at this point feel much like a victim, nor does she feel like she wants to put herself at risk by teaching socially privileged people about social injustice, the roles available to her feel limited and frustrating. Since Eric does not at this point feel much like a culprit who puts up obstacles in the way of people whose social characteristics are different from his, nor does he feel like adding more guilt to his already difficult life, the roles available to him feel alienating and frustrating.

I have had students who to some degree or another share some of Eric's and Cassandra's characteristics and reactions. These students withdraw from conversations in class about social privilege and social disadvantage because they do not want to serve as the usual suspects for a given social identity. They have had experiences in the past where diversity, inclusion, and multiculturalism—all buzzwords for a more just and equitable social system—have meant that their own social identity becomes oversimplified, ignored, or misunderstood.

Gabrielle Rosenstriech, a researcher who analyzed a wide variety of diversity training programs, stated that "An explicit conceptualization of how the multiple elements of identity come together to produce subjects is, however, entirely lacking or at best ambivalent in most diversity training programs."[4] What Rosenstriech means is that an account of how people actually develop their social identities and how multiple social factors influence their identities is either left out or not clarified in most diversity initiatives.

Fortunately, there are a number of philosophers and social theorists who have been working on more complex and authentic ways to represent social identity and the relationship between identity and social systems. This work has resulted in what is called an *intersectional model* of social identity. Unfortunately, this important work on intersectionality has not really made its way into many of the mainstream diversity and inclusion programs in business and professional settings or in our public schools and universities. Intersectionality is a theoretically powerful way to understand the complexity of the relationship between social identity and social structures and can provide a way back into the discussion for people like Eric and Cassandra and others who are suffering from diversity fatigue. So, what exactly is an intersectional model of identity?

Patricia Hill Collins, a sociologist and pioneering scholar on intersectionality, explains in her groundbreaking 1990 book *Black Feminist Thought: Knowledge, Consciousness, and the Politics of Empowerment,* that

Figure 2.1: Photo of
Patricia Hill Collins

our social identity does not exist in a hierarchy of individual properties but instead exists as an intersectional set of properties whereby race, class, ethnicity, gender, sexual orientation, religion, socioeconomic status, and dis/ability interlock around systems of power, privilege, and disadvantage.[5] As individuals, we experience our identity on a personal level. However, our microlevel experience is importantly related to a history and a set of social systems, a macrolevel, that positions us within what Collins describes as a "matrix of domination." Intersectionality allows us to see that social categories have historically only made sense when they reduced and limited the possibilities for identity. So, for instance, if our default schemata for the concept "person" is male, white, and heterosexual, then women, people of color, and same-sex partners lie outside the schema and can therefore be considered inferior or even socially deviant. Similarly, gender fluidity, racial fluidity, and sexual fluidity, which all challenge the static categories of social identity, become invisible as social identities.

Kimberle Crenshaw, a leading scholar in critical race theory and a professor of law at UCLA, uses the 1977 legal case *DeGraffenried v. General Motors* to illustrate the ways that limited and static social categories fail to capture the reality of people's experiences.[6] The case involved five plaintiffs, all black women, who claimed that the seniority system at General Motors was discriminatory not to blacks generally or women generally but to the intersection: black women. Because General Motors had hired and promoted black men as well as white women, the court ruled that there was no evidence of racial or gender discrimination. Yet as Crenshaw points out, "The paradigm of sex discrimination tends to be based on the experiences of white women; the model of race discrimination tends to be based on the experiences of the most privileged blacks. Notions of what constitutes race and sex discrimination are, as a result, narrowly tailored to embrace only a small set of circumstances, none of which include discrimination against Black women."[7]

Similarly, Collins's contributions to intersectionality grew out of her interest in the experiences of black women in the United States. Collins argued that black women experience gender oppression in ways that are different from white women. In addition, black women experience race oppression in ways that are different from black men. Collins recognizes that there are *some* overlapping aspects to gender and race oppression for black women in relation to white women and black men. However, she emphasizes that there are also some significant differences.

Patricia Hill Collins

Patricia Hill Collins is Distinguished University Professor of Sociology at the University of Maryland, College Park, and Charles Phelps Taft Emeritus Professor of Sociology in the Department of African American Studies at the University of Cincinnati. Collins's award-winning books include *Black Feminist Thought: Knowledge, Consciousness, and the Politics of Empowerment* (1990), which received both the Jessie Bernard Award of the American Sociological Association (ASA) and the C. Wright Mills Award of the Society for the Study of Social Problems, and *Black Sexual Politics: African Americans, Gender, and the New Racism* (2004), which received ASA's 2007 Distinguished Publication Award. She is also the author of *Fighting Words: Black Women and the Search for Justice* (1998); *From Black Power to Hip Hop: Racism, Nationalism, and Feminism* (2005); *Another Kind of Public Education: Race, Schools, the Media, and Democratic Possibilities* (2009); and *The Handbook of Race and Ethnic Studies* (2010), edited with John

Solomos. In 2008 Collins became the 100th president of the ASA, the first African American woman elected to this position in the organization's 104-year history.

For instance, when white feminists in the United States during the 1960s and 1970s were calling for more opportunities for women to get out of the kitchen and into the workforce, the message did not resonate for many black and working-class women in the same way. Many of these women had been in the workforce for decades, with a significant percentage working in the kitchens and homes of middle-class and wealthy white women. Working for pay had not liberated these black and working-class women from sexist oppression, nor did it allow them to gain any real measure of economic independence.[8]

So challenging social stereotypes about the appropriateness of women working outside the home was not a salient issue for black and working-class women as it was for college-educated white women. While gender inequity in salaries could be a common issue for both black and white women, the additional fact of salary disparities resulting from racism for black women and a lack of educational opportunities for working-class women would mean that these groups had additional disadvantages as compared with wealthier white women.

Rather than understanding social identity as a list of oppressed or privileged categories ranked from highest to lowest, Collins encourages us to think instead of the complexity of social identity and the ways in which the intersection of our identities results in connections and potential coalitions among different social groups. On some issues—the right to vote, for instance—women identified simply as women because they were being denied the right solely on the basis of their gender identity. On other issues, however, gender may be too simplified and reductive a category to capture social experience. White working-class and poor women have different experiences of race privilege in the United States than white middle-class and wealthy women. Heterosexual women experience social privilege in terms of their sexual identity in ways that bisexual and lesbian women do not. Collins reminds us that our social identities are always constructed in relation to, and in many cases at the expense of, others. No single social category is more oppressed in the sense of standing apart from all the others. As the great Caribbean American writer and civil rights activist Audre Lorde said, "there can be no hierarchies of oppression. I have learned that sexism and heterosexism both arise from the same source as racism."[9]

The network of social advantages and disadvantages we have all inherited is the result of a history of violence, subjugation, struggle, and transformation. Much of what makes up our social identity in this wider sense has very little to do with anything we have chosen or decided to do. Our gender, how we are perceived by others in terms of race and ethnicity, the people we are sexually attracted to, and the socioeconomic class that we were born into are all aspects of our identity that have consequences we did not choose. Yet in virtue of these same social identities, we are afforded different and dynamic benefits and losses without having done anything to deserve either. The recognition of this dynamic aspect to social identity is the first skill involved in being an intellectually empathic thinker: knowing that social identity is intersectional (and not simply reductive or additive).

We cannot be reduced to just single social and monolithic categories, nor do our experiences of social privilege or disadvantage simply increase or decrease because we belong to a variety of social categories. All women do not experience sexism in the same ways, though there are discernable patterns to their experiences. Race, ethnicity, class, religion, and sexual orientation all play a role in how sexism operates and is experienced. In addition, just because a group has historically experienced oppression or disadvantage does not mean that members of that group will always have it worse off socially when that aspect of their identity intersects with other aspects.

For instance, while African Americans have experienced a long and painful history of social injustice and women have been prevented from equal rights and equal access to social goods, it does not follow that African American women are doubly oppressed simply because they occupy the intersection of both "African American" and "woman." To be clear, it does not follow from this intersection of oppression that African American women have it better off than other women either. Rather, the intersectional analysis of social identity demands that we see privilege and disadvantage as being more contextual rather than as additive.

To see this point more clearly, consider the issue of negative body image. Many women in the United States suffer from negative body image, resulting in anxiety, depression, compulsive dieting, and eating disorders.[10] Yet in a recent study of one thousand African American women, the majority (66 percent), reported positive body image and high self-esteem, even among those women who would be considered overweight by government standards.[11] On the other hand, survey data of white women who are of average weight or thin showed that a minority (41 percent) reported positive body image and high self-esteem. One proposed explanation about the differences in body image among African American and white women is that since the ideals of beauty reinforced in mainstream media, from Disney princesses to fashion supermodels, have mostly excluded African American women, these women have had more opportunity to develop their own definitions of beauty within black culture. In this way, and with this issue, the intersection of "African American" and "woman" creates a unique space for resistance that challenges social disadvantage rather than simply adding up the two categories as doubly worse.

An intersectional account of identity does mean that there is not a need for identity-specific resources, programs, or even relationships. Though our identities are complex and we can experience social advantages and disadvantages at the same time, this does not mean that there has not been a very direct and targeted attack on specific identities historically. In other words, social and historical reality has in fact treated us all in reductive, oppositional terms such as male/female, white/black, straight/gay, Christian/non-Christian, able/disabled, and wealthy/middle class/poor. Given this reality, it is important for us to be able to analyze and challenge the oppressive dimensions of these terms. However, this does not mean that we cannot also work to break open these oversimplified and divisive categories so as to create new ways of understanding social identity and experience.

Eric, who struggles in virtue of his socioeconomic class and personal history, does not feel like he has any particular social advantages. In fact, when he looks for social programs to address his struggles as a white working-class divorced father who is also responsible for two elderly ill parents, he is at a loss to see how his race or his gender provide any benefits. Of course, Eric is right that there are no particular resources advertised as benefits for straight white men, but there are ways in which his race, gender, and sexual orientation do afford him significant unearned social advantages. For instance, though Eric is worried about maintaining his job, economic data clearly show that as a straight white male, he is likely to earn more than women, gay men, and heterosexual men of color doing the same work.[12] In addition, in virtue of his race, gender, and sexual orientation, it is less likely that Eric will be among the unemployed than it is for a woman or a man of color. However, if we consider educational level, the fact that Eric has only completed some college courses and has not received a bachelor's degree means that his chances of being among the unemployed are higher than they would be for those who have earned a bachelor's degree (or an advanced degree).[13] Moreover, the state that Eric lives in plays a role in how well he does economically and how secure his job is relative to men of color and women doing the same work.

Eric's economic advantages in terms of race, gender, and sexual orientation intersect with facts about his level of education and the geographic region where he resides, so it is an oversimplification to say that he benefits across the board on the basis of his race and gender. Yet it is also an oversimplification to say that Eric's intersectional identity dilutes his race, gender, and heterosexuality privilege. There are still distinct ways that Eric is likely to experience social privilege in virtue of being male, white, and heterosexual relative to women, gay men, and heterosexual men of color. These advantages can include Eric's not fearing sexual harassment or violence because of his gender or sexual orientation, not wondering what kind of message his wardrobe sends out about his sexuality, not worrying about whether his failures will be attributed to his race or gender, not being denied rights on the basis of his sexual orientation, and a host of other daily accumulative fears, concerns, and injustices that he might face were he not a white heterosexual male.

Because social privilege is most often invisible to those who have it (remember the point in chapter 1 about not noticing how beneficial it is to have a working car until something goes wrong), Eric doesn't *feel* any of these advantages; for him, they are simply part of the background. He does, however, notice his social disadvantages and his personal challenges. His lack of a college degree, the instability of his job, the troubled economy in his region, his battle with sobriety, and his parents' ill health are all at the foreground of his estimations of how hard things are. Since Eric can't see his privilege and since all he has heard about diversity and multiculturalism are oversimplified tropes about "can't we all just get along" and "white men have all the power," it is not surprising that he withdraws from discussions and events having to do with these initiatives.

This phenomenon, of not seeing one's social privilege, brings us to the second skill required for being an intellectually empathic thinker: understanding that social privilege is mostly invisible to those who have it.

Consider Cassandra, who is aware of the obstacles she faces as a biracial lesbian and a single mother but who has chosen to avoid labels and group identification and forge her own sense of identity and community through her friendships and her faith. Cassandra has never considered herself much of a joiner, and the qualities and characteristics that make up who she is, intersecting borders of race, religion, sexual orientation, and gender, have led her to resist social and political groups organized around one or two social categories. Cassandra sometimes feels that her social identity falls through the cracks when diversity and inclusion are the focus of public discussions. She has not felt at home in social groups organized around race, gender, sexual orientation, or family. The only exceptions are her church and the few close friendships she has cultivated over the years. Like many people who wish all this talk of race and gender and diversity would just go away, Cassandra would prefer that people be evaluated as individuals on the basis of their actions rather than their social identity. In this way Cassandra shares the desire for a color-blind society, but her desire is not rooted in her belief that diversity initiatives are "racist," as with Berliner and Hull quoted earlier. Rather, Cassandra has been asked too often to speak for all women of color and all lesbian women when she has been among a majority of white and heterosexual people concerned with diversity. She understands that her experiences do not represent the experiences of all the people who share her social identity, and she is fairly certain that diversity initiatives are mostly superficial window dressing rather than real social change.

Cassandra, as I have described her here, is resistant to diversity work not because she is naive or because she wants to silence disadvantaged groups but rather because the reductive categories of social identity do not seem to capture the reality of her social experience. When she is faced with a census form, for instance, she feels misrepresented by any choice she makes regarding race. Even though she can check both "white" and "black," she feels like she is neither. When she identifies as a Christian, she usually has to qualify her remarks so as to distinguish herself from the anti-LGBT views of some religious conservatives. When she identifies as a lesbian, she has reservations about limiting her sexual identity to women since she did have a loving and sexual relationship with the father of her child. The option "bisexual" does not resonate for Cassandra now because she feels that it fails to capture her current relationship with her girlfriend. For Cassandra, this frustrating history of having to check one box, so to speak, has motivated her to create her own sense of identity and community.

Cassandra, then, is tired of discussions about diversity and inclusion in public settings such as this middle school parent meeting. She is certain that a commitment to diversity in this specific context will amount to some halfhearted effort at a food festival or a global fashion show. Worse, Cassandra knows that by pointing out the social disadvantages she has faced in her life, she risks being assaulted with the defensiveness that comes from those who have to face their social privilege, often for the first time. It is not worth it for Cassandra to have to take that kind of risk just so that others can learn. As a result, she withdraws from public efforts to examine diversity and social difference.

Cassandra's decision is reasonable given her experience, but there are still ways that she may not be taking into account her own privilege and the opportunity to build connections and challenge social divides. Though Cassandra has had to struggle to forge an identity and a community that resonates with her sense of self, she had the advantage of doing so within a stable middle-class environment. She went to schools that were well resourced, and she managed to get a scholarship to a local private college because of her good grades and compelling personal narrative. Though she had a child at a young age, her mother was willing to share the child care responsibilities so that Cassandra could finish school. In college, Cassandra took a variety of courses and met a wide range of people who encouraged her self-exploration and supported her critiques of prevailing social categories. She managed to join and then drop out of clubs and organizations oriented toward African American students, LGBT students, feminist causes, and Christian groups. Though she never strongly identified with any one of these and her experiences were not always positive, Cassandra drew strength from elements in every one.

Cassandra's ability to explore her identity in this way is not, however, an option for everyone. The economic stability provided by her middle-class status and college education has meant that Cassandra has had more autonomy with regard to shaping her identity than many poor or working-class people would have. In addition, her mixed-race status and light skin meant that she could pass in circumstances as being something other than black, thereby accruing less of the social presumptions that confront many black Americans. Her bisexuality too meant that she could avoid some of the social land mines that face homosexual adolescents in their journey to sexual authenticity. Cassandra's boyfriend and pregnancy and the birth of her son construct her as a natural mother in ways that don't call into question the legitimacy of her maternal ties. All of this is not to say that Cassandra has not faced significant social challenges. Rather, what I want to draw out is that Cassandra's fatigue with the public conversation about diversity is in part the result of her having advantages that some of the other women, people of color, and LGBT people in the room may not have had. Cassandra is tired because she is over it and has earned a more nuanced way of looking at who she is. However, there is still the larger question of who she is in relation to everyone else and what she might gain from thinking in these more relational terms. Too, there are ways that Cassandra's experiences with a border identity could shed light on the experiences of others who may not have had the chance to explore the intersectional nature of their own experiences.

What Eric and Cassandra share is a desire to withdraw from these public events aimed at diversity. Both believe that their life experiences will be misunderstood and oversimplified. Eric does not understand why he should examine his social privilege, since he doesn't feel particularly well off. Cassandra does not understand why she should feel solidarity with social groups who have historically been disadvantaged. Each default to thinking of their identity in more individual terms, and so they miss the relevance of history, power, and politics to their sense of self and to their relationships with others. Despite the many ways that we feel uniquely individual, many important aspects of our identity are social. Unfortunately, the social categories that we are lumped into have a history of injustice and opposition. Admitting that we have social identities and that they are more complex than we have been led to believe can help us to both understand the history we have inherited *and* build new connections and collaborations with a variety of social groups.

If diversity, multiculturalism, and other efforts aimed at increasing our understanding of social identity incorporated a more robust conception of intersectionality, then Eric and Cassandra might trust the process more. The loss of Eric's and Cassandra's perspectives in diversity initiatives is significant. Eric and Cassandra both have had experiences that bring to life the complexity of the intersection of race, gender, class, and sexual orientation. Eric is not simply an oppressor, and Cassandra is not simply oppressed. Eric has social advantages that are hard for him to see, but the obstacles and struggles he faces socially are not insignificant. Clearly it is even harder for Eric to see these advantages if he feels that he is being unfairly judged at the outset. Cassandra may not be considering the ways in which she has both benefitted and struggled because of her multifaceted social identity. Yet if she feels that she is positioned at the outset as simply marginalized while at the same time feeling that she has worked hard for her satisfaction and success, it is not surprising that she is tired of what she sees as the diversity and multiculturalism bandwagon.

Initiatives aimed at diversity and social justice should begin with an intersectional account of social identity. By avoiding the monolithic additive view of social properties, we move away from thinking that some people are better or worse off simply on the basis of one or two of their social properties. An intersectional framework also creates an opportunity to build trust so that individuals can begin to assess their social experiences without feeling like they are being positioned at the outset in ways that may be unfamiliar or unfair. As we have said, thinking intersectionally about social identity does not mean that race or gender or socioeconomic status or religion or sexual orientation are not in and of themselves relevant categories for understanding the myriad ways that rights and goods have been unequally available. There are real statistical differences between whites and blacks, for instance, when it comes to wage disparities.[14] There are clearly identifiable health disparities between wealthier Americans and poorer Americans.[15] And there are significant differences between Muslims and Christians with regard to the obstacles they face in practicing their religion in the United States.[16] While these disparities are real and in most cases unjust, it would be a mistake for us to conclude from the data that any single individual black Muslim living at or near the poverty level *feels* worse off or more oppressed as compared with any individual white Christian person in the middle class. Rather, the data show that being white, middle class, and Christian in the United States means that you will face fewer obstacles in the pursuit of health, wealth, and freedom of religion than would be the case for a poor black Muslim. The white middle-class Christian who benefits from the lack of social obstacles does not, most likely, *feel* like an oppressor and probably attributes any success he or she has had to personal hard work and good sense. This is the way that social privilege can remain *invisible* to those who have it. We chalk it up to our own efforts or judge it as just normal from the perspective of our own limited experience. The point is that we need to distinguish social benefits and obstacles from the way people personally experience those benefits and obstacles. People who face social obstacles because of one or two of their social identities may benefit in other ways because of a third or fourth aspect of their social identity. For this reason, they may neither face nor even feel like they are in a perpetual state of social disadvantage or advantage. Rather, social advantage and disadvantage can intersect in complex ways that wind up producing complex experiences for individual people.

As we said at the end of chapter 1, invisibility of privilege means that some people in virtue of their social identity will have easier access to certain rights and goods without seeing that it is the result of their identity. To use a simplified metaphor, their race, economic status, sexual orientation, or religion can function as a kind of free EZ Pass on the road to social rights and goods. Think of heterosexuality as a road and of all the destinations open to people in American society who are straight. If you are in a heterosexual relationship, you can openly express affection to your partner in public, share stories with friends and coworkers about your relationship, be welcomed in long-standing traditions and rituals, know that your children will not be stigmatized because of their parents' relationship, and choose to marry and adopt with your partner. The road to these destinations is easy to travel for heterosexuals not because some heterosexual road commission set it up at some specific time in the past but because it was forged deeply into the social fabric after centuries of hammering by the most powerful political, cultural, religious, and economic forces. Social privilege, then, seems normal or just the way things are for those who can get around easily. The philosophies and ideologies that went into the creation of these roads and that make them easy for some to travel on and more difficult or even impossible for others is the least visible to those who travel with ease. Anyone who can't get around—gay and lesbian people, for instance—are viewed as having some personal failing that requires their need for a special inroad rather than as fellow travelers who are being unfairly excluded by the way the system of roads has been set up.

Having a metaphorical EZ Pass does not guarantee that those with one will be successful or even reach their social destinations. But it does mean that they won't have to worry about getting stopped along the way or pressured to give up something they value to get there. In other words, though our economic, political, legal, religious, and cultural institutions are set up to make it easy for heterosexuals to travel through life, it does not guarantee that all heterosexual couples will be happy or successful (and clearly a 50 percent divorce rate makes this evident). Rather, it means that the obstacles will be more personal and will be derived from individual choices rather than social roadblocks. On the other hand, for gay and lesbian couples without these publicly sanctioned highways, there are both predictable and unpredictable stops and checkpoints that make the journey longer, fraught with difficulty and frustration, and in some cases may even shut roads down. That is why social disadvantage is often easier to see than social privilege. We tend not to notice the systems, structures, and mechanisms when they work for us. But if something breaks down or prevents us from moving forward, the obstacles become very tangible.

Distinguishing between social structures and personal experiences will help us be sensitive to the fact that while privilege is often invisible to those who have it, social disadvantage is not always experienced as personal unhappiness or victimization for those who face it. In addition, lacking the metaphorical EZ Pass is not a guarantee that an individual or social group will never make it down the road to rights and goods, nor does it mean that they can never get there successfully. However, the frustration and anger that can often accumulate for those who have to face arbitrary roadblocks and checkpoints while others sail by should be understandable given the unjust aspects of the system. Larger roadblocks and more public discrimination, such as prohibitions on gay marriage and adoption or racially motivated decisions about hiring and promotion, often combine with microaggressions, or more subtle forms of bias and discrimination, to make daily life a struggle for groups who face social disadvantage.

Though the EZ Pass metaphor is a simplified one (to complicate it, we could investigate the origins of the tolls and passes and consider how those with power have benefitted from a system with controls and checkpoints), it does illustrate how discrete social properties can function in systematic ways to yield unfair costs and benefits for members of different social groups. Seeing these costs and benefits and how we perpetuate them is a tremendous step forward in terms of thinking critically about social justice. We have a whole history of activists, civil rights workers, suffragists, artists, and scholars to thank for naming these roads and checkpoints and providing a way for us to see how we play a role in their continuation. Yet while the work of identifying our role within these inequalities is significant, it can all too easily be used to divide social groups into victims and culprits. Owning an EZ Pass despite having done nothing in particular to earn it does not mean the owner has consciously set out to harm anyone. Not owning an EZ Pass despite having done nothing that should make the journey harder does not make a person a victim. Rather, it is evidence of a system of social injustice that thrives upon a victim-culprit dichotomy and discourages us from thinking about the intersectional aspects of our identities.

The Guilt Filter and the Blame Filter

Identifying social inequalities and seeing how we are affected by them and how we maintain them can challenge the guilt-anger, victim-culprit, and blame-shame dichotomies, allowing us to work instead toward mutual understanding. The process of effectively diagnosing social problems through a more critical analysis of the history of privilege and power is among the most important steps we can take in the service of social justice. However, there is a temptation when doing this work to take the guilt or the blame that inevitably arises with the territory and let it take over all of our perceptions and analyses. White guilt, for instance, can become a badge of honor for white people who despite their good intentions can wind up obscuring the experiences of people of color and reframing them as experiences of victimization or powerlessness. I remember attending a conference once where three African American professors were presenting evidence they had recovered on African American women in the antislavery movement. After presenting several case histories as well as the importance of research on African American women during this period, the professors asked for questions and comments from the audience. It so happened that for this particular session, the overwhelming majority of the audience was made up of African American scholars. However, the first hand that went up belonged to a young white woman. She said, "I am so moved by your research, and as a white woman working on a PhD in history, I want to know—what can I do to help you?" The cringe from the audience that followed the question was palpable. The problem with the young woman's question was that it assumed that the presenters, experts in their field, were in need of help and could somehow benefit from this young graduate student. While the question was most likely motivated by a sincere respect for the value of the presenters' research, it nevertheless undermined their authority and reified power differentials on the basis of race.

The problem with white guilt or any version of socially privileged guilt is that it replaces the work of actually gathering data with a distorted lens that merely reaffirms the existing inequalities. An intersectional analysis of identity can relax the guilt filter and allow us to take social experiences in a less distorted and more dynamic way. If the young woman at the conference presentation saw things in more than black and white terms and along more intersectional dimensions, she might have recognized the presenters' intellectual authority and professional status rather than seeing them as simply noble victims in need of help that she was not really qualified to offer.

Interestingly, in response to the student's question, one of the presenters said, "Maybe you could talk to your white colleagues in history about what you see as important within our research." It was not that the presenter sought to make the research a black and white issue, but the student (however well intended) wound up doing so. Given that the discussion went there, it made sense that the presenter instructed the student to use her race privilege to educate other white students about the value of the research, since her help could clearly apply there rather than to the African American researchers.

Along the same lines, the recognition of social disadvantages can sometimes create a blame filter through which we judge all social experiences. Seeing how others are privileged in ways that we are disadvantaged and for reasons that have nothing to do with how hard they, or we, have worked should produce a healthy sense of righteous indignation. However, the direction that indignation should take and how often it actually matches up with the facts of our social experience are altogether different matters. For instance, women who experience a consciousness raising in terms of gender disparities and who come to see the ways in which pornography, sexist media imagery, violence against women, wage gaps, and unequal divisions of labor in the domestic sphere all create obstacles on the journey toward equal rights and respect may become justifiably indignant. Indignation is a very reasonable reaction to injustice.[17] It is interesting to note, however, that in the history of Western philosophy, reason has often been conceptualized in opposition to emotion. The duality between reason and emotion aligns with other dualities that lie deep within our conceptual history, such as mind and body, good and evil, and the oppositional social dualities we have been considering. Men of color and women have often been associated with weaker or negative properties as part of their side of the dualities; emotion, body, and evil and that association has been used as a justification for preventing their access to education, politics, and the economy. When men of color and women have been angry or indignant in American history, their anger has often been construed as hysterical or dangerous and not as justified and reasonable. Compare this with historical narratives of the American Revolutionaries for instance, who were seen as both reasonable and just for rising up in indignation against the unfair policies of a tyrannical monarchy. Reason and emotion do not necessarily work in opposition, but they have often been characterized that way when men of color and women voice indignation and anger at the injustices they face.

Thought Experiment: Reason versus Emotion

Reason has had a long history of being contrasted with emotion in Western philosophy. Reason has been considered much more valuable in the quest for truth, and emotion has often been described as getting in the way or tempting us away from truth. For example, in *The Republic* Plato argued that the human soul was made up of reason, spirit, and appetite. Appetites that are inflamed by emotion and desire are maddening and irrational, according to Plato, and should be subdued with the power of reason. This idea of reason as being in opposition to emotion has led to popular expressions such as "leading from the head" (reason) and "leading from the heart" (emotion). However, there is good evidence for considering how reason and emotion work together, especially in our understanding of concepts and cognitive schemata. Can you think of ways that your judgments necessarily combine reason and emotion? How does critical thinking benefit from the integration of reason and emotion?

So, critical thinking in the service of social justice should make room for the role of anger and indignation in identifying obstructions to opportunity. However, the temptation exists to translate that anger into blame and apply it to a multitude of complex situations where it may not be justified. The feminist who sees sexism in every interaction or the person who sees racism as the sole cause of every social problem sees a single aspect of injustice everywhere and hence nowhere specifically. The reasonable anger that arises in response to understanding the injustices that one has faced in virtue of her or his social identity and unjust social systems should not close off the possibility that in some cases, that identity or injustice may not be playing a role in a difficult situation or with a particular person. Injustice certainly exists, and we should err on the side of developing our sensitivity to injustice rather than defaulting to a skeptical attitude. However, even starting from that vantage point, it does not follow that *every* situation and *every* interaction can be understood simply on the basis of sexism, racism, or any other reductive form of bias or discrimination. Moreover, seeing every situation or interaction in terms of these discrete categories of injustice fails to incorporate an intersectional account of identity. Even if gender bias is playing a role in a particular context or with a particular person, there will still be ways that it intersects with race and class and sexual orientation to create a complex social dynamic. White middle-class feminist women in the United States who support reproductive rights may interpret conservative policies aimed at reducing access to abortion as an attack on women. While it is clearly true that restrictions on reproductive rights negatively affect women in general, it is also true that they have severe consequences for poor families and people of color who disproportionately live in poverty. Because poorer women have more unplanned pregnancies and less access to birth control and rely more heavily on publicly funded reproductive health services, they and their families are made more vulnerable by a lack of publicly funded options.[18] Having to save for a private abortion can take time for poorer families, and the more time passes, the less safe and available the options. So, an attack on women's rights is also an attack on poor families and people of color. Recognizing the intersections between gender discrimination, socioeconomic disparities, and racism shows how white women's concerns, even white middle-class women's concerns, are intimately connected to poor families and men and women of color.

Rather than resorting to a uniform blame filter, we should look to see how evidence of injustice connects us to other groups so that we can think in terms of shared obstacles. Rather than being attuned only to the bias and stereotyping that affects us and the groups to which we belong, we should use our ability to identify bias as a step toward thinking intersectionally. The bias we experience has a relationship to other forms of bias and stereotyping inflicted upon others. The blame filter prioritizes only what affects us without allowing us to see the complexity in our relationship to others. Relaxing that filter is one step toward seeing the wider system of privilege and disadvantage.

If we reconsider Eric and Cassandra in light of this discussion, there are more effective ways to invite them into diversity discussions and initiatives. By starting with an intersectional analysis of social identity and then framing discussions of diversity around the ways that power and privilege can be situational and context sensitive, we recognize the complexity of both Eric's and Cassandra's experiences. By distinguishing their more personal and dynamic experiences from the public institutions of power and privilege hardened by the social inequalities of our history, we can account for the ways that social identity is both relational and omnipresent. We have some choice in how we define ourselves, but there are still significant ways that our identity comes from the outside in. When Eric feels alienated from discussions of white male privilege, we can understand his reaction because the economic and psychological challenges he faces weigh so heavily. Nevertheless, in virtue of his race and gender, Eric has a social EZ Pass that allows him to travel more efficiently on some but not all public access roads. The invisibility of privilege can be made apparent to Eric without discounting the struggles he faces in his life. Furthermore, relaxing the guilt filter that clouds his perceptions when diversity is raised will enable him to identify his privilege without positioning him as the culprit responsible for harms that he does not believe he has committed. Eric's privilege does not mean that he is never disadvantaged socially, nor does it mean that those who do not share his same privileges are victims in need of his superior assistance. Intersectionality combined with a relaxation of the guilt filter can create a way for Eric to come back into discussions of diversity without feeling like he is misunderstood or at risk.

Cassandra's fatigue with diversity also stems from feeling misunderstood and not finding herself in the available categories. She has moved on, in a sense, from a focus on the ways that institutions of privilege and power present obstacles. Cassandra has managed to forge a sense of herself and her identity that feels creative and empowering. Nevertheless, those institutions still remain and affect others who have less opportunity to work around them in the ways that she has. While Cassandra does not feel like a victim, discussions about diversity often make her feel like she needs to be the spokesperson for difference and marginalization. And she is wary of the anger and single-mindedness she experienced firsthand when she engaged in public discussions about social identity.

By starting from the point of intersectional identity and freeing Cassandra from the burden of having to speak or represent an entire social group, we make room for the complexity of her identity. Cassandra does not have to take on the role of victim to describe and diagnose the ways that social disadvantage has operated in her life. If we make a distinction, as we did with Eric, between how Cassandra *feels* about her life as compared with how she is *treated* within social systems of advantage and disadvantage, we can expand the victim-culprit dichotomy. Additionally, by identifying and appreciating justified anger, we can still encourage participants in the discussion to work at relaxing the blame filter somewhat so as to avoid oversimplified and indiscriminate accusations of bias against people who are participating. In so doing, we earn back credibility from someone such as Cassandra whose past negative experiences of social identity caused her to withdraw from diversity discussions.

Eric and Cassandra represent two ends of the disengagement spectrum. Why is it important to include them in discussions about diversity, inclusion, and multiculturalism? Eric and Cassandra represent important standpoints regarding who is left out and left feeling misunderstood in these conversations. Their withdrawal is symptomatic of the way that the media, business, and social and political institutions frame diversity and social difference. These differences are generally presented as either a happy patchwork of different colors or a dangerous set of oppositions rife with personal and political land mines. Either way, these presentations fail to highlight the ways that individual social identities are in fact multiple, embedded in systemic dynamics, and interlocking. Eric's and Cassandra's experiences, then, complicate social identity for the better, and their inclusion demands that we think in terms of coalitions and solidarities rather than simple categories and oppositions. Scholar, author, and activist bell hooks in a discussion of the issue of black self-determination writes:

> There is no monolithic black identity. Many black families have expanded to include members who are multiracial and multiethnic. This concrete reality is one of the prime reasons that nationalist models seem retrograde and outdated. While black self-determination is a political process that first seeks to engage the minds and hearts of black folks, it embraces coalition building across race. . . . It also

recognizes the importance of black people learning from the wisdom of non-black people, especially other people of color.[19]

Relaxing the guilt and blame filters, moving past culprit and victim dichotomies, and understanding the intersectional aspects of our own identities will provide us with a way to embrace coalition building across our differences. Acknowledging that we have a social system that unjustly bestows EZ Passes on some people in some contexts and puts up roadblocks for others, is a necessary first step to thinking critically and empathically about social differences.

Questions for Review

1. Why is a color-blind world problematic?

2. What is diversity fatigue? How does it relate to the false dichotomies discussed in the introduction?

3. What is an intersectional model of social identity? How does it challenge monolithic and uniform conceptions of race, gender, class, sexual orientation, religion, and dis/ability?

4. In what ways is Eric socially privileged? Why is it hard for him to see this?

5. In what ways is Cassandra socially disadvantaged? Why is it hard for her to identify this way?

6. How do the guilt and blame filters get in the way of thinking intersectionally about our identity?

Questions for Further Thinking and Writing

1. Are the categories of social identity essential, universal, and absolute? Why or why not? Would it be better if we did away with these categories?

2. Describe the metaphor of the social EZ Pass lane. On what roads in life or in what ways does your social identity allow you to move uninterrupted while others are stopped or detained? Be specific and draw from a wide array of areas in your life (economic, political, religious, personal relationships, media images, social and cultural aspects, etc.).

Additional Resources

Michelle Norris's Race Card Project, http://theracecardproject.com/about-the-race
-card-project/, provides a wonderful window into attitudes on race in the
United States, including the harms caused by those claiming color blindness.

Professor Kimberle Crenshaw has two excellent lectures online dealing with intersectionality and color blindness. Both were part of the 2011 W. E. B. Du Bois
Lecture Series at the Hutchins Center for African & African American Research
at Harvard University. The first, "Intersectional Interventions: Unmasking and
Dismantling Racial Power," is available at http://hutchinscenter.fas.harvard.edu
/node/1125. The second, "Global Iterations of the Du Boisian Knot: The Problem
of the 21st Century Is the Problem of the Color-Blind," is available at http://
hutchinscenter.fas.harvard.edu/node/1124.

Gina Crosley-Corcoran is the author of the Feminist Breeder Blog, at http://the
feministbreeder.com/explaining-white-privilege-broke-white-person, and has
written a thought-provoking piece titled "Explaining White Privilege to a Broke
White Person," which helps to make sense of privilege for someone such as Eric,
described in this chapter.

There is an online Tumblr called Microaggressions, at: http://microaggressions.tumblr
.com, where people post some of the small daily biases and injustices they face
in virtue of their social identity. There is also a comment section, which specifically states that "Our comment section is for people to LEARN from one
another."

3 | Arguments and the Adversary Method

> Reading online comments makes me want to give up on humanity. There is just so much racism and sexism and downright nastiness. I used to think it would be a great window into a lot of different points of view. Now I realize so many people are actually just mean and stupid and I want to shut that window and not look back.
>
> —Student comment

A Window into Our Irrationality and Hate?

In chapter 2 we considered why someone like Eric or Cassandra might disengage from conversations about diversity because of their frustration with how others framed their identity. Given the limited and oversimplified categories of identity, Eric and Cassandra couldn't find the complexity of their own experiences in the context of the debate. For that reason each opted out, taking flight in the fight-flight dichotomy.

In this chapter we will consider those circumstances where people actually decide to get involved in conversations about social issues by "fighting" and giving and reacting to arguments. The term "argument" has two different meanings that often get tangled up together, especially when people discuss social identity and social differences. The first meaning involves an angry or heated disagreement, such as a quarrel or a (verbal) fight. The second meaning of "argument" refers to a set of statements including a reason (premise) in support of a conclusion (the arguer's point of view). This second meaning of argument is like a justification or an effort to make a case, in the legal sense of the term. Traditionally in logic and philosophy it is this second sense of "argument" that is the primary focus, and its connection to the fighting sense has been downplayed or dismissed.

It is important to understand that arguments in the second sense do not have to become arguments in the first sense. When we argue an issue and provide reasons for our beliefs, we don't have to become hostile or angry.

Similarly, when we express our anger or hostility we can do so effectively without giving reasons or justifying our beliefs. Yet in ordinary conversations and debates between people, the first sense of argument often gets tangled up with the second so that simply shouting or name-calling can wind up substituting for giving reasons and offering justifications. To add to this entanglement, we live within a culture where political blogs, talk radio, and cable news shows (across the political spectrum) engage extensively in insults, mockery, name-calling, and belittling as a way of "arguing" their political points.[1] In addition, a variety of researchers and cultural analysts report that incivility, bullying, and rudeness are on the rise in almost every area of our lives, including business, education, and interpersonal relations.[2]

When it comes to issues of social identity and social difference, it can seem particularly hard to find arguments that rely on reasons and justification rather than insults and hostility. As we have established so far, issues of social identity and social difference are personal and so can affect us on gut levels. At the same time, they are imbued with a history of inequality and opposition, which constrains not only our choices but also our concepts and our language. However, the fact that there are two meanings for the term "argument" and that these meanings often get tangled up is also a matter of history. While philosophers have long advocated for the "dispassionate evaluation of reasons supporting premises,"[3] there has nevertheless been an adversarial element to arguing even in the logical sense.

In this chapter we will explore the adversarial history of argument and consider the ways it works in combination with the very personal and oppositional nature of social identity to raise the temperature in dialogues about social differences. When these "hot" reactions enter the sphere of anonymous online comment forums, a perfect storm of aggression and defensiveness develops, bringing out our worst argumentative tendencies. Like the student quoted above, we might come to the conclusion that the nastiness we read in online comments is evidence of a basically racist, sexist, bigoted culture that is hopelessly beyond reason and not worthy of our empathy or compassion. On the other hand, we could consider how the anonymous nature of online comments and debates poses particular problems for dialogues about social issues. What I hope to show in this chapter is that what we are reading in online comments is not so much a window into people's core beliefs but a distorted carnival mirror reflecting back some of the most limited and oppositional aspects of social identity discourse. Rather than it being a reason to give up on humanity, we should see it instead as a prime reason to transform our standard ways of discussing and debating issues of social difference and social identity.

The process of transformation, however, should begin with a clear understanding of the history of argument and its role as the very foundation of logic and critical thinking. Traditionally, argument in the second sense (providing a justification) involves examining the reasons or premises that arguers give to support and justify their point of view or conclusion. Trudy Govier, author of *A Practical Study of Argument* and a prominent scholar in argumentation theory, explains that a good argument begins with these three components:

   a. *Acceptability* or believability of the content of the premises as well as the source of the premises,
   b. *Relevance* of the content of the premises to the content of the conclusion, and
   c. *Grounds* or sufficient reasons for believing that the conclusion is true.[4]

So, for example, if I make the argument that we should lower tuition rates (the conclusion) because it will lead to all students getting A's in all their courses (the premise), you could object to my argument on the grounds that it is not an acceptable or believable premise (a). If I argued that we should lower tuition rates because it would give my friend Sam the extra money she needs for a fabulous vacation, you could object to my argument on the grounds that while my assertion is believable, it is nevertheless irrelevant to the conclusion (b). Finally, if I argued that we should lower tuition rates because so many students want lower tuition rates, you might agree that the premise is believable and even related to the conclusion but object that it does not provide a strong justification (c).

A good argument from the point of view of logic and critical thinking is, at the very least, one where the premises are acceptable, relevant to the conclusion, and able to provide grounds for the truth of the conclusion. Arguments in this sense differ from mere statements of belief or opinion because they are joined by the reasons used to justify the belief or opinion. If someone says "The current war is wrong!" he or she has not presented an argument but merely stated a belief or point of view on a controversial issue. To make it an argument, the speaker would have to add the reasons that justify her or his opinion. Once the speaker has done that, her or his opinion becomes a conclusion. Of course, as evaluators of the argument we have to judge whether or not the reasons (premises) presented are believable, relevant to the issue, and provide grounds for the arguer's conclusion.

These minimal criteria for a good argument are important to uphold and help to guide us in argument analysis. Yet when it comes to arguments that involve social identities such as race, religion, gender, sexual orientation, etc., these minimal criteria are often abandoned because the argument so quickly deteriorates into a hostile fight or disagreement. Rather than presenting believable, relevant, justifications for their point of view, many people resort to incredible statements, irrelevant reasons, and unjustified assumptions, even raising their voices (or writing in all capitals) with the intent of intimidating anyone who disagrees. We see examples of aggression posing as arguments when incredible or irrelevant claims are shouted by television commentators who yell in each other's faces, when people shout each other down in public debates and community forums, and especially in online comment sections following news stories and editorials about race, gender, religion, and other social difference issues.

These are arguments only in the first sense because the arguers make no effort to really engage with the issues and provide evidence and justification. *Pseudoreasoning,* which is the term we will use for persuasion that does not meet any of the criteria for a minimally good argument, makes it seem like evidence is being presented to support a conclusion, but on closer inspection, the evidence falls apart.

While a lot of pseudoreasoning involves appeals to our emotions, emotion is not the main problem. Even good arguments that meet all of the criteria above can get heated and emotional. As we said in chapter 2, anger can be a very rational response to injustice and unfair treatment. Similarly, more positive emotions such as compassion, empathy, and respect can all work productively with well-developed premises to create good arguments. Emotions in and of themselves are not the problem with pseudoreasoning. Rather, it is when emotions are used as a substitute for reasons and the emotions are irrelevant to the issue at hand that we get pseudoreasoning rather than a minimally good argument. When emotions work in conjunction with reasons and are relevant to the conclusion, they can do important work in emphasizing the significance of an issue and the consequences of accepting or not accepting a conclusion.

So, why do we often encounter pseudoreasoning in debates about social issues, and why is the emotion so often hostility and defensiveness? To understand why these emotions often arise in social difference contexts, it is useful to look back on our history of argumentation to assess what we have inherited from the classical and medieval periods of Western civilization.

Argument as an Adversarial Method

In his book *Fighting for Life: Contest, Sexuality, and Consciousness,* Walter J. Ong, a Jesuit priest and professor of English literature and humanities, chronicles the history of aggression in Western philosophy, from the ancient Greeks through the rise of Christianity and monasticism in the Middle Ages to the Renaissance and then seventeenth-century Enlightenment.[5] Ong's account begins with the Socratic method, which is the idea that if we put forth the utmost opposition to a reason, it will yield our best chances for getting to the truth. For instance, if my reason for believing that the war in Iraq was justified is because my history professor told me that it was, someone using the Socratic method would subject my reason to a slew of objections. Isn't it possible that my history professor could be wrong? Isn't it possible that I misinterpreted my professor? Is a history professor's opinion even relevant to the issue of whether or not the war was justified? If I cannot adequately answer these objections, my reason diminishes in value and thus fails as a justification for my conclusion. The more I am able to withstand these objections and provide consistent supporting statements, the greater my justification.

Ong points out that in the all-male monasteries and early universities throughout Europe in the Middle Ages, the predominance of the Socratic method created the conditions for an almost militaristic approach to reasoning and argumentation. Ong explains that during this time, young men considered eligible for intellectual study (women were considered unfit) were often forcibly taken from their families and cloistered together, facing brutal punishments for any infractions of the monastery rules. The hardships that these young men faced encouraged a mutual bond and an us-against-them adversarial attitude toward their teachers. Ong goes on to suggest that the centrality of oral disputation and examination pitted students against teachers as opponents engaged in a verbal battle favoring the most self-confident and aggressive disputant. While matters of relevancy, coherence, and consistency played a role in these battles, on their own they were insignificant if they were not couched in an overarching attitude of arrogance and disdain for one's opponent.[6]

Given that these early monasteries and the subsequent cathedral schools in Europe provided a model for higher education, the common style of argument became a model for reasoning in academia generally.[7] It is important to remember that the only people eligible for arguing in this academic sense were the male children of European nobility and then male children of the rising European middle class. David Noble, a historian of science, has noted that "The Latin Church is the great fact of modern civilization and it is here that the curious culture which shaped modern science took place. Here Orthodoxy invented heresy and then identified it with women, so that a world without women emerged. A society composed exclusively of men, forged in flight from women, and intent upon remaking the world in its own half-human image."[8] Noble notes how scholarly men associated women with all the properties that were in opposition to reason, such as emotion, the body, subjectivity, particularity, and evil. This association was used as a justification for the exclusion of women from institutions of learning and power. So, if a woman demonstrated an aptitude for argument and disputation, she was viewed as a heretic or as hysterical and never scholarly.

Women were not the only people missing from this academic world. Men of color, particularly African men, were stereotyped in opposition to the apparently "civilized" nature of white European men. Kate Lowe, a professor of Renaissance history at the University of London, explains that in the mid-fifteenth century and through the early seventeenth century, a record number of sub-Saharan Africans were forcibly taken by Portuguese traders and transported to Europe to be slaves. Lowe notes that at the same time, the whole idea of civilization became critical to the European self-image. "It is paradoxical," she writes, "that in order for a definition of 'Whiteness' to crystallise among Europe's different identities, it may have been necessary for Renaissance Europeans to encounter Black Africans in the flesh. The timing of this encounter had serious detrimental consequences for black Africans (in addition to the brutality of slavery), since they were categorised and stereotyped in opposition to Renaissance standards and ideals."[9] While women were deemed irrational, men of color were deemed uncivilized and so were excluded from the realm of academia and justified argument. When men of color attempted to argue in the intellectual sense, their efforts at disputation were taken as insolence and violent aggression. So, the overarching arrogance and disdain for one's opponent that was part of academic argumentation was only for those "rational" and "civilized" European white men of privilege. For anyone else—women, men of color, the poor—it was insubordination and hysteria.

Walter Ong and David Noble's work as well as the work of philosopher Janice Moulton and linguist Deborah Tannen have contributed to our understanding of how the seeds of aggression and opposition in arguments and debates have grown alongside the development of universities, the scientific method, and the rise of technology and the information age.[10] This aggression and opposition also constructed women and men of color in aggressive opposites to the ideals of intellectual life.

The very words we use to describe arguments and debates reveal these strong undercurrents of aggression and opposition. In their now classic 1983 book *Metaphors We Live By*, George Lakoff, a cognitive linguist, and Mark Johnson, a philosopher, show how our use of metaphors influences the way we view and understand a variety of human experiences, including argument and debate contexts.[11] Lakoff and Johnson begin the book with the "argument as war" metaphor to show how the very term "argument," even in the logical sense described earlier, is so often conceptualized as a battle. They note phrases such as "He attacked my idea," "I defended my position," "I countered her attack," "I shot down his reasons," and "I won the argument."

This "adversary method," as philosopher Janice Moulton called it in her very important contribution to this topic, is problematic not simply because it favors particularly aggressive personality traits that are encouraged in privileged white men and discouraged in women and in men of color, but because the adversary method winds up getting in the way of a genuine effort at evaluating reasons and providing justifications.[12] Moulton explains that because the method relies on isolating and highlighting disagreements and examining individual claims, arguers must raise objections by citing counterexamples and inconsistencies to each individual claim. With the focus shifted to specific claims, the issue of the debate is narrowed to such an extent that it can often risk being disconnected from a whole host of important and related matters. Moulton notes how philosophers, for example, continue to revive ancient debates about the logic of claims for God's existence while ignoring contemporary issues about the relationship between religion, morality, and politics.[13] Similarly, pundits today who analyze arguments about climate change will often do so by isolating particular data or restricting the focus to a narrow range of conditions rather than considering wider systemic claims and implications. As a result, the isolated evidence becomes detached from a whole host of related data as well as the broader issue of environmental damage.[14] To deny arguments about the increase in Earth's temperature by saying something like "Well, 1934 was actually the hottest year on record so it can't be that temperatures are getting hotter!" isolates one fact and fails to consider the broader systematic data. The record-setting heat of 1934 reflects temperatures in the United States and not global average temperatures, which is the relevant data set for proponents of climate change. One reason climate debates remain controversial is that the evidence for the increase in Earth's temperature and its link to human causes requires thinking about evidence in complex and systemic ways. This is unlike the traditional adversarial method of argumentation that treats premises in isolation and refutes by way of counterexamples.

Similarly, the adversary method discourages us as critical thinkers from coming up with ways to improve arguments rather than knock them down. Because we view those with whom we argue as opponents and not collaborators, we are not positioned to hear their claims with any openness or willingness that would enable us to see how their conclusions are related to our own. Our impulse when faced with opponents is to have them fail, so even if we recognize something reasonable in their view or we have ideas about how they might improve their argument, the adversarial method discourages us from making such moves because in strengthening my opponent's position, I render myself more vulnerable. This is why the false dichotomies of victim-culprit, guilt-anger, and winner-loser seem to be our only options when social identity and social difference are at issue.

Philosopher and argument theorist Catherine Hundleby has raised significant concerns about how the adversary method, as it is employed in logic and critical thinking textbooks, actually undermines the development of logical and critical thinking skills.[15] In her sampling of thirty textbooks published between 1998 and 2008, Hundleby concludes that an overwhelming majority go beyond recommending a minimally oppositional method (starting by dividing an issue into for and against positions), and instead actively encourage an "Adversary Paradigm." The term "paradigm" refers to a broad encompassing view or set of ideas that work together to create a particular kind of interpretation. An "Adversary Paradigm" treats argumentation as a battle of wits with only two sides and one winner. Hundleby writes that "The Adversary Paradigm creates problems in philosophy. The broad influence of the Adversary Paradigm reinforces forms of social exclusion and dominance."[16]

Hundleby's point is not that opposition to an idea is always a bad thing. As she explains, oppositional stances have been rightly taken in response to injustice. However, a framework that takes opposition as the *only* viable method and treats those with whom we disagree as opponents or enemies winds up giving priority to the loudest and most aggressive voices in the room (or the online debate) rather than the ones that are most credible or true. Given that aggression and opposition have traditionally been encouraged as masculine behavior and discouraged as nonfeminine behavior and as being socially acceptable for those in assumed positions of authority and condemned when shown by those with less power, the adversarial method can silence the voices of those who are not aggressive, who are not encouraged to be aggressive, or who would risk significant social losses for being aggressive. In debates about social differences that means silencing or shaming a whole host of people, including women, people of color, the poor and working class, the young, the old, and the disabled, all of whose voices are needed to effectively understand and assess social issues.

Arguments Online

Argument, along with its adversarial and oppositional history, have moved beyond the monastery and the university and into our social and political institutions. And even more recently, argument has moved into the virtual world with the advent of the Internet, social media, and online forums. On the face of it, these technological options for argument seem like they should create new opportunities for debate that are more inclusive and more democratic. Yet what many of us have discovered instead is that online comment sections produce some of the most hostile and poorly reasoned arguments we find anywhere. Some of this could be attributed to our increasingly hostile and "uncivilized" culture. Some of it could be the intractable nature of racism and sexism and social difference. Before we consider the causes, let's consider some of the effects.

In a post titled "Why We're Shutting Off Our Comments," *Popular Science*'s online content director Suzanne LaBarre detailed how comments on the Internet are actually bad for science at large.[17] LaBarre cited a study led by University of Wisconsin–Madison professor Dominique Brossard in which 1,183 Americans were given a fabricated story on nanotechnology and were asked how they felt about the subject, both before and after reading fake comments. By reading both civil and "vile-trolling" responses, the study found that people were swayed far more by negativity. "Simply including an ad hominem attack in a reader comment was enough to make study participants think the downside of the reported technology was greater than they'd previously thought," wrote Brossard and coauthor Dietram A. Scheufele in an op-ed piece in the *New York Times*.[18]

Ad Hominem Arguments

The Latin phrase *ad hominem* means "to the man" or "to the person." An ad hominem argument is an example of a *logical fallacy*, or an argument that fails to meet the ARG (acceptable, relevant, and grounding) conditions of a minimally good argument. The problem with ad hominem arguments is that they target the person rather than the relevant issue. For example, someone with a disability says, "I think we should consider a different location for our event because this one will not accommodate people with disabilities." I respond, saying "Oh, you're just saying that because you're disabled." With this response, I have committed a version of the ad hominem fallacy. Rather than considering the evidence—that the location will not accommodate people with disabilities—I shifted to something about the person who presented the evidence. As we will see in chapter 5, there are a variety of ad hominem fallacies that have been chronicled through the centuries. We humans have been very inventive in coming up with ways to personally attack each other rather than focusing on the evidence.

Popular Science is not alone in trying to manage negative comments. The popular video site YouTube instituted a new ranking and personalized system of commenting to address what one journalist described as "a hotbed of spam and idiocy."[19] The new system requires commenters to log on using a Google+ account, and commenters can decide who among their "circles" can see the comments. Video posters on YouTube can also edit comments, and readers can rank comments so that relevant issues stay near the top of the discussion. The goal of the new system is to reduce anonymity and add accountability and evaluation to YouTube conversations.

What most social media users know is that if an issue arises that has anything whatsoever to do with race, gender, sexual orientation, or religious differences, the online comments will proliferate and take on significantly negative and hostile tones. These comments can range from outright hate-filled speech to hostile biased accusations to inconsistent and faulty reasoning. Looking to online comments, then, for examples of good reasoning can be like entering a hornet's nest to find a butterfly. The chance of one being there is not impossible, but it is unlikely. And as you search, you will be stung multiple times and have to absorb some very nasty venom. As a friend of mine once remarked after reading through more than one hundred comments following a news story about the mosque planned in proximity to Ground Zero, "I had to stop reading when my eyes began to bleed." It can feel like that. Approaching online debates about social issues with an open heart and a presumption in favor of human rationality can be dangerous. These kinds of comments are not even attempts at ad hominem or adversarial arguing; they are simply venomous outbursts. You are not prepared when you encounter comments such as

- "Trayvon's mother is a crack ho." (Comment on news story about Trayvon Martin's parents.)
- "You are an ignorant hypocritical slut. I hope you get cancer." (Comment in response to an opinion piece on a tech blog.)
- "The libtards keep saying that two faggots are 'normal.' If they're normal why can't they have kids." (Comment on a story about gay adoption.)
- "Repuglicans are neo-Nazi facists." (Comment on a story about Mitt Romney.)
- "When will Americans learn that Mooslims are psychotic terrorist f**ks who hate women." (Comment on an article about American Muslims after 9/11.)

As people concerned with thinking critically about social issues, what conclusions should we draw from the prevalence of these kinds of comments? Like the student quoted at the very beginning of this chapter, should we conclude that open and public debate actually provides a window into the hatred and negativity hidden in the hearts of our fellow citizens? Before we jump to that conclusion, it is worth taking a look at some of the research conducted by John Suler, a psychology professor at Rider University who studies online behavior. Suler describes a variety of factors that lead people to respond very differently in anonymous online communications than they would in face-to-face interactions.[20] Suler's research reveals that because commenters are not known or seen by their audience and since they are not obliged to remain in the conversation for any duration, they tend to imagine their audience as a set of characters with qualities and values that they (the commenter) creates. Given this made-up audience, Suler argues that commenters start to view their own participation in the conversation as a type of game where the stakes are not very high and the consequences are minimal to nonexistent.[21] By treating commenting as a game with characters, commenters can try on different roles and take different positions with no accountability to anyone in their audience. In acting out this way, the commenter is never directly responsible because he or she always has the option of claiming "That's not really me" or "I don't really think that." This kind of distancing between what people do and who they believe they are is what psychologists call *disassociation*.

Disassociation combined with the additional false belief that everyone who reads your comments is equal in terms of expertise and authority leads Suler to the conclusion that there is an *online disinhibition effect.* That is, people interacting online are likely to take on personas that they would rarely exhibit in face-to-face interactions. Since their assessment of who they are communicating with is often a caricature absent of the kind of sensitivity and nuance they generally apply to people in face-to-face meetings, they feel no accountability for their remarks. The online disinhibition effect means that we are most likely getting very little evidence from online comments about what lies close to the core of a commenter's web of belief—that is, the kind of beliefs the commenter would continue to defend if he or she were engaged in a face-to-face debate. This is not to say that these comments don't betray some ugly attitudes held by the commenter. However, their appearance in anonymous blog posts means that the low-stakes nature of the claims will not require any real defense. It is far more revealing in terms of core beliefs to see what lengths people will go to in order to defend in the face of disconfirming evidence.

So, are these anonymous comments giving us a window into people's true beliefs or real self? Suler addresses this question directly:

> Each media allows for a particular expression of self that differs— sometimes greatly, sometimes subtly—from another media. In different media people present a different perspective of their identity. The self expressed in one modality is not necessarily deeper, more real, or more authentic than another.[22]

Returning to the metaphor of the hornet's nest, one thing we can take away from Suler's research is that the venom we find in many online comments may not reflect commenters' true beliefs or real self as much as they reveal one aspect of people's media self-expression. This is not to say that this aspect of self is false. Rather, it is important to recognize that the self expressed in an anonymous media comment should not be viewed as more real or more essential than the self expressed in other contexts. "We contain multitudes," as the poet Walt Whitman said, and this means that we may express aspects of ourselves that are inconsistent and even contradictory. Anonymous online expression is a particular kind of context where people can try on risky personas with few consequences. Yet the question remains, why should this persona take on such a hostile and ugly quality when the issue is social identity and social differences?

To answer this question, we should start by recognizing the very oppositional and constricted nature of our social identity language. Because we have little opportunity to think and talk about the intersectional aspects of our identity, the very terms we use set us against each other. Add to this the adversarial history of dialogue and debate as well as the false dichotomies of victim-culprit, anger-guilt, and shame-blame that are inherent in our conceptions of social difference, and you start to see the conditions brewing for a perfect storm. Put these conditions in the context of anonymous public forums on topics having to do with race, gender, sexual orientation, and religious differences, and you get an explosion of vitriol and aggression that replaces critical thinking and analysis. The kind of hate-filled speech that caused my student quoted above to want to "shut that window and not look back" is, I believe, the result of people's pent-up frustration with social differences and their lack of tools for thinking and reasoning effectively about social identity and social power. Rather than ignoring these comments or bemoaning the lack of intelligent life on the planet, I think it is important for us to see them as symptomatic of the structural and institutional constraints of social inequality and the personal and emotional costs of social divisions. When I read comments such as these, I see the suffering behind the hate. And I mean suffering not just in the sense of individual suffering but also in the larger sense of a social malady or affliction. Our language and our social and political systems carry with them a history of opposition, aggression, and inequality. This history impacts our beliefs on both conscious and unconscious levels. Yet the contemporary narrative of our society today is that we are better. We are apparently postracial and postsexist and postinequality. Our public institutions celebrate this apparent transformation with such words as "diversity" and "inclusion." So if you do not experience the world as "post" all those oppressive things, then there is some failing in you rather than in the institutions. This willful unseeing, to use Sara Ahmed's phrase again, represses experiences of inequality and opposition and projects instead a happy and colorful image of difference. But these differences are not simply about color and race and a rainbow world. They involve the intersections of race, gender, class, sexual orientation, religion, and ability (as well as other identities). They include social privilege and social disadvantage and estimations of winning and losing power as well as the need that groups have to preserve their identities and values. Given that all of these concerns challenge the happy diversity narrative, they have to be rerouted and expressed in alternative forums such as politically polarized news programs, satirical cable news shows, social media, and online comments sections. While these forums provide some outlet for people's frustration with the happy diversity model, they too contribute to the oversimplification and polarization of these issues by prioritizing adversarial styles of argument or treating the problems like impossible jokes with no chance for social change. Online comments in particular allow people to channel their own individual frustration in a public and still anonymous low-stakes forum.

Consider a recent case involving feminist blogger and media critic Anita Sarkeesian that illustrates the type of anonymous online response.[23] Sarkeesian was interested in "tropes," or stereotypical portrayals, of women in popular culture and so started an investigation into different mediums. She decided to choose video gaming as one of the sites for analysis and mounted a web campaign to raise funds for a series of short films that she planned to produce on the topic. The issue was "Whether or not video games portrayed women in stereotypical or biased ways." To answer this question, Sarkeesian needed to purchase or rent a wide selection of video games. In addition, she wanted to set up a poll to survey video game users' attitudes about female characters. To do all of this she needed to raise some money for research, so she set up the web fund-raising campaign to introduce the project and her plan for researching the issue.

Sarkeesian's web campaign was met with an avalanche of negative comments on her fund-raising site, the YouTube page where she posted the video announcing the project, and her online blog. The anonymous comments included ad hominem attacks and abusive language:

"You are a dumb bitch."
"Stupid Jew!"
"If you are such a feminist why do you have long hair and wear hoop earrings?"
"You alienate guys for being guys. You are an ugly girl hiding behind feminism and trying to spoil other people's fun."[24]

These kinds of comments targeted Sarkeesian herself and used name-calling, insults, religious and gender bias, and speculation about Sarkeesian's motives rather than an engagement with the reasons that she gave for undertaking the project. Ad hominem and abusive attacks such as these, aside from being disrespectful and cowardly, are also significantly illogical, since they are not relevant to the reasons that Sarkeesian presented for why she wanted to undertake the research.

We can attribute some of these attacks to the disinhibition effect described above by Suler. That is, commenters have created bogey men (or bogey women, as in Sarkeesian's case) with all the worst qualities the commenter associates with that particular social identity. So when Sarkeesian identifies herself as a feminist interested in analyzing the tropes about women used in video gaming—a still majority male activity[25]—she is recast by many commenters as a man-hating shrew out to destroy a great source of pleasure and virtual community in the name of women's superiority. If much of the commenters' anger really stems from their fear of the monster they created, then why not express the fear instead of the anger? If the online disinhibition effect explains the tendency for commenters to take on a role and cast the people they are addressing as characters, couldn't the role be more compassionate and the characters more likable?

Given the lack of opportunities and tools for engaging in honest dialogues about social identity and social differences, anonymous online comments become the release valve for a frustrated segment of the society. As comments become less about presenting information and evidence and more about contempt and derision, participants shelter themselves within their own beliefs, and further debate becomes unproductive.[26] The anonymity of online forums masks not only the speaker but also the audience. This lack of face-to-face contact contributes to the dehumanization of participants in online forums, and dehumanization in turn fuels opposition and aggression. Research on social bias and prejudice shows that "dehumanized groups are thought not to experience complex emotions or share beliefs with the in-group."[27] Sociologists Margaret Zamudio and Francesco Rios found in their research that though "race talk" was viewed as socially unacceptable, "racist talk" was still widely practiced by individuals when they thought their conversations were in private.[28] Anonymous Internet forums with a focus on controversial issues of social identity present a strange new context. On the one hand, it is a relatively risk-free, unaccountable open space that encourages the dehumanization of opponents in a public debate while, on the other hand, commenters write from the intimate space of their homes and personal computers, lending a private quality to the experience.

So, rather than concluding that the hostility in online comments is evidence of the essential racism, sexism, etc., in the hearts of our fellow citizens, I would suggest instead that we see it as the result of a variety of interrelated and unique factors. First, that people are complex and multifaceted and what they say in anonymous online comments might only reveal some limited aspect of their web of belief. Second, the model of argument that we have inherited encourages aggression while downplaying other emotions, such as empathy and compassion. Third, issues of social identity and social difference can only be adequately addressed when people in the discussion are accountable to each other. Trust is necessary for admitting and describing experiences of bias and discrimination and is also necessary for those who want to understand how they may be contributing to the problem. Immediate anonymous online communication cannot create that kind of trust if commenters can fly in and fly out without any responsibility to each other. Fourth, the strangely public-private nature of online discussions means that they can encourage our worst tendencies to dehumanize and publicly humiliate others while, at the same time, giving us the illusion that we are engaged in a private conversation. What we should conclude from these four factors is not that irrational hate-filled people surround us everywhere but instead that people are suffering from a history of adversarial argument and painful social injustices. What we lack are effective methods for thinking and reasoning about social differences. Given this, anonymous online discussion forums are probably the worst contexts for trying to work out these issues.

Moving from an Adversarial Model to a Cooperative Model

So, where does this leave us? If we view the prevalence of venomous speech on the Internet not as a window into society but instead as a distorted carnival mirror, this will hopefully restore some of our confidence in the possibility of public forums for discussion and debate about controversial social issues. We began this chapter by considering the two senses of "argument" (verbal fight and logical justification) and how they seem to blend when the issue involves social identity and social differences. We acknowledged the preponderance of poorly argued, aggressive, downright nasty comments that surface in public forums and online debates when social differences are the focus. Rather than seeing this as evidence of the pointlessness of debates about social issues, I am suggesting that we instead recognize the unique conditions surrounding these social issues, which ignite extremes of aggression and defensiveness. Getting a handle on the aggression and hostility in online debates about social issues is a first step toward understanding why most of these debates are not actual efforts at critical thinking or social justice. Ad hominem and abusive attacks are so common in these forums because they are the easiest form of adversarial reasoning. However, rather than seeing this as a hopeless sign for the future of debate, we should instead recognize the unique conditions that surround social issues in online forums. When the perfect storm of aggression and defensiveness meets the worst possible context of anonymous commenting, our most hostile and disaffected tendencies are drawn out and highlighted.

Given that we can't change the history or the context, how can an intellectually empathic critical thinker work against these negative factors to promote constructive and effective dialogues about social issues? To answer this question, let's remind ourselves of the first two skills involved in intellectual empathy that we established in chapter 2: knowing that identity is intersectional and understanding that social privilege is mostly invisible to those who have it. Given the discussion we have had in this chapter about arguments, the adversarial method, and the climate of anonymous online forums, it is time to introduce the third skill involved in intellectual empathy: cooperative reasoning.

Cooperative reasoning involves thinking and reasoning cooperatively about social identity and difference, because when we reason in an adversarial manner, we fail to access the relevant feelings, experiences, and data that are all necessary for understanding the oppressive aspects of social identity. We need to think through these issues together, and this means hearing about how each of us experiences social systems and social categories. There are far too many structural pressures working against the opportunity for us to talk together. As we have noted thus far, history, language, media, and political and educational institutions, each in various ways, constrain and oversimplify our social experiences. Cooperative reasoning begins by acknowledging these pressures and reducing their impact on our dialogues and discussions.

Cooperative reasoning is the recognition that not all arguments have to be battles aimed at persuading and winning. Arguments about social identity and social differences should be efforts at establishing mutual respect. This would make anonymous online debates significantly less than ideal forums, since these contexts lend themselves to dehumanizing attitudes that are common with bias and prejudice. Arguments about social identity and difference should establish some base level of mutual recognition for each other's vulnerability and humanity in the face of social pressures.

Cooperative reasoning should also be sensitive to our experiences of cognitive dissonance, or the state of having contradictory beliefs as well as beliefs that do not seem to match up with reality. Paul Gorski, a professor at George Mason University, writes that

The most important revelation of my life as a social justice educator-activist is that I am a facilitator for people's cognitive dissonance. This realization has changed virtually everything I teach about poverty, racism, sexism, imperialism, nationalism, heterosexism, and other oppressions, not because I want to protect the feelings of those who are experiencing cognitive dissonance related to one or more of these issues, but because everybody experiences cognitive dissonance related to one or more of these issues.[29]

Thinking and reasoning about social differences and injustice can lead to cognitive dissonance because of the strong reactions we may have to new information that conflicts with our sense of ourselves and how the world works. People who are experiencing cognitive dissonance often feel hostile, surprised, confused, or withdrawn. Gorski recognizes that though cognitive dissonance is difficult to experience and work through, it is nevertheless common for anyone who thinks and reasons about social privilege and disadvantage. This provides him and his students with the opportunity to think together about the experience of cognitive dissonance, since it is a state they will all experience at some point in their discussions and debates. If we can work to cooperatively manage cognitive dissonance together, we move past the impasses that can block our access to relevant social evidence.

Cooperative reasoning also encourages reflection, or metacognition. What I mean by this is the ability to think about what we think. Metacognition allows us to reflect on the obstacles in our own thinking so that we might get comfortable with being uncomfortable. Knowing that everyone has been shaped in different but predictable ways by living in a socially stratified culture allows us to face this reality while still working together to challenge its affect on our system of beliefs.

Finally, cooperative reasoning contributes to revealing the false dichotomies that constrain so much of our thinking about social identity and difference. Rather than seeing ourselves as winners or losers in a debate about social identity, cooperative reasoning instead positions us as collaborators working together to uncover and understand our social beliefs. Philosophy professor and argument theorist Michael Gilbert provides a very thoughtful and well-developed model of cooperative reasoning in his book *Coalescent Argumentation*:

> Coalescent argumentation posits agreement as the goal of successful argumentation wherein the object is not to identify what is wrong with an argument, but what are the points of agreement and disagreement. Furthermore, coalescent argumentation views an argument not as an isolated artifact, but as a linguistic representation of a *position-cluster* of attitudes, beliefs, feelings, and intuitions.[30]

In Gilbert's model of coalescent argument, the point is not to win but instead to wind up agreeing. If we think of our web of belief again, Gilbert's model seeks to find points of intersection between our webs as well as points of disconnection. The task of argument is to then find out the reasons for our disconnection by sharing our beliefs, attitudes, feelings, and gut reactions, all which contribute to what is in our web and where it is located. These beliefs and attitudes may not wind up being justified upon review, but if our goal is not to win but instead to reach a point of agreement in our arguments, then understanding in the light of evidence is the reward.

You are no longer a culprit and I am no longer a victim if we are working together to understand how we have both been shaped by history. Similarly, the adversarial move of challenging your claims by presenting one counterexample or attacking one reason is not reasoning cooperatively. Instead, we recognize that systems of belief are complex and intertwined with structural pressures as well as personal feelings. Reasoning cooperatively means that I look not for exceptions to your point of view but instead for ways that my views connect with yours. If your reasons don't add up for me, then I consider evidence that would strengthen your view. In other words, I work to make your view more rational for me, and you work to make my view more rational for you. This does not mean that we swap positions if we started with different views on an issue. What it does mean is that we work together to strengthen and support each other's views so that we consider different perspectives and the best available evidence.

To see how cooperative reasoning works in practice, consider an excerpt from a dialogue that occurred between two students in one of my classes. We will identify the students as Kim and Sara. The dialogue begins when Kim is asked to describe a belief she has about a social group other than the ones to which she belongs:

> Kim: I work at a community pool, and I've come to believe that Arab American men are really arrogant. I think it has something to do with how they view women in their culture. Every time I remind them that they have to shower before going in the pool or that they can't bring food on the deck, they give me this look. They just seem really dismissive because I am a white woman.
>
> Sara: So, Kim, I am assuming that you are not Arab American?
>
> Kim: Yes.
>
> Sara: Also that you see Arab Americans as not white?
>
> Kim: Yeah, I guess so. I mean, I think Arab American men act dismissive toward all women but especially to white women.

Sara: Well, I am Arab American, and your generalization bothers me. But before I say why, let me just say I appreciate you taking the risk of saying this. I know you could have said nothing and kept this belief to yourself, but you offered it up for discussion.

Kim: Thanks. I hope you don't think I'm a total bigot for saying this. It is just a kind of stereotype I formed, and I wanted to see what other people thought.

Sara: Well, one thing I wonder is if there were some other things these men had in common. Is it the same men or different ones each time?

Kim: Well, they're all in their early twenties. It is usually the same group of guys. They just act really arrogant and dismissive when I remind them of the rules—like I am speaking a foreign language.

Sara: I could see why that would bother you, but do you think it might be more about their age rather than their ethnicity? Also, maybe they're acting like you're speaking a foreign language because they might not be native English speakers. Have they responded to you in English?

Kim: No. That is the problem. They are always speaking Arabic, and so I have never gotten more than a shrug and an eye roll from them.

Sara: I don't know. I mean, I think you can't really generalize from these young guys to all Arab American men. I also think it is easy in your case to attribute this to them being Arab rather than them being dismissive guys who may or may not even understand English. My concern is that if they were guys who looked like your friends or family, you would chalk it up to them being jerky guys, not jerky white guys.

Kim: Yeah, I get that. I guess I really don't have other examples of Arab American men except what I see on TV or in movies. You know, Sara, I want you to know that I appreciate you taking the chance to think about this with me, since I can imagine it must have made you feel uncomfortable.

Sara: It does, but it also doesn't surprise me. There are a lot of stereotypes out there about Arab American men that are unfair. You know, I had a friend visiting once from Lebanon, and I walked her past a tailgating party near the university stadium. This friend was Muslim, and she didn't drink or smoke. What she saw was a group of all-white fraternity guys drinking and swearing and knocking each other down playing football while a sorority group sat behind talking quietly amongst themselves. Her conclusion was that white

American college men were dangerous and dominant and the women were submissive. I had to talk through that one with her!

Kim: So, I guess it is a matter of who is seen as being different. I have to think about whether my judgment really was based on my not being able to see these guys as just guys and not Arab American males.

Sara: Yeah, I mean, these particular guys might be behaving badly. I'm not about to defend all Arab American men, because it is silly to try and defend an entire group's behavior on anything. But what I do think is that if these guys are being jerks, it is not because they are Arab American.

At a variety of points in the dialogue, Sara could have adopted an adversarial model of argumentation, chipping away at Kim's claims and reasoning. Sara could have said "Well, my father and my brothers are Arab American men, and they are not sexist!" Or she could have argued that Kim failed to consider other possibilities besides ethnicity rather than letting Kim consider age on her own. Kim also considers how her generalization is based on a small sample but is still reinforced by the wider culture. Sara supports Kim's point by noting the stereotypes that encourage Kim's way of thinking. Sara then offers the example of her own friend visiting from Lebanon to let Kim know that she understood how the 'othering' that Kim was applying to the men at the pool was not just something that a horribly biased person would do. Sara was letting Kim know that most of us are susceptible to problematic stereotypes and generalizations, even people we like. Both speakers found an opportunity to remind the other that they knew this kind of conversation was difficult and risky. Both offered some reassurance. Kim faces some cognitive dissonance but also recognizes that she has to engage in some metacognition to consider how her belief developed. Sara admits that Kim might be right that the guys were behaving badly but not because of their ethnicity.

In this dialogue, Sara and Kim wind up with better information and more developed reasoning skills. An adversarial dialogue would have shut down this conversation much earlier, confirming the worst assumptions that each had about the other. Cooperative reasoning, then, is an attitude of openness and a willingness to take in new information and consider how it might coexist with our firmly held beliefs. Approaching reasoning and argumentation not as a battle but instead as a cooperative process means that we could prioritize asking why someone might have come to believe something that seems contrary to what we know rather than immediately looking for ways to show that it is wrong. We could offer information or evidence that would help to make sense of another's point of view rather than simply looking for any weaknesses or points of conflict. We could consider how our own web of belief might change if we incorporated new or different information, and we could reflect on our resistance to change our beliefs. This process does not mean that we have to wind up being persuaded of something that lacks good evidence. It also does not mean that we can't disagree or even have conflicting points of view. What it does mean is that we have to approach dialogues about social differences not with the intent to win but with the goal of relaxing our defenses and cooperatively assessing the relationships between our social beliefs and the social systems of privilege and disadvantage.

Approaching argumentation from a cooperative perspective rather than a combative one is not an easy thing to do. The topics are personal, and the beliefs associated with them are often tied up with lots of unexamined emotional content that we have inherited from our families of origin, the culture around us, and false information within our own web of belief. In the dialogue above, we can imagine that Sara may have felt initially defensive and was either angry or hurt by Kim's description. Yet if we remind ourselves that all of us hold social beliefs that could potentially anger or hurt others, we can relax our blame filters. We all get something wrong when it comes to beliefs about individuals and social groups. Some of this is the result of the ignorance of privilege, and some of it is just ignorance and a basic lack of experience and information. If we view each other as collectively imperfect and sincerely trying to learn, we can work at arguing more cooperatively. This does not mean that if Sara did feel defensive or hurt or angry that she is wrong for having these feelings. Instead, cooperative reasoning encourages us to examine those reactions in the same metacognitive way that we should examine our beliefs. Our reactions do not have to lead us to jumping to conclusions about others. Sara could be hurt without coming to the conclusion that Kim is a bigot. Sara could even describe her feelings while still seeing herself as collaborating with Kim. Similarly, Kim should be able to hear Sara describe her feelings without jumping to the conclusion that Sara is incapable of reasoning through the issue. To use Michael Gilbert's phrase, an argument is a "position-cluster," and while it contains feelings, it still contains beliefs and reasons, and we should be prepared to consider the complexity.

In the next chapter we will discuss some of the common biases that contribute to the errors and unprocessed emotions in our web of belief. For now, let us just appreciate that we have inherited a long history of adversarial reasoning and understand that intellectual empathy is an effort to create alternatives to the argument as war metaphor.

So, we will be committed to dialing down the aggressive and poorly reasoned attacks and lifting up the standards for cooperation and consensus. In this way, intellectually empathic critical thinkers can help to create a new climate surrounding debates about social issues. By modeling this kind of cooperative consensus-based reasoning, we create new possibilities for public reasoning about social issues. However, once we reduce the hostility, we still need to work at identifying the common mistakes that occur when thinking and reasoning about social differences.

Questions for Review

1. What are the two meanings of "argument" that often get tangled up together?

2. Describe each of the three criteria for a minimally good argument:
    *   Acceptability
    *   Relevance
    *   Justification

3. Is the problem with pseudoreasoning that it involves appeals to our emotions? Do emotions always get in the way of good reasoning?

4. What were the historical justifications for excluding women, men of color, and poor and working-class people from engaging in intellectual and academic arguments?

5. What is the adversary method? How does it get in the way of thinking and reasoning about large systemic issues such as social identity and difference?

6. What is an ad hominem argument? How is this different from adversarial reasoning?

7. What are the four elements of cooperative reasoning?

8. Describe Michael Gilbert's notion of argument as a position-cluster.

Questions for Further Thinking and Writing

1. What differences do you see between the adversarial model of argumentation and the cooperative model? Consider a time in your life
   when you argued cooperatively rather than in an adversarial way.
   What were the advantages? What were the challenges?

2. The risks for reasoning cooperatively are different when the issue
   highlights one person's social privilege and another person's social
   disadvantage (think of Kim and Sara from this chapter). Can you
   think of a time when an issue related to your social identity prompted
   an argument? Did the argument highlight your social privilege or
   disadvantage? How did you react? Reflecting on it now, did you react
   in a way to promote cooperation? If so, what did you do? If not, what
   could you have done differently?

3. Reasoning cooperatively requires that all participants be committed
   to the goal of agreement, not winning. What are some signs that
   you should withdraw from an argument that is not proceeding in a
   cooperative way? In other words, when does cooperation become too
   risky?

Additional Resources

The Centre for Research in Reasoning, Argumentation, and Rhetoric (CRRAR), http://www1.uwindsor.ca/crrar/, at the University of Windsor has some excellent resources on critical thinking and argument theory, including books, news, and conferences. The center cooperates with a variety of international critical thinking and argumentation organizations to bring together some of the best research and scholars in the field.

PBS's Open Mind video series has a talk by Deborah Tannen on her book *The Argument Culture*. The video is available at http://www.ovguide.com/video/the -open-mind-the-argument-culture-part-i-0aa1fb64fb0f11e29cd01231392275ac.

Professor Catherine Hundleby has an excellent blog at http://chundleby.com with resources on critical thinking books, including three steps to choosing a text.

RAIL, http://railct.com/rail-resources/, a blog on reasoning, argumentation, and informal logic, has a whole host of news and resources related to these topics.

Professor Michael Gilbert's web page "Argumentation Theory," http://www.yorku.ca /gilbert/argthry/argtyhry.html, includes several resources related to his theory as well as his writings on argumentation theory.

4 | Cognitive Biases

Individual Habits and Social Beliefs

In chapter 3 we considered how the history of argument and debate was linked with aggression and the idea of conquering your opponent. We also considered how this history combines with the strong emotional content of our social identity to create fertile ground for pseudoreasoning. We considered how cooperative reasoning, the third skill of an intellectually empathic critical thinker, provides us with a better model for thinking and reasoning about social identity issues as compared with the adversarial method. Yet even if we work to argue cooperatively about social identity and social differences, there are still some common habits we are all prone to when forming and organizing our beliefs. In this chapter we will look at some of these habits and the ways they can work against our ability to reason cooperatively, critically, and empathically when it comes to social differences.

The mistakes we will consider here affect our ability to take in information and form acceptable beliefs. Psychologists and argument theorists use the term "cognitive bias" to refer to the ways that individuals are prone to particular kinds of habits when we take in and process information. There is a second type of pseudoreasoning called *fallacies* that we will consider in chapter 5, and these occur in outward expressions when we communicate and interact with others. Both cognitive biases and fallacies can seem persuasive, despite the fact that they often contain false, misleading, or irrelevant information.

We have the ancient Greek philosopher Aristotle to thank for doing some of the very first work documenting fallacies.[1] Knowing how important public dialogue was to public policy, Aristotle sought a way to organize the mistakes that people made in speeches, arguments, and debates so that those mistakes would be easy for ordinary citizens to identify. When it comes to cognitive biases, we have the psychologists Amos Tversky and Daniel Kahneman to thank for their pioneering work in the early 1970s.[2] Tversky and Kahneman were interested in whether people actually reasoned according to rational choice theory, a popular model for understanding human behavior in economics and political science. What they discovered instead is that many people seem to use *heuristics,* which are rules that make processing information simpler for the brain but nevertheless systematically introduce errors in our reasoning.

Keeping in mind the web of belief, let's consider some of the common cognitive biases that can affect the way we take in and position beliefs within our weblike system. Remember that beliefs positioned at the core of our web are practically impossible to revise because a change at the core will have dramatic repercussions for the structure of the entire web. Beliefs that lie more on the periphery are much easier to revise because they have less influence on the entire structure. We said that confirmation bias, a cognitive bias we are already familiar with from chapter 1, works to reinforce and strengthen connections in our web because it motivates us to take in information that is consistent with our existing set of beliefs. At the same time, confirmation bias works to exclude or dismiss information that is inconsistent with our web of belief. This means that our cognitive habit is to not seek out information and evidence that could disconfirm our already existing system of beliefs. This habit has some practical value. If we take in available information and begin to form a coherent web of belief, then we move through the world more efficiently (though not necessarily more effectively) if we do not have to attend to every counterinstance and contrary occurrence. The young child who has come to believe that Brussels sprouts taste bad does not ordinarily waste time considering whether this belief may be false, nor does the child seek out different kinds of Brussels sprouts experiences to test her or his belief. Like most of us, the child holds on to that belief until something forces her or him to challenge it, leading the child to either reconsider or seek out new evidence. While this is an efficient strategy for preserving beliefs, it can mean that we miss out on important evidence as well as experiences that could challenge our beliefs. So, though cognitive biases can have practical value, they are not always aligned with good critical thinking.

When it comes to beliefs about social identity and social issues, there are several cognitive biases that appear with frequency in dialogues and debates. Again, these biases (and the same will be true of fallacies) only become *bad* habits when we rely on them at the cost of gathering and considering actual available evidence relevant to an issue under consideration. In other words, biases and fallacies are *context sensitive.*

For instance, if I asked you to go out and find as much information as possible confirming a particular belief you had about Mexican immigrants in the United States and you came back with a whole host of evidence that did confirm your belief about Mexican immigrants in the United States, you would not be guilty of a confirmation bias. The evidence is relevant because I asked you specifically to retrieve information that would confirm *your* belief. If I asked you to gather information about the situation of Mexican immigrants in the United States in general, the bias would occur if you only retrieved information confirming the beliefs you have about Mexican immigrants. The issue in the former case is whether or not you found evidence to confirm your beliefs about Mexican immigrants in the United States, and the issue in the latter case is whether or not you found credible evidence about Mexican immigrants in the United States in general. The point of carefully attending to this distinction is that when the issue involves some aspect of social identity, it is quite common for people to mistake evidence for their own beliefs as relevant evidence in general. If you are not considering all acceptable evidence, even evidence that does not align with your own beliefs, then you are not thinking critically.

Seven Cognitive Biases in Arguments about Social Differences

Let's start by considering seven of the most common cognitive biases that cause people to misread or misinterpret evidence so as to support their existing web of belief. These are (1) actor-observer bias, (2) in-group bias, (3) group polarization, (4) out-group homogeneity effect, (5) status quo bias, (6) false consensus bias, and (7) hostile media effect.

Actor-observer bias refers to the tendency to judge our own behavior as resulting from the particular circumstances we are in rather than some general fact about our personality. Yet when we judge other people, we are more likely to attribute their behavior to their character rather than to external, situational factors. Interestingly, researchers have found that people tend to succumb less to actor-observer bias when it comes to judging the behavior of close friends and family members.[3] The explanation is that when we know more about people's beliefs, desires, and motivations, we are more likely to account for the external forces that impact their behavior. The less we know, the more likely we are to attribute their behavior to internal factors. This gives us further evidence for why online dialogues and debates between strangers can be breeding grounds for faulty reasoning. A good example of actor-observer bias can be seen in this comment following an article that appeared on CNN online following a story titled "The Return of the Welfare Queen." The commenter DebbieIndiana states:

I am a single mother and when my daughter was little I decided to go back to school to earn my nursing degree. I was in a tough situation financially and so I applied for food stamps. I used them for a time but I got off them once I could earn a decent living. Most of these people today though on food stamps just want a free handout and they expect everyone else to take care of them.[4]

This commenter is able to see the structural reasons that led to her temporary need for food stamps, but when it comes to others she attributes their use of food stamps to laziness and an unwillingness to work. Notice that the claim referring to "most people" does not provide any evidence to justify the belief that welfare recipients "want a free handout and everyone else to take care of them." Rather, it seems that DebbieIndiana is biased in favor of a structural explanation to make sense of her previous difficult circumstances but is not biased in favor of a structural explanation for strangers in a similar situation. In this way, actor-observer bias can lead to far more compassionate interpretations of our own behavior and the behaviors of those close to us and far less empathic interpretations of the behaviors of those we do not know personally.

Similarly, *in-group bias,* which refers to our tendency to prefer people whom we believe belong to the same groups that we do, can lead us to minimize or discount people whom we believe belong to groups with which we do not identify. It does not seem necessary that we have to have overt negative beliefs about out-group members for social bias and stereotyping to play a role in our thinking. As social psychologist Marilyn Brewer put it in her summary of the evidence, "Ultimately, many forms of discrimination and bias may develop not because out-groups are hated, but because positive emotions such as admiration, sympathy, and trust are reserved for the in-group."[5] In-group bias is context sensitive in the sense that the groups with which we identify can vary in significance and priority depending on the context. For instance, if we attend a sports event, our identification with fans of the team we prefer will be more prominent during the game than our identification with other groups to which we belong. Similarly, when we are not at the sporting event and are instead at an ethnic festival celebrating our cultural heritage, our identification with the sports team will be far less prominent.

Because in-group bias is sensitive to context, it can lead individuals and groups who might not ordinarily prioritize a certain aspect of their identity to suddenly become consciously aware and protective of that identity. If the issue of gender is raised, for instance, a group of people who ordinarily have a lot in common could suddenly shift to identifying with only those who share their gender. If a debate about gender arises, the third cognitive bias, *group polarization,* can play a role. Group polarization refers to the way our individual beliefs and attitudes can become more extreme and more rigidified in the presence of other members of our social group. In other words, our tendency to identify with others in our social group can lead us to a common view that is more extreme than an average view. The outcome of in-group bias is that arguments within and between groups wind up generating extreme beliefs and attitudes rather than midpoints between extremes.

If we include the *out-group homogeneity effect* in our analysis, we can see why many people tend to judge as extremists those with whom they debate and who are outside of their social group while judging those within their own group as having more varied and nuanced perspectives. Out-group homogeneity effect refers to the tendency to see those in the out-group as all alike and interchangeable and even expendable while viewing the in-group as made up of unique and diverse individuals.

The combined effect of in-group bias, group polarization, and out-group homogeneity can lead to dialogues such as the following that occurred between three posters commenting in Time Magazine Online (December 2012) on an article about gun violence:

> LuvMyGuns: It is not guns that need to be controlled in Chicago, it is some of its citizens who think their answers to most everything is pulling a trigger. Obama's gun control laws will only wind up punishing legitimate citizens who own firearms.
> DionysBeer: Removing guns from gangs makes it harder for them to kill as many people. I'd think even the most ardent gun fanatic would see a value in taking guns from gang members.
> CliffCabbage: Chicago has some of the strictest gun control laws in the country and it is the murder capital of the United States. Obviously gun control laws aren't effective at getting guns away from gang members.
> LuvMyGuns: Exactly!
> DionysBeer: We have laws that prohibit drunk driving. People still drive drunk so do you propose that we give up those laws? Of course not, you still support the laws because it is better than not having any!
> CliffCabbage: Yeah but we don't take away cars or alcohol from people if they are caught driving drunk. We punish the people driving.

These new gun control laws are going to make it easy for the government to take my guns.
LuvMyGuns: Anyone with common sense can see that gun laws
don't work!
DionysBeer: You NRA shills are all the same. You need a gun to prove
your masculinity and hide that fact by using words like "freedom"
and "patriot."[6]

The dialogue begins with LuvMyGuns stating that more gun control laws
will not lead to a decrease in violence in Chicago and will only serve to
restrict or punish those who legally own guns. DionysBeer makes the point
that making guns harder to obtain will result in fewer guns in the hands
of gang members. CliffCabbage then enters the discussion and makes the
point that Chicago has some of the strictest gun control laws in the nation
and yet has one of the highest rates of gun-related violence. LuvMyGuns
sees this as supporting evidence and exclaims "Exactly!" LuvMyGuns now
has an ally in the debate. DionysBeer then makes the point that drinking
and driving laws, which have not eliminated drunk driving, have nevertheless reduced the number of incidents. CliffCabbage retorts that those laws
are not analogous since they do not restrict the use of alcohol or driving but
instead punish the person driving under the influence. With CliffCabbage
and LuvMyGuns aligned as members of an in-group, their position, as
expressed by LuvMyGuns's statement "gun laws in general will not work" is
now more extreme than LuvMyGuns's original claim that Obama's efforts at
gun control may wind up punishing noncriminal gun owners. The transition to this more extreme position can be attributed to group polarization.
DionysBeer ends the debate employing the out-group homogeneity effect
by casting all those who oppose stricter gun laws as all alike and simple-
minded. No doubt DionysBeer views him/herself and those who share his/
her views on gun control as more sophisticated and nuanced in their thinking and less monolithic than those "NRA shills."

Our fifth cognitive bias, *status quo bias,* refers to an unjustified preference for the current state of affairs. The mistake here is thinking that any
change is equal to a loss. Unless we evaluate available evidence, we cannot
assume beforehand that a change in the current conditions will result in a
negative outcome. We can see evidence of this bias in many public reactions
to the changing demographics in the United States. The Pew Research Center has reported that by 2050, whites who are currently 70 percent of the
U.S. population will make up only 47 percent of the population.[7] The largest
growth in population will come from Hispanic and Asian groups, and a

much smaller proportion of these groups will be foreign born as compared with 2005 data. By 2025, the rise of the immigrant population in the United States will surpass the peak of immigration nearly a century ago. Estimates are that by 2050, one in five Americans (19 percent) will be immigrants as compared with one in eight (12 percent) in 2005. In response to these predicted changes, some white Americans have voiced their anxiety and even fear that they will face oppression as the new minority. Sociologist Charles Gallagher, who researches white racial attitudes, was baffled to discover that many whites find themselves to be an embattled minority group following the news of changing demographics.[8] Comments such as the following by "SKACALL2010" sum up this anxiety:

> I wouldn't say we're oppressed. . . . But I definitely see it coming down the road. We have a harder time getting jobs and getting into college because we're white, and because public colleges (and many private ones) give preference to other races. Many companies are more likely to hire you if you're not white, and most levels of government have diversity policies that require them to give hiring preference to people who aren't white. We have a whole system devoted to making it harder for white people to survive in America. It's so sad![9]

We can say several things about this anxiety relative to the status quo bias. One, if a group has benefitted from being in the majority, a change in that status will be anticipated as a coming loss rather than as a neutral or positive outcome. What is worth noting is that this expectation is a bias rather than the result of considering available evidence. If whites have not had advantages in virtue of being a racial majority, then why worry about shifting to a minority status? The worry reveals that there is a belief that by shifting from majority to minority status, whites will lose advantages. This anxiety is expressed by SKACALL2010 in the comment above when s/he says that it is "harder for white people to survive in America." Is this reasonable in light of the available evidence?

Let's consider the claim that it is getting harder for whites to get jobs. According to the Bureau of Labor Statistics, the unemployment rate for black male college graduates 25 and older in 2009 was twice that of white male college graduates, with a rate of 8.4 percent as compared with 4.4 percent. A 2009 study published in the *Journal of Labor Economics* found that white, Asian, and Hispanic managers tended to hire more whites and fewer blacks than did black managers.[10] The Economic Policy Institute reports that between March 2013 and February 2014, nationwide unemployment rates were 5.8 percent for whites, 8.1 percent for Hispanics, and 12.0 percent for blacks. These elevated rates have grown since 2007 along with the racial disparities. In 2007, the nationwide unemployment rates were 4.1 for whites, 5.6 for Hispanics, and 8.3 for blacks.[11]

For the past four decades through good economic times and bad, the black unemployment rate has been roughly double that for whites. The disparity is evident across education levels and occupations, which complicates efforts to close it. It is simply not true that it is harder for whites to get jobs because they are white as compared with other racial and ethnic groups, and there is no evidence to suggest that it will become harder. This is especially so when we consider how important friends, networks, and connections are for getting a job. The more people who are established in positions of management and leadership, the more chances are that people they know and connect with will fill open positions. Of course, this is not to say that merit alone can never win out over personal connections, but if someone does not feel like the right fit from the point of view of a manager, it will be harder for merit to prevail.

What about the concern that it is becoming harder for whites to get into college because of affirmative action policies and the changing demographics of the population? Research has shown that only the top 20 percent of colleges actually consider racial preferences when making admissions decisions.[12] This is because these colleges receive many more applications as compared with available slots, and the admissions criteria are very rigorous. Other things being equal (grades, test scores, writing samples), an underrepresented racial minority might take preference over a majority student for a coveted slot in the same way that a talented athlete or musician would. Assuming that 15 percent of students selected at these schools are black or Hispanic and that absolutely all of them are accepted based on their race (given comparable test scores, grades, etc.), this would make affirmative action just 3 percent of all selective college admissions in a year.

University of Chicago economist Brent Hickman discovered a similar estimate in his research.[13] Hickman found that affirmative action reduces nonminority enrollment at the top one-fourth of schools by about 4.2 percent a year. This means that at a university such as Harvard, which received 35,000 applications for admission in 2011 and accepted only 6.2 percent (2,065 students), if we assume that 60 percent (1,239) of those students are white (a conservative estimate), affirmative action would give roughly 34 seats to nonwhite students (4.2 percent of the remaining 826, or 40 percent, accepted) that could have gone to whites. Remember that 35,000 students overall applied. So, if fewer than 2 percent of all accepted students benefitted from affirmative action and this rate is only relevant at the most elite colleges and universities, why is it so common for whites to feel that they are being cheated in college admissions by affirmative action policies?

In a paper titled "Affirmative Action and Its Mythology," Harvard economist Roland Fryer and Brown University economist Glen Loury explain this feeling by drawing an analogy with parking.[14] Suppose a single unused parking space in front of a popular restaurant in a crowded city is reserved for disabled drivers. Nondisabled drivers who observe the unused space while trying to park might resent this policy, imagining that it prolongs their parking search. But when parking is tight it is likely that, even if the disabled space were not reserved, it would have already been taken by the time any given driver came along. The result is that many nondisabled drivers will overestimate their chance of getting the unreserved space if only it were not reserved for the disabled. Hence, the perceived policy favoring the disabled is seen as a high cost for the nondisabled, despite the fact that the policy has a negligible effect on the mean duration of a parking search. So too, Fryer and Loury argue, are the perceived costs to whites from racial affirmative action in higher education.

In other words, even though it is unlikely that we would ever get that spot right in front of the restaurant, the fact that it is specially earmarked for someone other than us means that we overestimate its value while we are driving around looking for a spot. In the same way, many whites overestimate the few benefits and protections afforded to nonwhite Americans. This overestimation combined with the status quo bias helps us to understand the anxiety that many white Americans seem to have about changing demographics. However, this anxiety and biased thinking can significantly get in the way of actually considering the available evidence. Moreover, it generates comments such as that by "BRAVI," a commenter following a CNN news story titled "Are Whites Racially Oppressed":

> You don't have to be a Tea-Partyer or a white supremacist to see that the US has a ton of programs supporting minorities and uplifting and celebrating minority communities (scholarships, community and student groups, etc.) but few if any designed specifically for whites. For example, I currently attend a top-100 American university, am white, and receive ZERO aid despite my parents having average income. I also know of many other white students who receive zero financial aid, and whose parents live fairly humbly. However, I have African American friends who are dropped off by their parents in shiny new Mercedes and have huge flat-screens in their rooms,

and they've told me they receive significant financial aid. Is it wrong that whites feel like a dispossessed majority when any attempts to celebrate our identity are labeled racist, and such injustices as that listed above occur on a daily basis?[15]

BRAVI makes two substantive claims in this comment. The first is that the United States, while having "tons of programs" to support and celebrate minorities, has "few if any designed specifically for whites," and if whites participate they are labeled racists for celebrating their racial identity. Second, while there are ample scholarship and financial aid opportunities for minorities, BRAVI claims that there are "ZERO" for whites. Let's take each of these claims in turn.

First, is it true that there are no programs to support and celebrate whites? One aspect of racial privilege, as we discussed in chapter 3, is that it is often invisible to those who have it. People who identify (and are identified) as white are more likely to pick out their ethnicity rather than their race when asked "What are you?" For example, many whites with European ancestry will respond by saying "I'm Italian" or "I'm half German and half Irish" rather than "I'm white." It is a feature of privilege that those who have it experience an incredible range and variety within their privilege but see a monolithic "them" when they perceive others. The idea that "they" all "look alike" or "sound alike" or "believe the same thing" is perpetuated by people with privilege who do not have to really learn about the complexity and variety of nonprivileged groups. So while BRAVI may feel that there is nothing specifically that celebrates whiteness in our culture, he ignores the preponderance of European American festivals, clubs, societies, and holidays. Moreover, when we celebrate our nation's history, our leaders—our most beloved statesmen, writers, scientists, and artists—are overwhelmingly white (and male). The few recent examples of nonwhite leaders, athletes, and artists who are celebrated are notable because of a long history in which such accomplishments were rendered almost impossible because of racist laws and policies.

BRAVI's second claim—that there are no scholarships for whites—also fails to account for "white" being equated with European American. Many of the clubs, societies, and European American organizations referred to earlier award scholarships to their members' children and members of their community. In fact, Mark Kantrowitz, a financial aid analyst, explains that "while there are very few private scholarships that are explicitly targeted at white students as a category, white students receive a disproportionately greater share of private scholarships and merit-based grants. White students receive more than three times as much in merit-based grant and private scholarship funding as minority students."[16] In the case of private scholarships, while the focus is not on white students, the scholarship sponsors tend to establish funding for characteristics, activities, and talents of interest to them. These factors in turn tend to resonate for students with backgrounds similar to the sponsors. So, scholarships for equestrian sports, water sports, winter sports, golf, archery, rodeo, and wrestling tend to go to white students rather than black, Hispanic, or Asian students. Similarly, private scholarships based on a European national origin or heritage such as German, French, Czech, Danish, Polish, Italian, Irish, etc., will predominantly or exclusively go to white recipients. State scholarships from areas with a large majority of white residents such as Montana, Idaho, North and South Dakota, Wyoming, Utah, Maine, New Hampshire, Iowa, and Nebraska will award scholarships to local residents who happen to be white. Finally, scholarships based on field of study and even religious affiliation will break down along race lines, with a larger majority going to white students.

In terms of merit-based scholarships, Kantrowitz attributes the disproportionate number received by white students again not as overt discrimination against students of color but instead as the result of economic and educational disparities based on race. Middle-class and wealthier students are likely to be white and more likely to have access to educational resources and well-funded schools. This too is the outcome of a long history of racial discrimination and institutionalized racism that made it much harder for nonwhites to have access to education and equal opportunity. Yet when middle-class and wealthier white students are recipients of merit scholarships, they tend to attribute their success to their own innate intelligence and hard work rather than the advantages they had in virtue of their wealth and social privilege. This is not to deny that white recipients of merit scholarships have worked hard. Rather, their hard work was bolstered by the advantages of growing up in middle-class and wealthy communities where the vocabulary, the school systems, the cultural reference points, and even the social and recreational activities closely matched the requirements for higher education. In addition, having parents who have navigated the college experience themselves and can provide tutors and extra help for what may be lacking means that success is in part the result of some unearned advantages.

When people with social privilege mistakenly attribute their success solely to their own hard work rather than to unearned structural advantages, they also mistakenly perceive anyone who has not achieved success as lacking innate intelligence and the ability to work hard. This explains why someone like BRAVI may feel that there are no scholarships for whites because merit scholarships are given out on the basis of merit, which from his mistaken point of view has nothing to do with race or class.

The group biases involving in-group bias, group polarization, and out-group homogeneity effect and the status quo bias work together to create the erroneous assumption that whites are suffering at the expense of special rights and privileges afforded to nonwhites. The presumption that a right or privilege afforded to a minority group will take something away from the majority is all-or-nothing thinking. Yet if we look at our nation's history of affording rights, it is often the case that what was considered a special right for a particular social group winds up translating to a broader human right.

Consider maternity leave, which was a hotly contested legal matter throughout much of the 1970s and 1980s.[17] Opponents to protected maternity leave argued that it was extending a special right to a subset of the labor force. Defenders of the measure argued that pregnant women were not a special interest group but instead were a normal part of the working population. This led to a public reconceptualization of what constitutes a "worker." The question arose, Does the idea of a lone adult male who neither becomes pregnant nor has any family responsibilities present an accurate picture of the typical worker? The decidedly negative response to that question extended the discussion of maternity benefits to a broader public discussion of family responsibilities that led to the 1993 Family Medical Leave Act. This federal law extended job protections for qualified medical and family reasons, including personal or family illness, family military leave, pregnancy, adoption, or the foster care placement of a child. So, what was initially seen as a special right just for pregnant women actually provided an opportunity for a broader discussion about human rights and the concept of worker rights. If we are only capable of an all-or-nothing reaction to proposals for extending rights and benefits, then we lose the opportunity to reflect on our concepts and revise our beliefs.

As intellectually empathic critical thinkers, what should we learn from these examples of group biases and white perceptions of shrinking opportunities and unfair advantages afforded to nonwhites? Should we just chalk it up to prejudice, selfishness, and flat-out racism? Perhaps in some cases the answer is simply "yes." But I would argue that in most cases the answer is likely more complex and nuanced. In addition, by adopting a more intellectually empathic perspective we could solicit more relevant evidence, which would in turn give us a better understanding of these seemingly irrational and biased beliefs.

118 | Intellectual Empathy

The first step toward doing this is recognizing that whites, like other racially identified groups, are neither all the same nor all equally privileged.[18] Poor and working-class whites are often pitted against poor and working-class people of color when it comes to limited rights and goods. I have often found, for instance, that more of my white students who come from poor and working-class families will object to rights afforded to undocumented immigrant workers than will white students who come from middle-class and wealthier families. This may be so in part because poor and working-class whites have good reasons to feel that there is already so little opportunity to go around that when rights are afforded to noncitizens, it is perceived as a loss of resources they should have as citizens.

Another factor contributing to the feeling that many whites have that there are opportunities for everyone else but them is their thin ancestral history and mixed or unknown ethnic identity. Many white Americans are the descendants of European immigrants who came to the United States fleeing religious persecution, war, poverty, and famine. Those histories were often painful in their own right, and though many of those immigrants had the advantage of assimilating into white Anglo-Saxon systems of privilege, there were still costs. Native languages were suppressed, customs and traditions eroded, and family histories were often lost or destroyed, just to survive. The result is that for many white Americans, their knowledge of their ancestral history only goes back one or two generations, and their sense of a specific culture and tradition is unclear or absent. While this does not compare to the horror of the kidnapping, enslavement, and persecution that devastated so many African American families or the violence committed against Native Americans, there is nevertheless loss and pain in the histories of many who today are considered to be white Americans. As we said earlier, when asked their ethnicity, many whites in the United States will say things like "I don't know, some German, French, Scottish on my mother's side and Italian, Irish, English on my father's side," reflecting the patchwork identities of successful assimilation. But with that success comes the costs of not having an ancestral home or a history tied to a specific place or culture. For this reason, many whites may overestimate and even resent efforts to value racial and ethnic identities. Efforts to celebrate Chinese culture or Indian heritage or African American history can be reminders to whites that they have had to give up more specific ethnic or racial identities. So, it may seem—incorrectly—that there are all sorts of ways that "everyone else" is valued and they are not.

The point I want to make, then, is that despite data and evidence to the contrary, many whites still believe that there are fewer opportunities for whites and that nonwhites seem to get special treatment in terms of social benefits. Rather than judging this as simply racist, I suggest that we instead consider how the invisibility of privilege can combine with class differences as well as a loss of ethnic and racial history to create the mistaken impression that everyone except for whites is afforded special opportunities.

Another bias related to beliefs about groups is *false consensus bias*. This cognitive bias occurs when we overestimate how much people agree with our beliefs, opinions, preferences, and values. This does not mean we assume that everyone believes what we believe. Rather, we assume that what we believe is the common view and is much more widely held than any evidence indicates. False consensus bias operates in interesting ways with regard to group beliefs and dynamics. For instance, group members who are prone to false consensus bias come to believe that others in the wider population share their group's collective opinion. Since people generally do not seek out disconfirming evidence for their beliefs (confirmation bias), the effect of false consensus goes unchallenged.

For example, when a friend of mine who taught at a college in New England decided to take a new job at a small college in the rural South, he was shocked to find so many faculty members who regularly attended church. This friend was an atheist, and in the community he left, all the intellectual and creative people he knew did not identify with any organized religion, nor did they regularly attend religious services. So, my friend came to believe that scholars and artists and intellectuals did not participate in organized religion. Of course, his belief remained unchallenged as long as he remained within that community but was significantly tested when he relocated. The experience led him to revise his web of belief, particularly those beliefs having to do with the relationship between intelligence, creativity, and religion.

The final cognitive bias that we will consider is *hostile media effect*, which was first documented by Stanford psychologists in a 1985 study.[19] The researchers recruited 144 Stanford students with differing views about the crises in the Middle East. The students initially filled out questionnaires detailing their general knowledge of the massacres of Palestinians in Sabra and Shatila in 1982. The students were also asked about their general sympathies toward either the Palestinians or the Israelis. The researchers then divided the groups into pro-Israeli, pro-Arab, and neutral cohorts. These groups viewed identical news clips about the incident in groups of 6–12. After the viewing, students were asked to fill out forms regarding the objectivity and fairness of the news segments. This included such things as the percentage of favorable, neutral, and unfavorable references to Israel as well as an estimation regarding how many neutral viewers would change to more positive or negative views about Israel.

The results of the study showed that the cohorts who were nonneutral saw the news reports as biased in favor of the other side. Pro-Arabs thought that the programs applied lower standards to Israel and focused less on Israel's role in massacre. The pro-Israeli group saw exactly the opposite. Both groups felt that the personal views of the news staff were in opposition to their own. Further analysis showed that the two groups actually "saw" different news programs. The pro-Arabs heard 42 percent opinions favorable to Israel and 26 percent unfavorable. The pro-Israeli group saw 16 percent favorable and 57 percent unfavorable. Besides being perceived differently, the program content was also evaluated differently. Perhaps most interesting is that the more knowledgeable students were about the incident, the more they believed that the media presented biased content.

One of the things we can learn from this study is that charges of bias against the media may come most forcefully from those who have the strongest beliefs and the most information regarding a social or political issue. Yet even though these same people might possess relevant evidence about the issue, those at either end of the extreme will perceive the very same information as unfavorable to their view as well as factually inconsistent with what they know. This may seem like the opposite of confirmation bias in that knowledgeable people with strong beliefs will attend primarily to news reports that run counter to their beliefs. Yet this is not so different from confirmation bias if we assume that the starting assumption for those with strong beliefs is that the media is biased. If this is assumed, then it makes sense that those susceptible to hostile media bias will attend to evidence that confirms their belief that the media is biased. That is, these folks are not actually looking for evidence to counter or disconfirm their beliefs about the social or political issue but instead are looking for evidence to confirm their belief that the media does not objectively report the news.

Questions to Counter the Effects of Cognitive Biases

So, what conclusions should we draw from exploring these seven cognitive biases? First, there is a lot of evidence to show that these biases occur frequently in the thinking of ordinarily reasonable people. This means that we should pay careful attention to whether the biases are operating in our own arguments and the arguments presented by others. Second, the prevalence of these biases should put the following questions at the forefront of our thinking and reasoning about issues related to social differences:

- When I explain my problems and the problems facing people like me, do I attribute those problems to external conditions rather than to my own behavior? And when I explain the problems facing people who are not like me, do I attribute those problems to their behavior rather than external conditions?
- Do I prefer the people who are like me in circumstances where identity becomes the issue? Do I have the tendency to take a stronger position than I would normally when I believe that people like me are under attack? Do I believe that people like me are much more reasonable and varied in their opinions about our social group and that those who are not like me are much more rigid and extreme?
- Do I prefer that things remain the way they are in terms of race, ethnicity, religion, sexual orientation, dis/ability, and immigrant rights because changes will bring about worse conditions for me (and people like me)?
- Am I confident in my social beliefs because most everyone I care about and spend time with shares these beliefs (rather than because I have actually challenged or tested them by seeking evidence outside of my family and friends)?
- Do I pay attention to media reports that I judge to be unfair to me and people like me and ignore those that I believe to be in favor of other groups?

By carefully keeping these questions in mind and paying attention to how we take in and process information, we can reduce the effects of cognitive biases in our beliefs about social differences. In the next chapter we will consider fallacies, the pseudoreasoning that affects the way we construct and present arguments when trying to communicate our social beliefs to others.

Questions for Review

1. What is the difference between finding evidence to support your belief on an issue as compared with finding evidence about the issue in general? How does the failure to make this distinction contribute to confirmation bias?

2. Give an example from your own experience where one of the following cognitive biases played a role in your thinking:
    -   Actor-observer bias
    -   In-group bias
    -   Group polarization
    -   Out-group homogeneity effect

3. What are some of the fears that white Americans have about becoming a minority in the near future? How is this related to the status quo bias?

4. How has the transition from maternity leave to the Family Medical Leave Act demonstrated the way that a special right can become a human right?

5. What is one of the conclusions we can draw from the study of pro-Israeli and pro-Arab viewers of news reports on the massacres of Palestinians in Sabra and Shatila in 1982?

Questions for Further Thinking and Writing

1. Describe the analogy that economists Roland Fryer and Glen Loury make between white attitudes about affirmative action and a parking spot reserved for the disabled. What are the strengths of this analogy? What are the weaknesses? Can you think of a better analogy to make the same point?

2. Choose one of the questions in the section "Questions to Counter the Effects of Cognitive Biases" toward the end of this chapter and write a response reflecting on a particular experience when you were subject to a cognitive bias in your own thinking. What would you do differently now?

3. Is there a cognitive bias that was not covered in this chapter or not documented in the psychological literature that you think is important to consider when thinking and reasoning about social identity and differences?

Additional Resources

Daniel Kahneman, one of the pioneering researchers on cognitive biases, presents an excellent overview of some of his work in a lecture titled "Biased Biases" at the History and Rationality Lecture Series at Hebrew University in Jerusalem. You can find the lecture at http://www.youtube.com/watch?v=3CWm3i74mHI.

Antiracist essayist, author, and educator Tim Wise has done a significant amount of work on white anxiety and resentment regarding changing demographics. You can find his website with a variety of resources at http://www.timwise.org. Wise also gave a talk at Google titled "White Like Me: Reflections of a Privileged Son," which is available at www.youtube.com/watch?v=oV-EDWzJuzk.

For some historical background on the Civil Rights Act of 1964 and equal employment, see the National Archives, http://www.archives.gov/education/lessons/civil-rights-act/.

5 | Logical Fallacies

Ad Hominem: The Common Variety

In chapter 4 we established that cognitive biases are habits we form when taking in and processing information. These habits have advantages in some contexts but can also prevent us from examining evidence that is not already within our web of belief. In this way, cognitive biases can become bad habits that limit our critical thinking abilities. In this chapter we will consider logical fallacies, which are common argument patterns we rely on when expressing the reasons we have for our point of view. Like cognitive biases, these patterns are not always bad. However, in contexts where a common pattern relies on unacceptable or irrelevant evidence and distracts our attention away from what is relevant, the pattern is a logical fallacy.

Philosopher and argument theorist Christopher Tindale in his book *Fallacies and Argument Appraisal* provides an excellent overview of fallacy research and notes:

> One thing the recent literature has made very clear is that fallacies are far more complex, and thus deserving of much fuller analyses, than the traditional textbook treatments have suggested. Two things have reinforced the recognition of how complex fallacies really are: The first of these is the appreciation that many of the fallacies are failed instances of good argument schemes or forms. Hence, we cannot dismiss all *ad hominem* arguments or *Slippery Slopes*, for example, because there are circumstances under which such reasoning is appropriate. The second feature that reveals the complexity of fallacious reasoning is the recognition that to evaluate fallacies fully we need to consider aspects of the context in which the argumentation arises. In many instances this involves the details of a dialogue between participants in an argumentative exchange. In other cases we must sift through what is available of the background to a dispute, such as the history of exchanges between the participants or the beliefs of the audience.[1]

What we learn from Tindale is that fallacies are, first, argument patterns that are problematic in some contexts but actually reasonable in others. Second, context includes the arguer's background, her or his history of arguing related to the topic, as well as the beliefs of those evaluating the argument. In this way, fallacy analysis is complex and context sensitive and benefits from self-awareness, an understanding of privilege and power, and a commitment to cooperative reasoning. These are all skills that as intellectually empathic critical thinkers we work to develop. And because fallacies have this complexity, as we work through this chapter we will first consider the problematic contexts that give rise to a fallacy and then consider a context where the same pattern would not be logically fallacious. This kind of analysis, which forces us to move from simple fallacy labeling to thinking about fallacies in a dynamic and context-sensitive way, provides us with more opportunities for thinking critically and empathically.[2] Our focus will be on ten of the most common logical fallacies that occur when people reason and debate about social differences.

The first and arguably the most common fallacy we will consider is *ad hominem,* which was introduced in chapter 2 and is Latin for "to the man" or "to the person." Because this fallacy is so prevalent and so easy to commit, there are several variations. For our purposes, we will consider just two of the basic varieties. The first and most obvious variety occurs when an arguer attempts to refute another argument by simply attacking the source of the evidence rather than the evidence itself. When the attack is directly related to the personal characteristics of the source, then it is an *ad hominem–abusive attack.* An ad hominem–abusive attack occurs when someone tries to refute another's argument by calling that person "stupid," insulting the person's appearance, or putting down the person's race, ethnicity, sexual orientation, etc., rather than reasons. As we saw in the case of Anita Sarkeesian, the feminist blogger described in chapter 3, much of the comments aimed at her by critics were in the form of ad hominem–abusive attacks.

The second variety is *ad hominem circumstantial.* A person who tries to refute another's argument by claiming that the opponent's circumstances and social standing are relevant to an argument commits an ad hominem–circumstantial fallacy. For instance, if there is a question of whether or not a particular business practice is unfair to women and a woman argues that it is, any person who said that the woman's argument must be wrong, just because she has something to gain, would commit the fallacy. Similarly, if an initiative has been proposed to benefit women and a particular woman did not support it because she did not like the details, any person who claimed that she should support it because she is a woman would commit an ad hominem–circumstantial fallacy. The lesson to learn here is that a person's particular characteristics and social identity are irrelevant to the reasons the person has given in support of her or his position. It is the responsibility of any arguer to address the reasons in an argument and not the person giving the reasons. This is because as in the cases just described, a woman can give good reasons for why a policy might negatively impact all women even if she stands to gain from overturning the policy. Similarly, even a woman can object to a policy that seems to benefit women on the basis of the problems she finds in the reasons given to justify the policy. Just because someone stands to gain or lose if we accept her or his conclusion, it is still irrelevant to whether or not the reasons the person gives are credible, relevant, and justifying.

Credibility and Ad Hominem Circumstantial

It is worth taking a moment here to say something about credibility. We said in chapter 3 that the first step in evaluating an argument is to judge whether the premises are acceptable or believable. I want to add here that we also need to evaluate whether the source for the evidence is credible. For instance, if you claim that drinking cow's milk is tantamount to drinking poison and I ask you for the source of that claim, I am asking for a credible reference. If you reply that the claim comes from your vegan friend who feels so much better since cutting out dairy, then the source does not measure up to the weight of the claim. In other words, even if your vegan friend does feel so much better after eliminating dairy from his diet, it does not follow that drinking cow's milk is tantamount to drinking poison. To substantiate that claim, the source must include evidence from a large sample of many more individuals, controls for different digestive systems, and repeatable studies over time that demonstrate the effects of cow's milk on the human body. The source for such a broad claim that is inconsistent with what many people take to be common knowledge (that milk is generally good for the human body) should meet our very strictest standards for careful long-term study. This is not to say that it can't turn out to be true that cow's milk is tantamount to drinking poison (I am not making this claim, only mentioning it for the purposes of this example!) but only that it would require more than your friend's testimony to be believable. Another way of thinking about this is that your friend is not an expert on the matter of the effects of cow's milk on the human body.

However, it is also a mistake to think that just because the claim runs counter to common sense and is so broad and far-reaching as to require expert credibility, any expert will do. We would need to appeal to experts whose area of expertise is directly relevant to the claim in question. In addition, there would have to be a certain amount of objectivity to these experts in terms of their investment in the truth of their expert judgment. So, for instance, assuming that their methodologies are sound, a biochemist whose salary is paid exclusively by the dairy industry and argues for the safety of cow's milk could be deemed less credible than a biochemist who does independent research, earns a living from grant money, and argues for the safety of cow's milk. This is because the dairy industry biochemist has a stronger vested interest in her conclusion being right. Her salary depends on it. The independent researcher is not tied to a single for-profit source of funding. Of course, all of this is not to say that the dairy industry biochemist cannot be right and the independent researcher wrong; it is just that our standard for evidence should go up when the source's credibility goes down. It would be reasonable for us to want to see more corroborating evidence for the dairy industry's research as compared with the independent research.

It may seem that our demand to weigh the credibility of a source runs counter to what we said about the ad hominem–circumstantial fallacy. Wasn't the point of that discussion that we can't refute a claim just because a person may benefit from our accepting her or his claim? Isn't it wrong to be skeptical about the dairy industry biochemist because we are addressing her circumstances rather than her conclusions? The answer is that it is not fallacious to be skeptical about the dairy industry's biochemist and to require further evidence. Rather, we commit the fallacy when we decide that the dairy industry's biochemist is wrong (rather than doubtful or less credible). That is the difference between assessing credibility and committing the ad hominem–circumstantial fallacy. In the case of credibility, we want to determine if the source of the claim is sufficient for establishing the likelihood of the claim. For that reason, we need to determine if the source has the relevant experience and in some cases expertise for making the claim. However, to rule out the source as not credible simply because he or she will gain from our accepting the claim is to commit the fallacy.

Now, how does all of this connect to social identity and intellectual empathy? I wanted to make the distinction between credibility and ad hominem–circumstantial because when the argument has to do with social issues and social identity, many people can easily slip from assessing a speaker's credibility to flat out denying that a speaker has any credibility at all. For instance, in numerous cases in my classroom where social difference is the topic, I have seen students report an incident to the class where they believed they faced racism or sexism or some other form of bias and discrimination, only to have their classmates deny it. Given that the rest of the class was not present for the incident and that the person offering the example experienced it firsthand, why is it so typical for so many members of the class to deny the speaker's experience?

One explanation for what is going on is that the students who deny the experience are sliding from a reasonable assessment of a source's credibility to an unreasonable ad hominem–circumstantial fallacy. Just because individual circumstances may directly relate to someone's argument, it does not follow that the person's claim should not be believed. Rather, if the person has a history of reliability, if we do not have direct evidence that runs counter to the person's claims, and if her or his evidence is based on firsthand direct experience, the person should be believed. To see this more clearly, consider again the claim that dairy is tantamount to poison. We said that such a broad claim required much more evidence than your friend's experience to make it believable. However, if the claim was "My friend said that drinking milk *for him* is tantamount to drinking poison" and it was based on his direct firsthand experience with drinking milk, then his claim should be believed unless we have evidence that he does not reliably tell the truth, unless we know that dairy has not been a problem for him, or if we find out that he has not really kept track of how he has felt before and after ingesting dairy. If none of these conditions hold, then your friend should be considered credible. In fact, the standard in logic and critical thinking is to assume that people are credible unless we have a reason to believe otherwise. And this is a standard that most of us use ordinarily in our day-to-day lives. If I ask a man on the street what time it is and he tells me "It's 4:45," then I believe him unless it seems highly unlikely that it is 4:45. But if that sounds about right, I don't demand further evidence or judge that he is probably lying or delusional.

Yet when people report on direct firsthand experiences of bias and discrimination, they are often met with knee-jerk reactions of doubt and dismissal. So why do these kinds of reports raise such high demands for credibility? I believe that the answer is twofold. First, hearing about bias and discrimination triggers the blame-guilt dichotomy we discussed earlier in chapter 2. When we hear that someone with a social identity different from our own has been discriminated against, we wonder whether we are being included in the problem. Since we don't feel (or at least like to feel) like we are part of the problem, it is easier to conclude that the discrimination didn't really happen. It is easier to chalk it up to a mistake on the part of the person reporting it than to take on blame and guilt for something we were not directly involved with. However, when listening to reports of bias and discrimination, we need to remain aware of the fact that blame/guilt and denial are not the only reactions available to us. While we may not have directly contributed to the bias or discrimination, we are still part of a social system where bias and discrimination operate. Just because we may not directly see it does not mean it is not there. Remember that social privilege is often invisible, and many people tend to socialize and spend time with people who share many of their social characteristics. For these reasons we can fall under the mistaken assumption that since we are not affected by something, it does not really exist. That is why those with different social characteristics often meet reports of bias and discrimination with skepticism. If my web of belief does not include injustices on the basis of my gender or race or religion or sexuality or ability, then recognizing that others are so affected means revising my web of belief. Given that these beliefs lie closer to the core of our web since they are connected to our identity, it may be easier for some people to simply deny the reports and leave their web intact. For others, they might make minor revisions in their belief system by judging the report to be true but deciding that it is just a single case of a sensitive person encountering a sexist, racist, etc., jerk. This judgment leaves the majority of the web intact, since it does not require thinking systemically and holistically about bias and discrimination. This judgment also allows us to avoid considering how we might be playing a role in such a system so we can avoid blame/guilt.

Second, it seems that very few people are sympathetic to someone who is "complaining." A person sharing a story of discrimination is often heard by others as blaming other people for her or his own problems. This can be true even for those people who belong to the same social groups as the speaker. Remember Cassandra in chapter 2 who developed diversity fatigue after participating in various social justice groups. Those who do not share the speaker's social identity and even those who do can be too quick to blame the person rather than the social system. Of course, this is understandable given American culture. We have all inherited a "pick yourself up by your bootstraps" ethos whereby if you work hard enough and remain disciplined, you can accomplish anything. While that characteristic of our culture has produced some great successes, it obscures the way that merit alone is often not enough, especially when there are intentional roadblocks and checkpoints for some people and not others (think of the EZ Pass we talked about in chapter 2 and the denial of equal opportunity in our country's history). Furthermore, the bootstrap ethos makes dependency seem like a bad thing, when in fact dependency is just part of life. We are dependent as infants and children, we are dependent when we are ill or injured, we are dependent as we get older, we are dependent when we need help. We depend on and trust our family and friends, coworkers, food producers, health professionals, teachers, law enforcement, fire and safety professionals, and on and on. Dependency and mutuality are essential for thriving, and yet dependency often gets stigmatized in the American culture of independence. This is not to deny the value of independence, but it should not come at the cost of devaluing our need for each other. Furthermore, it should not come at the cost of failing to see how erosions in that dependency and trust are often misinterpreted as complaining or being too sensitive.

The automatic doubt we have about the person we interpret as "complaining" about bias and discrimination may have more to do with our resistance than the person's lack of credibility. Philosopher Miranda Fricker calls this kind of doubt a "*testimonial injustice*" and describes it as when "a speaker receives an unfair credibility deficit on the part of the hearer due to a prejudice on the hearer's part."[3] What Fricker is describing are those cases where we dismiss a person's claim of discrimination because we prejudge the person to be trying to gain something or because we judge the person to be a whiner. However, such prejudgments cause a double harm to the person who has actually been discriminated against. The person now has to face both the experience of discrimination and our skepticism or denial of that experience, thereby leaving the person doubly harmed. Fricker says that when we are doubted with regard to our firsthand direct experiences, we suffer not simply as arguers but even more fundamentally as humans.[4]

As intellectually empathic critical thinkers, we will avoid inflicting this kind of double harm and injustice by being attentive to our capacity for knee-jerk dismissals of those who report discrimination and bias. Does this mean that we can never judge someone to be "playing the race card" or "the gender card" or that sometimes people really do fail to see how their personality and communication style might be causing more problems than their race or gender or religious identity? It does not. However, as intellectually empathic critical thinkers, we should come to that conclusion only after we have reflected on our own potential for bias as well as any evidence related to the person. Relevant evidence would only become apparent after we answered questions such as the following:

Does this person have a history of unreliably reporting their experiences?

Does the person attribute racist, sexist, homophobic, etc., motives to everyone uniformly rather than to more specific contexts and individuals?

Does the person lack allies? That is, does the person dismiss others who may not share the same social identity but who nevertheless act to support the person's struggles?

Does the person lack self-awareness?

Does the person never admit that he or she might be wrong?

The answers to these questions require time and careful consideration, but if they turn out to be mostly "yes," then there might be good reason to doubt such an individual's report of bias or discrimination. However, notice how much more information, history, and consideration would go into making that judgment. It is far from the automatic "What a whiner" or "It was probably just you" that so many reports of discrimination are met with. And even if there is good reason to question the speaker's credibility, it would still be fallacious to conclude that her or his claim is simply false. Even people who lack credibility may sometimes be right. For that reason, assessing a source as lacking credibility means that we are justified in seeking out more evidence to determine if the claim is credible. It does not mean, however, that we are justified in denying the claim just because the person has something to gain (which would be the fallacy of ad hominem circumstantial).

Finally, it is worth noting that skepticism and doubt about reports of bias and discrimination are often given much more attention than actual cases of bias and discrimination. In a recent study looking at ten years of reported sexual assaults on a college campus, the data showed that only 5.9 percent of reported cases turned out to be false allegations.[5] Even though 94.1 percent of reports turned out to have merit, many people still focused on the few false reports. Why do so many people seem to focus on false reports rather than on legitimate cases of sexual assault and harassment as well as racial, ethnic, and religious discrimination? The answer, I believe, has to do with the guilt-blame response that so many people feel is both inevitable and unfair. Remember that most people with social privilege have a hard time not only seeing their privilege but also feeling that their privilege gives them any real power. In many cases when privilege intersects with disadvantage, as in the case of Eric described in chapter 2 who is a white male but is also working class and not college educated, his social power is contextual and situational rather than consistent and ever present. If Eric hears a black coworker report an instance of racism perpetuated by another white coworker, Eric's identity as a white person is now highlighted.

It is not surprising, then, that accepting the report will somehow feel personal for Eric, as if he too is somehow implicated. Yet Eric has done nothing wrong as far as he can see, so why should he feel bad? Moreover, from Eric's standpoint, everyone has it tough. Why should we be so sensitive to race issues when every day Eric feels that he faces indignities from his boss, his neighbors, and the culture at large. Finally, Eric knows that there are policies protecting people from racial discrimination at his company, and he realizes that if such an accusation were made against him, it could mean public humiliation and even the loss of his job. Balancing these considerations, it is easier for many people to blame the person making the report than it is to accept it. The focus on false allegations serves to reinforce this choice because it protects the status quo and draws attention away from the more significant number of reports that have merit.

So to reiterate, as intellectual empathic critical thinkers we will treat reports of bias and discrimination the way we would treat all firsthand reports of direct experience, as credible and with a presumption in favor of their truth. We will work against defensive reactions of guilt-blame and denial and be open to hearing the evidence that a person presents. We will keep in mind that social privilege often obscures social disadvantage so that even if we have not seen or experienced what someone else reports, this does not mean it does not exist. Our goal in these cases is to become what philosopher Miranda Fricker calls "virtuous hearers," meaning that we hear reports of bias and discrimination with an awareness of the moral costs of denying their truth. We "reinflate" credibility to where it should be without our biases and defensive reactions.[6] In chapter 7 we will return to the notion of virtuous hearing and consider how the skills of intellectual empathy can play a role in developing this virtue.

Similarly, when reporting our own experiences of bias and discrimination, though we may face resistance from our hearers, we should do what we can to reduce their guilt-blame response and their tendency toward denial. Of course, this is not to say that we should be taking care of people who doubt us by making sure they feel safe. Doing so can just reinforce the power differentials that lead to biases and discrimination. Rather, what I am suggesting is that as intellectual empathic critical thinkers we recognize that when social differences are the issue, defensive reactions can often get in the way of seeing and hearing the evidence. If we start by assuming that people who are not like us can *never* see what we see or that they are too biased to ever admit that there is a problem, then we close off the possibility of thinking critically together. It is all too easy for things to get personal when we recount our experiences of bias and discrimination, but this can go both ways. While someone hearing a report of bias can often take it too personally, the reporter is also capable of transferring her or his anger and pain onto the hearer. This is especially so if the hearer shares social characteristics with the original offender. This kind of transference only heightens the climate of defensiveness. So, just as we need to be virtuous hearers, we also need to be responsible reporters. And just as we should assume that a speaker is credible unless we have demonstrated evidence otherwise, we should also assume that a hearer is sincerely interested in justice unless we have evidence otherwise.

Thought Experiment: Credibility and Testimonial Injustice

Miranda Fricker in her book *Epistemic Injustice: Ethics and the Power of Knowing* argues that testimonial injustice undermines a person's capacity as a knower, contributes to broader systematic inequalities, distorts people's identity formation, undermines their self-confidence, robs them of potential knowledge, and stunts their intellectual development. Can you think of a time when someone did not believe something you knew to be true? What were the power dynamics involved? What did it feel like not to be believed? Can you think of a time when perhaps you did not believe someone because of that person's race, gender, ethnicity, sexual orientation, or dis/ability rather than the evidence he or she gave? What do you think contributed to the credibility deficit that you assigned to that person? Are there times where you may have assigned a credibility excess to someone based on social factors?

Back to Logical Fallacies

Now that we have established some basic things about ad hominem fallacies and credibility, we can move on to the rest of our fallacy list. The second fallacy we will consider is *appeal to tradition*. This fallacy occurs when an arguer claims that a particular belief or practice is right because it has a long history and tradition. The reason this line of thinking is fallacious is that just because something has a long history and tradition does not justify why it should continue. When we call a belief or practice into question and ask whether or not it should continue, it is circular to answer by saying "Well, it has always been this way!" What the question demands is a reason for why it should continue. For instance, someone asks, "Should we reconsider our public policy of educating children according to their age and instead look at other factors like interests or abilities?" The response is that "Our public educational system has always organized children by their age." Even if this is true, it is not a justification for why we should continue the practice. What we would need to adequately address the question is evidence that the practice itself makes sense relative to our educational goals.

Appeal to tradition makes our list of fallacies because it tends to come up in arguments about social differences and social identity. For instance, if someone argues that the changing demographics in the United States (an issue we considered in chapter 4) was a sign that the country was in decline and gave as the reason the fact that the United States has always been a majority white country, then that person would have committed an appeal to tradition. The fact that the country has historically been a majority white country is not a justification for why it should remain so unless the only goal for our country is to maintain a majority white population. Changing demographics are a reflection of changes in immigration (from European immigration in the late nineteenth and early twentieth centuries to more recent immigration from Mexico, Central America, and Asia).[7] Though it is difficult for people who have long been a majority to imagine being in the minority or to have a belief or practice that has long been a source of benefit and comfort called into question, it is nevertheless fallacious to use that stability and comfort as a reason for why things should stay the same. This is especially true when the belief or practice provides stability and comfort for some while increasing the costs and discomfort for others. Many all-male domains such as universities, corporations, and sporting and economic clubs provided significant benefits and comfort to the men who were able to take advantage of them. In these spaces, mainly white middle-class and wealthy men were able to establish relationships and networks that helped to increase their wealth and public power. However, the fact that women and men of color were prohibited from participating as equals in these spaces meant that they could not access the same benefits and comforts. In addition, the benefits and comforts were often maintained through the labor of working-class and poor men and women as well as the mothers, wives, and daughters of the privileged men. When reforms were proposed to address the injustice of these practices, tradition was often invoked as a reason for why they should be maintained. Fortunately, tradition was not sufficient to justify "men only" and "whites only" policies that were understandably comfortable for some people but a source of suffering for others.

Keeping in mind Tindale's point about the complexity of fallacies, it is important that we understand how tradition can be appealed to in a nonfallacious way. For example, if the issue in question is whether a certain practice was a tradition that was worth keeping, then appealing to the history of that practice and its value would not be fallacious. Some families and friends have a favorite movie that they watch together every year. If one year a person in the group wonders why they should all watch it again, considering that everyone has already seen it, the others may present evidence about how it has become a tradition. This kind of evidence would place a higher value on being together and sharing memories rather than on the quality of the cinematic experience. If everyone in the group agrees that traditions matter, then the issue is whether watching this movie annually is a tradition worth keeping. Unlike the case of a majority white population, where the issue was whether changing demographics were a sign of the nation's decline, in this case tradition is neither unjust nor irrelevant to the matter.

The next fallacy we will consider is *hasty generalization*. This fallacy occurs when an arguer reaches a conclusion about a group on the basis of a small or unrepresentative sample of that group. For instance, if I conclude that all Toyota cars are unreliable on the basis of the one Toyota I just rented or on the basis of several very old and worn models, then I have committed the fallacy. The point is that the target group in my conclusion, all Toyotas, is much larger and more varied than the small and unrepresentative sample in my premise.

When it comes to debates about social differences, hasty generalization is a common logical fallacy. For instance, if I concluded that the Muslim religion forbids women from wearing cosmetics in public based on what I was told by two Muslim friends, that would be a hasty generalization. Islam is a complex and varied religion, and there are differences among followers just as there are differences among practicing Christians and Jews and Buddhists. Religion, like gender, race, ethnicity, and sexual orientation, is a way of classifying large and diverse groups of people who, while they may share some things, are nevertheless multifaceted. To draw a conclusion about the beliefs and practices of the whole group based on a very small sample is to mismatch the weight of the evidence to the weight of the conclusion. In the same way, to draw a conclusion about the whole group by appealing to an unrepresentative sample of that group would be another way to commit the fallacy. If you concluded that Americans positively support gay and lesbian relationships based on your experience talking to people in the Castro in San Francisco (one of the largest and most politically active gay communities in the country), then your generalization is hasty given the unrepresentative sample. The point, then, for our purposes is to pay special attention to generalizations about social groups because they often hide the group's real complexity and variety. In many cases, arguers will selectively choose a subset of the group to defend a conclusion about the entire group despite the fact that the subset is either too small or unrepresentative.

Like cognitive biases, which can have practical value, hasty generalizations can also be an efficient way to reach a conclusion. In cases where the stakes are very high or the risk is great, it might be more practical to go with a small or biased sample rather than taking the time to acquire larger and more representative evidence. If I eat at a particular restaurant and get food poisoning, it does not seem unreasonable for me to cross the restaurant off my list of places to dine. However, it may have been just one ingredient in that one dish that caused the illness and not the food or kitchen quality overall. Still, the vivid memory of the food poisoning and its association with the restaurant will outweigh the logical demand to obtain more representative evidence. This is understandable, but it does not mean that further evidence could not and should not be obtained if, for instance, the restaurant was undergoing an inspection. In that case, eating one meal in the dining room would be insufficient to determine the overall quality of the food and the kitchen management. So, while we may reach hasty generalizations in our own lives when it comes to very good and very bad experiences, we should not forget that an undue reliance on this argument pattern is logically problematic and insufficient if we explore issues beyond our own pleasure or displeasure.

The fourth fallacy on our list—*fallacy of anecdotal evidence*—is related to hasty generalization because it deals with generalizations and unique or unusual personal examples. Fallacy of anecdotal evidence occurs when an arguer denies the truth or plausibility of a generalization based on her or his knowledge of a counterinstance. For example, a person who denies that smoking causes lung cancer and other serious health problems because Uncle Joe smoked three packs a day and lived to be ninety commits the fallacy. While it may be true, the case of Uncle Joe does not falsify the truth that in general, smoking does cause lung cancer and other serious health problems. Generalizations and percentages reflect patterns across groups. This does not mean that the pattern is true for every member of the group but rather for a statistically significant number. The fact that there are members of the group for whom the pattern does not hold is not evidence that the pattern is false.

This fallacy often comes up in debates about social issues when a statistical generalization is made that challenges people's biases and stereotypes. If you hear that unemployment is generally higher among blacks than whites even in cases where both groups share the same educational level and you respond "But I know this black guy that got a job over a white guy," the objection is fallacious. This is because individual counterinstances are not sufficient to falsify a general pattern. Of course, because we may not like what the generalization or pattern suggests, our minds seem to naturally go to the counterinstance. This is another form of defensiveness in an effort to protect our web of belief. However, before we do the work of objecting to an uncomfortable generalization, it would be worth our while to consider why we find it uncomfortable.

What work does the availability of that counterinstance do to sustain other beliefs we have? In the case of the person who is ready to tell us about Uncle Joe's long life as a smoker, what does the example provide in terms of preserving the person's web of belief? If the person is a smoker, knowing that it is possible to escape smoking's deadly effects most likely offers some comfort. However, by overemphasizing Uncle Joe's case rather than the large body of data on smoking, the person avoids looking at the much more likely fact that smoking will cause significant harm. Similarly, thinking that things are not as bad as the studies show because "I know a case where . . ." can be comforting but can also blind us to the real harms that are perpetuated regularly in our society. Anecdotal evidence provides a way to avoid integrating uncomfortable (but relevant) data into our web of belief.

When is anecdotal evidence not fallacious? In some cases where a very broad generalization is put forward, anecdotal evidence can narrow the generalization to reveal its actual scope and limits. For instance, if someone claims that "Every woman wants to be a mother" and then hears from a variety of different women who report that they do not have that desire, their reports, while anecdotal, still undermine the generalization about "every woman." Generalizations that begin with "all" and "every" are referred to as "universal" in logic and critical thinking. The problem with these kinds of generalizations is that they can be undermined with one counterexample. Keeping in mind that we want to practice cooperative reasoning (our third major skill as intellectually empathic thinkers), we will be wary of both making such broad universal generalizations and shutting down an argument because we can raise one counterexample. If we shift to modifiers such as "many" or "most" and specify that we are referring to our own experience, we can work together to make sense of the generalizations and particular experiences that make up our belief systems. The person above who made the claim "Every woman wants to be a mother" could have said instead "Most of the women I know have said they wanted to be mothers." A woman hearing this claim but who does not have this desire could point out her different view without shutting down the dialogue. By explaining that this does not hold true for every woman, she could still seek out reasons for why the person who made the claim found it worth reporting. Similarly, the person who made the claim could consider how it might feel for someone to be subjected to a generalization that does not feel accurate. When generalizations are made about social groups, we should always consider these three questions:

Who benefits from the generalization?
Who is marginalized or left out?
How does this perpetuate existing inequalities?

The next fallacy we will consider is *straw person* (or "straw man" as it was traditionally called), and this occurs when someone reformulates another person's argument in such a way that it is more vulnerable to objections and harder to defend. The idea is that a straw person is very easy to knock down. So, for example, if Sue argued for increasing our use of public transportation by reducing our reliance on personal automobiles and if I, upon hearing her, objected by saying "So, Sue wants to take away our cars so that we have to depend entirely on public transportation," I would have committed the straw person fallacy. Sue's original claim was that we should use public transportation more and personal automobiles less. But this is a much more modest proposal than Sue wanting to take away our cars and make us completely reliant on public transportation. This unfair interpretation of her claim makes it much more vulnerable to objections and counterexamples as compared with what Sue proposed in her original statement.

The straw person fallacy is unfortunately all too common when the issue involves social differences and social identities. For example, a news story about a transgender first grader who was born a boy but identifies as a girl reported that the child was initially prohibited from using the girls' restroom at her school. Michael Silverman, executive director of the Transgender Legal Defense & Education Fund, argued that "By denying the child the right to use the little girls restroom like all the other little girls at school it created an environment that was hostile, discriminatory and unsafe. . . . [The child] wants the same dignity, respect and opportunity, and deserves that, as every other student."[8]

In an online news and opinion website about the story, one commenter said that the argument amounted to "FORCING people to embrace and celebrate others' sexual/gender alternative lifestyles and that is NOT 'equality.'"[9] However, Silverman's original argument did not advocate for embracing or celebrating a transgender identity. Rather, he called for "dignity, respect, and opportunity." There is nothing inconsistent with affording another person dignity, respect, and opportunity while at the same time not embracing or celebrating that person's identity. By reinterpreting a group's demand for equal respect and opportunity as a demand for embracing and celebrating that group, the commenter makes the argument much less defensible.

Consider the difference between providing some meatless options at an important business luncheon for a coworker who does not eat meat versus everyone at the meeting embracing and celebrating vegetarianism. The first accommodation is respectful and affords an equal opportunity, while the second is just silly and excessive. And in the first case the accommodation requires very little effort and presents no obstacles to the rest of the attendees, while the second would require major challenges and life changes.

Even minimal accommodations, however, can feel like big sacrifices when groups with social privilege have to make room for equal opportunity. This difficulty is compounded when the people who are demanding equal access are perceived as being immoral or out to destroy what is good. Enslaved people who demanded freedom, women who demanded equal rights, LGBT people who demand respect and equal protection, people with disabilities who demand equal opportunity, and religious minorities who demand freedom from persecution are all examples of groups seeking equal access and opportunity and not mass conversion or social destruction. This shift from social reform to social destruction, which has a long history in debates about social identity and difference, leads us into a discussion of our next fallacy.

The next fallacy, the *slippery slope*, occurs when an arguer claims that accepting a certain position will soon lead to greater and greater disastrous outcomes, although there is no evidence connecting the position to this terrible outcome. Say, for instance, you ask a friend whether you might borrow his car. You have a good driving record, no history of stealing things, and are not under the influence of drugs or alcohol. However, your friend says no because he believes that you will not drive carefully and will wind up in an accident, thereby wrecking his car. Your friend has committed the slippery slope fallacy.

The slippery slope fallacy crops up in arguments about social differences because it reflects the anxiety and fear associated with social change and reform. As we saw with appeal to tradition as well as the status quo cognitive bias, even reasonable requests for accommodations and change can feel like major destabilizing overhauls to the people who have not had to make changes. Operating with a win-lose or zero-sum framework, many people who have not had to pay attention to their privilege will interpret a request for social change as an effort to strip away their rights. Extending "special rights," as they are often negatively described, means that those with "ordinary" rights will have to lose something. We see this in former senator Rick Santorum's claim that legalizing gay marriage will lead to the legality of "man on child, man on dog, or whatever the case may be."[10] We also see it in the argument by former Colorado governor Richard Lamm that "multiculturalism and encouraging immigrants to maintain their own culture and believing that all cultures are equal" will eventually lead to "the destruction of America," since no nation can withstand competing languages and cultures.[11] Both examples rest on the assumption that rights and opportunities afforded to some will mean a loss of morality and security for all.

Yet there is easily available counterevidence to both arguments that get lost as we slide down the slippery slope. In the case of gay marriage leading to pedophilia or bestiality, there is the obvious point that the latter cases do not involve consenting adults. In addition, Santorum compares the right to marry (which is legal for heterosexuals) to illegal sexual acts. One is a positive right available to some, while the other is a prohibited act restricted for all. For these reasons, the slide from extending that positive right to permitting generally illegal acts is unjustified.

In Lamm's argument, the point that no nation can withstand competing languages and cultures ignores the fact that for most of American history, "competing" cultures and languages were the norm. In seventeenth-century Manhattan, Dutch and English were spoken alongside Native American Lenape languages (Munsee and Unami) and west African dialects. In nineteenth-century rural Pennsylvania, English, Dutch, German, and Irish dialects were spoken.[12]

Globally, nations including China, India, Malaysia, Switzerland, Belgium, Guatemala, Pakistan, New Zealand, and many more have multiple official languages and cultures.[13] So, if there are obvious counterexamples to these arguments, why are they nevertheless put forward by seemingly reasonable people in positions of leadership? While we do not have access to the beliefs and motives of Santorum or Lamm, we can nevertheless try to make sense of their claims so that we might understand why slippery slope fallacies are so common. Clearly fear has persuasive power, since most of us actively avoid the things that frighten us or cause us harm. Many people are frightened of social changes even if the evidence fails to demonstrate a clear risk. Remember that with the status quo bias discussed in chapter 4, many people assume that change will bring about negative consequences, so they assume that the right thing to do is to maintain the status quo. In addition, if social advantage and disadvantage is framed within people's belief system as a zero-sum game of us versus them, it is not surprising that extending rights to groups who have not had equal opportunity will be interpreted as a loss and a takeover. For these reasons the disastrous outcomes predicted in slippery slope arguments capture the fears and anxieties that many people have about social change, so the arguments seem reasonable from an emotionally charged standpoint. Similarly, because many people feel that rights should not be extended to those they judge to be living an immoral life, public support is interpreted as an abandonment of the entire moral system. The fear that gay marriage will erode all sense of right and wrong is a prime example of this kind of reasoning. How might intellectually empathic thinkers counter these kinds of fears and draw attention back to the relevant evidence?

For starters, we should understand that these fears are close to the core of many people's belief systems, including perhaps our own. They are connected to and reinforced by the things that give significant meaning to people's lives, such as family, morality, religion, patriotism, and tradition. To give up or revise a belief about one of these areas means a radical revision within a person's web of belief. Given our human tendency to be conservative about changes in our web of belief, it is understandable that people become very protective and very afraid of changing even one or two of these core beliefs, since the revisions could be substantial. Yet we do know that people change these beliefs and in some important instances change them and still preserve their core commitments to morality or religion or patriotism.

For instance, a variety of recent longitudinal sociological studies each found that overall public opinion in the United States toward gay and lesbian people, starting with attitudes in the late 1970s, has become increasingly positive over time, with 2003, the last study, having the most positive responses.[14] Does evidence of a change in public attitude mean that people have had to radically revise their belief systems and give up their core beliefs?

If we consider that during this same time period the concept of homosexuality itself was undergoing radical revision, we might gain some insight as to how it could be integrated into individual belief systems without radical changes in core beliefs. In 1952, the American Psychiatric Association published its first diagnostic manual and identified homosexuality as a disease and a mental disorder.[15] The diagnosis reflected long-held beliefs in American society that homosexuals were social deviants. Given the intense negative perception of homosexuality, many gay and lesbian people remained closeted, unable to counter the misinformation for fear of retaliation. Yet by 1973 that diagnosis was rejected, and homosexuality was no longer considered by mental health professionals to be a mental illness. During the 1970s the gay and lesbian rights movement gained momentum in the United States, and more gay and lesbian people came out. Throughout the 1980s and 1990s and into the new millennium, more Americans were introduced to gay and lesbian characters in television shows, films, and novels. More gay and lesbian people in a variety of prominent and popular public roles also came out and revealed their sexual identity. More Americans came to know someone in their own personal lives who identified as gay or lesbian. Integral to bringing the issue of equal rights and protections for gay and lesbian Americans to national attention were the 1979 National March on Washington for Lesbian and Gay Rights, in which 75,000 people gathered in support of gay rights; the 1980 Democratic National Convention, where Democrats added the equality of gay and lesbian people to their platform; and the 1994 Employment Non-Discrimination Act. These created multiple and more accurate sources of information about gay and lesbian people, as compared with the very limited and distorted information available only three and four decades previously. In this way, the very concept "homosexual" went through a radical public reconceptualization, and this required Americans not to radically revise their core values but instead to replace a false belief with a true one in light of better evidence. While this kind of change requires some adjustments to the web of belief, it does not have to lead to the radical overthrow of core beliefs that one might suspect.

To see this more clearly, imagine that I believed that bird-watchers suffered from some kind of mental illness that caused them not only to watch birds but to also kidnap babies (this is a thought experiment, so please excuse the strangeness of the example). If I believed this, it would be reasonable and ethical for me to want to restrict bird-watchers' rights and keep them far from places where they could do harm. If someone objected by saying that "Bird-watchers should have equal rights and should be able to teach in our schools, work in our hospitals, run for public office, own businesses, etc.," I would be understandably outraged. How could we put so many small children at risk? What kind of moral and social order could make sense of giving rights to known kidnappers? To accept the plea for equal rights for bird-watchers would mean radically revising so many of my beliefs about what is moral, socially acceptable, and safe. Yet if I came to find out that I was wrong about bird-watchers being kidnappers, that it had been based on years of misunderstanding and limited evidence, and if I came to personally know a variety of different bird-watchers who had no kidnapping tendencies whatsoever, I would have good reason to change my negative belief about bird-watchers. Notice that in so doing I would not be required to make changes to my whole moral system. I could still believe that we should restrict kidnappers' rights and that it is right for me to avoid kidnappers. The revised belief is just that bird-watchers do not fall into the category of kidnappers, not that I have to see kidnapping as something deserving of equal rights.

In the same way, I would suggest that the majority of Americans who now support gay and lesbian rights have revised not their entire moral system but rather the false belief that a loving relationship with a person of the same sex is a sickness, or a deviance, or a public threat. What we can learn from this change in attitude is that some efforts at social justice are actually efforts at getting the evidence right rather than a requirement to destroy people's core values or overhaul their entire web of belief.

Following Tindale and keeping consistent with our efforts to understand the complexity of fallacies, when is the kind of reasoning employed in slippery slope patterns nonfallacious? Reasoning that links causes to effects is an important form of *induction,* a process whereby we try to find strong (but not certain) evidence for our conclusions. So, when we claim that one thing will lead to another and we have strong evidence for this, we are not arguing fallaciously. For example, if I don't return a library book, then I will accumulate fines on my account. If I accumulate enough fines, my borrowing privileges will be revoked. If my borrowing privileges are revoked, then I will not be able to take out new books when they come to the library. Because this chain of events is likely to occur, I decide to return my library book. Of course, the chain is not guaranteed. It could turn out that there is some glitch in the library's account system that deletes a record of my having taken out the book. This kind of possibility, though, is less likely than the library's system functioning properly. So based on the evidence, it is reasonable for me to return the book.

The difference between a strongly justified causal chain argument and a slippery slope fallacy is that in the case of slippery slope, there is a lack of evidence between the causes and the effects. In addition, slippery slope fallacies often predict disastrous outcomes that are not justified by the available evidence.

The fallacy we will consider next is *false dilemma,* which occurs when an arguer presents two options as if they are the only ones, while obvious alternatives are easily available. An actual dilemma is one where only two options exist. Either you are pregnant or you are not. You vote either guilty or not guilty. You either accept the job offer or decline it (assuming you cannot put the offer on hold). In these cases, there is no wiggle room, or possibility, for negotiation or alternative outcomes.

The fallacy of false dilemma occurs when an arguer treats a case that has a variety of alternatives as if there are only two possible options. For instance, if a student receives a failing grade on an exam and says "Well, this is the result of either my lack of intelligence or the poor environment in which I grew up," she commits the fallacy of false dilemma. There is an obvious third alternative: the student may not have studied and done the work needed to pass the exam. However, by presenting the two options as if they are the only ones, the student gives the impression that the failure cannot be the result of anything else.

The fallacy of false dilemma comes up in dialogues and debates about social issues and contributes to the false dichotomies described in the introduction. Like zero-sum games, either-or options oversimplify the available evidence and restrict the ways we can think about social identity and social issues. When someone says "America, love it or leave it," they are presenting us with a false dilemma. There are obvious alternatives, such as remaining in the country and working to change the things you may not love. There is also the option of leaving and nevertheless still loving America. However, by setting up the choice as loving or leaving, the claim makes no room for dissent from within. The false dilemma in this case is an effort to silence that third alternative.

On recent example of false dilemma in debates about social identity and social difference is the argument that if you fail to support a particular policy of President Barack Obama, then you are a racist. Louisiana Democratic Party chairwoman Karen Carter Peterson said on the floor of the Louisiana Senate in May 2013 that opponents of the president's Affordable Care Act are motivated by racism.[16] The problem with this objection is that it fails to consider the obvious possibility that critics are motivated by shortcomings with the plan itself. By leaving out this option as if it is not even a possibility, Peterson reduces the complexity of the debate to an oversimplified either-or scenario.

Why do seemingly reasonable people resort to false dilemma, especially when third and fourth options are so obvious? One way of making sense of the appeal of false dilemma is that when a person is in the grip of an argument, the adversarial nature of that context breeds a "you are with me or against me" dichotomy. As discussed in chapter 3, we have inherited the metaphor of argument as war. If an argument is perceived as a war, then there must be just two sides and two causes. To counter this oversimplification, intellectually empathic critical thinkers should recognize the grip of false dilemma while reminding the arguer that another less polarizing option is available. Similarly, when we find ourselves in the grip of an either-or presentation of the evidence, we should remain mindful of the fact that we may be overlooking some third important alternative.

The next fallacy to consider is *appeal to ignorance,* which occurs when someone argues for a particular conclusion on the basis of an absence of evidence. For instance, if I argue that cancer will never be cured because no one has found a cure, I have committed the fallacy of appeal to ignorance. It is worth noting with this fallacy that two opposing conclusions can be drawn from the same evidence. I could have just as well drawn the conclusion that since no one has yet proven that cancer cannot be cured, a cure is certain to exist. What we should conclude when the evidence is inconclusive is that the issue remains an open question. The logical thing to do, then, is to suspend judgment until relevant evidence is found.

We see the fallacy of appeal to ignorance come up in debates about social identity and social difference when arguers try to force conclusions on the basis of inconclusive evidence. For example, some non–Muslim Americans have argued that because Muslim Americans have not publicly condemned certain violent actions by radical Muslims, they must therefore support those violent actions. Yet an absence of condemnation is not the same thing as support. Along the same lines, to conclude that Muslim Americans oppose the violent actions of radical Muslims on the basis of their not publicly coming out in support of those actions would also be an appeal to ignorance. It would be more reasonable to conclude that most people do not support violence because it causes harm than to conclude that they do not support violence because they have not publicly voiced their support for it. The point is that a lack of evidence should not be used as evidence for any conclusion. So, why is this fallacy so common in the context of social issues?

One reason may be that when there is an absence of evidence, it is very easy for arguers to impose their point of view, since there is no counterpoint. If a particular conclusion is important to me and I see that no one has disproven it, it is easy enough for me to take that as a justification, since I already believe that the conclusion is true. Sentiments such as "silence is consent" and "a failure to work against something is working for it" reflect the judgment that by not taking a position, one actually does take a position. However, this is not entirely fair, especially since in many circumstances the relevant evidence may not be available to people. Calling people "sheep" because they do not take a stand on an issue fails to consider that they may not have the relevant evidence. Rather than resorting to name-calling, the intellectually empathic thinker should actively seek out this evidence and make it available for everyone's consideration.

Along the same lines, a failure to articulate a position on an issue may be the result of it seeming so obvious that people do not feel the need to voice their concerns. If a murderer is apprehended and happens to be a female professor, I would not feel the need to make clear that as a female professor, I do not condone her actions. My silence is not consent but instead is a result of my believing that there is no need to make such a statement, since being a female professor was not the cause of her committing murder. In the same way, many social groups are surprised when they are expected to come out against a terrible action perpetrated by someone who identifies with their group. Murderers who kill in the name of God are in fact murderers and are not acting on behalf of everyone who practices the same religion. Yet, Muslims are asked to account for murderers who happen to identify as Muslim. The Ku Klux Klan had an explicitly Christian ideology and stated its goals as "reestablishing Protestant Christian values in America by any means possible."[17] Yet many Christian Americans saw the Klan as a terrorist organization that had no connection to their values or their Christian faith.

Similar to false dilemma is *complex question*. This fallacy occurs when an arguer embeds a controversial assumption in a question so that a response to the question will confirm the assumption. For example, if I ask you whether you will finally admit that you are a drug user and you say "no," you have implied that you will continue to hide your drug use. Of course, if you say "yes," you imply that you will now admit your drug use. The problem is that I have not established whether or not you have concealed a drug habit; instead, I have merely assumed that in my formulation of the question. Complex question is related to false dilemma because both fallacies falsely constrain the options within a dialogue.

We see complex question in arguments about social issues that use premises such as "Since men are naturally better at science and mathematics, shouldn't we stop wasting resources on programs to get women into these fields?" and "Since illegal immigrants steal American jobs, shouldn't we work harder to stop them from getting into this country?" or "Why are we so hated in the Arab world?" In all of these cases, the question embeds the controversial claim as if it were true rather than requiring evidence. Like false dilemma and even appeal to ignorance, the use of this fallacy may have more to do with the confidence the arguer has that the embedded claim is true as opposed to intentionally wanting to deceive or trick the hearer. Our response to complex questions should be to divide the question and point out that while the speaker may be confident in the truth of the embedded claim, it still requires evidence. Similarly, we should be attentive to the fact that when we are convinced of a controversial claim, we too may smuggle it into a complex question, treating it as if the evidence is obvious. As often as we can, we should make it a habit to identify and make explicit the reasons that support our beliefs about social issues and social identity.

The final fallacy on our list is the *perfectionist fallacy,* which is a special form of false dilemma because it limits our options to either a perfect outcome or nothing at all. The perfectionist fallacy typically occurs when an arguer objects to a proposal on the grounds that the proposal will not lead to a perfect result. So, imagine that I was trying to choose the best option of care for my aging relative, and you suggested a nearby adult assisted living facility based on your knowledge of a resident's positive experience. If I asked whether his care was "perfect" and you replied "Well, it is pretty good" and I then rejected the facility on the grounds that it was not perfect, I would have committed the perfectionist fallacy. This is because perfection is an unrealistic demand when it comes to quality care. In fact, in most situations perfection is an unrealistic demand. The expression "The perfect is the enemy of the good" conveys the idea that quite often, a demand for perfection can often overlook what would actually be a good solution.[18]

This final fallacy comes up in arguments about social differences and social identity when proposals are put forward for solving social problems and are rejected because they will not provide a perfect solution. For instance, if someone argued against efforts at ending injustice and discrimination on the grounds that it was not going to solve all the problems of injustice and discrimination in the United States, the arguer would be committing the perfectionist fallacy. Even if it is true that the best efforts will not solve all these problems, it is still an open question as to whether those efforts can solve some of these problems. The arguer would need to provide evidence that addressed the inadequacy of the particular efforts rather than simply demanding perfection.

The appeal of the perfectionist fallacy may stem from the fact that it is easier to reject a proposal that calls for doing something about a big problem than it is to roll up our sleeves and get to work. Large-scale social problems can make people feel inadequate and overwhelmed. Just making a small difference can seem like more effort than it is worth, so why not focus on the insignificance of the effort? The problem with this way of thinking is that some good solutions that could make things better (but not perfect) get dismissed before they can even be implemented and assessed. As intellectually empathic thinkers, we should be committed to keeping an open mind about proposals for solving social problems. We should not let a demand for the perfect get in the way of our efforts to make things better.

Are there contexts where either-or reasoning is justified? If there are in fact only two options available, then it is not fallacious to appeal to just these two options. However, all too often when the issue involves social differences, either-or thinking gets in the way of our consideration of the variety of alternative possibilities and limits our potential to think critically and creatively.

Chapters 3, 4, and 5 explored the different ways that people can aggressively make mistakes when arguing about social issues and social differences. We looked at the hostility in debates as well as our tendency to employ cognitive biases and fallacies in our thinking and reasoning. In the next chapter, we will see where there are opportunities for establishing common ground in dialogues and debates about social differences, and we will explore the last two skills involved in being an intellectually empathic critical thinker.

Questions for Review

1. What is the difference between wanting more evidence based on a source's circumstances as compared with committing the ad hominem–circumstantial fallacy?

2. What is testimonial injustice according to philosopher Miranda Fricker? How does it cause a double harm to people who face social disadvantages?

3. Why are people so prone to the slippery slope fallacy when the issue involves social change? Provide an example from your own experience.

4. How does the change in public attitudes about gay and lesbian relationships show that social justice does not require radically revising our values but does involve changing from a false belief to a belief that is more accurate?

5. Are the ten fallacies that we considered in this chapter fallacies in every context? Why or why not? How does relevancy play a role in answering this question?

Questions for Further Thinking and Writing

1. Give an example from your own experience when you (or someone you know) used one of the following fallacies when reasoning about social identity and differences:

   - Appeal to tradition
   - Hasty generalization
   - Anecdotal evidence

2. Find an example from a news article, a political speech or debate, or some other public forum where the speaker committed a straw person fallacy related to an issue of social identity and difference. Provide some analysis for why the person may have been susceptible to this fallacy.

3. What does the expression "The perfect is the enemy of the good" mean from your point of view? How does this relate to the perfectionist fallacy?

Additional Resources

The Australian science education resource service techNyouvids has created a series of six two-minute videos on basic logic principles, including fallacies. The videos are aimed at middle and high school students but are also designed to resonate with adults. The animation and presentation are fun and well designed. The first in the series of videos is at YouTube, http://www.youtube.com/watch?v=iSZ3BUru59A.

The Internet Encyclopedia of Philosophy has a very useful article titled "Falacies," available at http://www.iep.utm.edu/fallacy/.

Professor Christopher Tindale at the University of Windsor has a homepage at http://www1.uwindsor.ca/ctindale/articles with links to several of his papers, including research on fallacies.

Philosophy Bites, an online resource of interviews with the world's philosophers, has an excellent interview with Miranda Fricker about her book *Epistemic Injustice*. A podcast of the interview is available at http://www.philosophybites.libsyn.com/webpage/category/Miranda%20Fricker.

6 | Finding Common Ground through Intellectual Empathy

What We Have Established So Far

So far we have established three of the five skills for becoming an intellectually empathic critical thinker:

1. Knowing that identity is intersectional,
2. Understanding that social privilege is often invisible, and
3. Working at reasoning cooperatively.

We also explored seven common cognitive biases that we are susceptible to when forming our beliefs about social identity and issues of social difference. In chapter 5 we considered ten common logical fallacies that are hard to resist when arguing about social identity and social differences. By paying attention to these cognitive biases and logical fallacies, we can more effectively employ the five skills of intellectual empathy. In this chapter we will add the last two remaining skills, and then in chapter 7 we will see how we can take intellectual empathy out into the world.

Everyone Has an Uncle Moe

At the beginning of any class I teach involving controversial social issues, I ask my students to raise their hands if they have a close friend or relative who would make them feel uncomfortable if the friend or relative came and spoke in front of our class about his or her views on race, gender, ethnicity, religion, or sexual orientation. Invariably almost every single hand in the class will go up. When I ask students what would cause their discomfort, they say things like "My uncle is a good guy, but if you hear him talk about Mexicans you would probably think he is a racist" or "My cousin has a good heart, but her views on gay rights are so ignorant." In other words, most of the students in the class have someone in their life who espouses social views about some other group, and these views if expressed publicly would invariably create discomfort. What lessons can we learn from this?

First, it is important to note that most of us have grown up around conversations in which social bias, stereotyping, and discrimination were part of the dialogue. This means that we all have examples of people whom we love and care about but who may nevertheless express beliefs and opinions that we find uncomfortable or false. For the purposes of discussion, I ask my class to refer to this person as "Uncle Moe." The reason I do this is so that when all of our hands are raised, we can look around and see that families of different races, ethnicities, religions, etc., are each saying something that we identify as socially biased. Someone in an Asian student's family might be saying something negative about Latinos, for example. And someone in the Latino family might be saying something negative about Muslims. And the Muslim family might be saying something negative about gays and lesbians, and so on. That is, someone in some family is most likely saying something about one of the social groups to which you belong. (Often it is white students who are the most surprised to find out that they are seen as a race by other racial groups and are sometimes the target of comments around some other family's dinner table.) We all seem to grow up hearing some biased, stereotypical beliefs expressed openly. The people who express these beliefs are also people whom we nevertheless care about and love.

The first lesson, then, to learn from this is that we share the common experience of having been brought up by adults with biased and stereotypical beliefs. Though the biases and stereotypes may be about different groups, we were all in a similar position as children hearing them. Just this fact alone can often create a sense of common ground among my students. As we all look around at each other with our hands raised, we realize that there are forces within our personal lives as well as in our public and professional lives that nurture and perpetuate these attitudes and beliefs. It is as if collectively we can come out about the sexism, racism, heterosexism, and religious bigotry that were sprinkled into our family gatherings like the seasoning in our food.

The second lesson to learn is that though we may disagree with some of Uncle Moe's social beliefs and attitudes, it does not follow that we don't love or care for Uncle Moe. This lesson reveals the complexity of our relationships with family and close friends and gets to the integrated nature of effective critical thinking. Good critical thinking does not separate rationality from emotion or the individual from his or her relationships. Rather, effective critical thinking integrates these in ways that value the complex dimensions of our experiences and balances reason with emotion, self-interest, and our concern for others. Family life and close personal friendships are two of the most important areas where we have to manage this complex balancing act.

Unfortunately, close personal relationships, which have long been associated with the private sphere of human activity, have generally been downplayed or ignored in much of the Western philosophical tradition.[1] Rationality and morality, two essential elements in thinking critically about social justice, have often been described in the history of Western philosophy as the kind of thing that a single individual (historically a property-owning adult white male) achieves by overcoming emotion and sentimentality to arrive at the objective Truth, with a capital "T."[2] The contemporary version of this idealized loner is the individual motivated by rational self-interest that is common to many mainstream economic models. As sociologist Mabel Berezin writes, "It is arguable that the project of modern social science from its European nineteenth-century origins to its contemporary variations defines emotion out of social action in general and economic action in particular."[3] Emotion, relationships, and subjective familial ties have a long history of being characterized by scholars as obstacles that get in the way of effective reasoning and moral decision making.[4]

However, from the point of view of intellectual empathy, healthy family relationships—the kinds built on trust, mutuality, care, respect, and constructive conflict—are a significant resource for developing methods of effective communication.[5] Most of my students express a real love and concern for the people in their families. Most of the students have healthy relationships with family members in the sense that they trust them, don't always agree with them, and may fight and argue with them but continue to care for and to be cared by them. If your Uncle Moe says something wrongheaded or biased, your first reaction is most likely not to write him off as being unworthy of your respect. We generally want to maintain our connection to the people we care about, so we try to resolve the inconsistencies between their good hearts and their offensive claims.

We might discover, for instance, that our Uncle Moe lacks some information and that when we present it he is willing to change his point of view. Or through conversation we may come to realize that our judgment of the wrongheadedness or offensiveness of Uncle Moe's claim was really a failure on our part to correctly interpret his claim. Or we may come to see that Uncle Moe's claim was made thoughtlessly or as a joke and that upon further reflection, he would not stick by it when expressing his more considered beliefs. And there is always the possibility that after some conversation, we might just come to the conclusion that on this issue, Uncle Moe harbors fear or anger that makes it nearly impossible for him to reflectively assess this belief or to fairly consider the counterevidence. If so, we may decide to flag that issue as a conversational land mine and tiptoe around it when we are with him. The point is that none of these possibilities can emerge unless we maintain a certain amount of trust and open communication with Uncle Moe.

Though many of my students may feel uncomfortable or strongly disagree with some of the statements their Uncle Moe makes, this does not render them incapable of having a relationship with him. Nor does it necessarily mean that they give up on trying to understand him. Yet for many of us, if a stranger, an acquaintance, a coworker, or a classmate says something at work, at school, or in a public gathering and we believe that it is biased and wrong, it can result in our immediately writing the person off as undeserving of any further attention or respect. This difference, between our treatment of Uncle Moe's claims and our colleague's or coworker's claims, most likely exists because we don't have the same level of trust and history with the person, nor do we feel any obligation to understand the person.

But just as we should begin with the presumption that people are reasonable, we should also begin with the presumption that people are trustworthy and that we do have an obligation to understand and make sense of their seemingly biased or stereotypical claims. This is not a recommendation that comes from being nice or because it will magically lead to us all getting along. Rather, from the point of view of intellectual empathy, we should assume these things because it puts us in a better position for gathering and sharing evidence. When we write off someone with whom we disagree or adopt a totally negative attitude toward that person, we have eliminated the possibility of learning anything from the person or sharing with her or him relevant evidence that we may have. Again, some people will not be capable of teaching, learning, or reflectively assessing their social judgments, but many more people will be capable in these areas. We don't want to give up on the many because of the insurmountable few. Our goal as intellectually empathic thinkers is not to create perfect public discourse but instead to create a more improved discourse. (Remember, we don't want to commit the perfectionist fallacy discussed in chapter 5!)

So, treat those who express social beliefs that you find uncomfortable, false, or even morally problematic like you would Uncle Moe, who makes you roll your eyes but with whom you nevertheless have to live. The advantage of starting from this perspective is that it puts you in a better position for gathering and sharing evidence. As I said above, this does not mean that we can never judge some beliefs and some people to be dangerous or irrational, but we should only come to that conclusion after sifting out the evidential opportunities from the dead ends. And as I've said, in my experience teaching critical thinking, there are far more opportunities with people than there are dead ends. If we start from the position that people with whom we disagree might be lacking relevant evidence, might have evidence that we lack, or might just have failed to consider evidence at the moment they uttered their claim, then we open ourselves up to the possibility of greater understanding. If after exploring these possibilities we find that a person is just simply too fearful, angry, biased, and unreasonable, we now have evidence for believing that he or she is not a credible source (on this topic), and we should flag that issue within that person's belief system and tiptoe around it as if it contained a land mine. Our goal then is to distinguish actual land mines from firecrackers and imaginary land mines.

The Principle of Conditional Trust

The principle of conditional trust, the fourth skill of an intellectually empathic thinker, involves accepting a principle that stems from what we have said thus far. The principle requires that when we are faced with a claim that we judge to be biased or stereotypical, we trust that the person who made the claim is reasonable and well intentioned, so we engage the person further to understand her or his reasons for making the claim. The principle assumes trust provided that the following four conditions are met as they emerge in the dialogue:

1. The person must be willing to consider relevant counterevidence to the claim if we are able to present it.
2. We must remain open to the person's relevant supporting evidence even if we don't like it or if it means that we were wrong about the person being biased.
3. If upon further reflection the person admits that he or she was simply being thoughtless or trying to be humorous, we reassure the person that we too have made such mistakes and that we understand how they happen.
4. Finally, the person reassures us that he or she will not distrust us in the future for raising the possibility that his or her claim was biased.

These conditions help to lower the stakes for both the person inquiring about the possible biased nature of the claim and the person making the claim. By committing ourselves to the idea that we are all a work in progress when it comes to being better people and more intellectually empathic thinkers, we can create more possibilities than the fight-flight and guilt-blame dichotomies described in the introduction. However, keep in mind that if either person in the dialogue fails in some way to meet one of these conditions when he or she is faced with it, conditional trust should be suspended and caution and skepticism should enter to replace it. A failure to meet these conditions when they arise is an indication that our dialogue partner is not sincerely engaged in an effort to think critically.

So, how would the principle of conditional trust operate in an actual dialogue or debate? Let's consider the first condition, where an individual makes a claim we judge to be biased or stereotypical. Imagine someone who says that "Muslims do not support equal rights for women." Such a claim on the face of it is problematic simply because it takes a large and multifaceted set of belief systems and collapses it into one monolithic category—"Muslims"—and then attributes a negative position to that entire group. The claim sounds like an instance of the hasty generalization fallacy that we discussed in chapter 5.

Imagine that we had accumulated the following bits of information. Approximately 1.6 billion people in the world identify as Muslim (about 23 percent of the world's population).[6] There are 49 majority Muslim countries around the world, and according to a report on the Pew Forum on Religion & Public Life, "They differ significantly by country and region in levels of religious commitment, openness to multiple interpretations of faith and the Sunni/Shia divide."[7] Suppose we had read an article in the *Washington Post* a few years back by John Esposito, a professor of Islamic studies, who wrote:

> When it comes to popular Muslim attitudes about women's rights, the facts aren't always what one might expect. Majorities of Muslims, some in the most conservative Muslim societies, support women's equal rights. According to a 2007 Gallup World Poll, majorities in virtually every Muslim country surveyed say women should have the same legal rights as men to serve in the highest levels of government. In addition, majorities of both men and women in dozens of Muslim countries around the world say that men and women should have the same legal rights.[8]

What we learn from piecing together the data is that while Muslims around the world share beliefs such as there is one God, Muhammad is God's prophet, and Muslims should fast during the holy month of Ramadan and give alms to the poor, beyond that there are some significant differences. Many Muslims who immigrated to the United States, for instance, did so because they were seeking greater freedom and opportunities for their families, including education for their daughters. Muslim women around the world have sought out leadership roles in politics, economics, and academic research, and their efforts have the support of the men in their lives. Of course this is not true in every instance and every case, but there is enough data to have undermined the myth that all Muslims do not support equal rights for women.

If we now imagine that the person who made the original claim did not have this information or seek it out—that is, if she did not know that there was variability in Muslim beliefs, that Muslim women held prominent social and political positions, and that many Muslim women sought legal and educational opportunities—and her justification was based solely on media depictions of the most fundamentalist Muslims, then we might understand why she came to hold the belief. However, rather than judging her to be anti-Muslim or bigoted, the first condition of the principle of conditional trust would require us to present her with the information we have and give her the opportunity to revise her belief. If after considering the evidence she does in fact revise her belief, then our trust was warranted, and the conversation provided an opportunity for us to share relevant evidence and dispel an unwarranted assumption.

Now, of course, this scenario assumes that we have the evidence. It is not always so easy to have the facts and figures at your fingertips when you are in the midst of a debate about social identity and social difference. Yet intellectually empathic critical thinkers should actively seek out counterevidence to social myths and stereotypes and get in the habit of collecting this data and regularly refreshing it. Again, this is not because it is a *nice* thing to do or the *politically correct* thing to do but because misconceptions and myths are the things that often sabotage our critical thinking skills in debates about social issues. By tending to our collection of facts and figures that counter social myths and stereotypes, we can more effectively meet the first requirement of the principle of conditional trust. Rather than just concluding that a biased claim means that we are dealing with a hopelessly biased person, we can remain in the dialogue, providing relevant information that may simply be missing from the other person's belief system.

The second condition of the principle of conditional trust arises in those circumstances where we judge an individual to have made a biased or stereotypical claim and it turns out that we are the one lacking relevant evidence. To see how this could play out, imagine that you are in a debate with someone who makes the claim that "Jews in the United States are wealthier than most other Americans." Your initial judgment of the claim is that it is biased because it takes Jewish people to be a monolithic group and attributes a property to all the members of that group. Like the case with Muslims above, this sounds like a hasty generalization that does not take into account the variety and complexity of the group in question. However, unlike the case concerning Muslims, the property attributed to American Jews is not a negative belief—the inequality of women—but rather the group's socioeconomic status. In this case the attribute in question—wealth—is something that can be measured independently of the group's beliefs and is not in and of itself something negative. But the claim smacks of bias and stereotyping because Jews have long been discriminated against and oppressed on the basis of their relationship to money. But what if you do not have counterevidence to this claim, as you did in the first instance? Still you say confidently, "Jewish people have long been stigmatized and mistreated on the basis of their relationship to money, so you shouldn't make that claim." Can this serve as counterevidence to the claim? While it is true, it is actually not counterevidence to the original claim. It is relevant information regarding bias and stereotyping against Jews but does not address the socioeconomic status of Jews in the United States. If we don't have counterevidence, or any evidence regarding the socioeconomic status of American Jews, the second requirement of the principle of conditional trust says that we have to withhold our judgment of bias and trust the claimant enough to ask her or him for supporting evidence.

Imagine that what the claimant tells us is this: According to a 2003 population report by the United Jewish Communities, the distribution of household income among Jews, especially at the high end of the income scale, reflects their relatively high education levels and high-status jobs. More than one-third of Jewish households (34 percent) report income over $75,000, compared to 17 percent of all U.S. households. Proportionally, fewer Jewish households (22 percent) than total U.S. households (28 percent) report household income under $25,000. The current median income of Jewish households is $54,000, 29 percent higher than the median U.S. household income of $42,000. In 1990 the median income of Jewish households was $39,000, which is 34 percent higher than the median income of $29,000 for all U.S. households.[9]

This data, our debate partner goes on to say, is consistent with the results of a longitudinal study conducted by sociologist Laura Keister on the role of religion in wealth and asset accumulation in the United States.[10] As it stands, on average Jewish Americans are wealthier than most other Americans (Jewish Americans are also older and better educated on average than other Americans). So, our debate partner asks "Does this mean that every Jewish person in the U.S. is wealthy?" and then says "No," explaining that median averages are the middle range in a set of given values. (Mean averages take the sum of all the given values and divide them by the total number of values. Mode averages are the most commonly occurring number in a set of values.) So, there are clearly Jews who are less wealthy as well as more wealthy than the median average. However, the person now concludes, the claim that Jews in the United States are wealthier on median average than other Americans is true.

By adopting the principle of conditional trust, we remain in conversation with the other person and gain the benefit of information that we did not have and would have missed if we simply judged the speaker to be hopelessly biased. In this case we also gain the benefit of seeing that while some stereotypes may have a relationship to actual empirical data, that relationship is distorted into caricatures that oversimplify or misrepresent the facts. While Jews in the United States may on average be wealthier than other Americans, this clearly does not entail that they are greedy, cheap, or manipulative. From the Middle Ages to the Holocaust, Jews in Europe were ostracized from most careers with the exception of tax collecting and money lending, and this added to the social, political, and economic strains that existed with Christians.[11] Fictional images of Jews as conniving merchants were perpetuated in stories, plays, cartoons, and later films.[12] So, the more recent fact of wealth accumulation by Jews in the United States can be used to revive harmful stereotypes that were used against Jews for more than a thousand years. However, the status of the original claim, that Jews in the United States are on average wealthier than other groups, is not in and of itself a biased claim, nor was the person who stated it revealing her or his anti-Semitic attitudes. By conditionally trusting the person who makes this claim and not simply dismissing the person as biased based on our interpretation of the claim, we gain the benefit of new evidence and a better understanding of the speaker's perspective.

Finally, let's consider the third condition where we should maintain a principle of conditional trust. A good example that illustrates this condition occurred when Barack Obama appeared on *The Tonight Show with Jay Leno* just a few months into his first term as president. Leno asked the president whether he had used the White House bowling alley.[13] Obama replied that he had in fact tried bowling but, given his low score, "it was the Special Olympics, or something." Though the audience laughed, many more people around the country who were watching, including Special Olympians and their families, were hurt and frustrated by the president's insensitive remarks. The comment was particularly egregious for some because it came just one year after the "A More Perfect Union" speech that Obama gave in March 2008 while on the campaign trail in Philadelphia. That speech, which was widely praised by politicians, news media, academics, and other groups across the country, was concerned with race and racism. Even Charles Murray, author of *The Bell Curve* and a member of the conservative think tank the American Enterprise Institute, said, "As far as I'm concerned, it is just plain flat out brilliant—rhetorically, but also in capturing a lot of nuance about race in America. It is so far above the standard we're used to from our politicians."[14]

Given the president's nuanced analysis of race, an analysis praised even by those outside of his political party, his insensitive remark about disability made him suspect for some Americans. In an ABC online news story about the president's Special Olympics remark, commenters said things like "Obama is a complete fraud" and "People who are so concerned with 'tolerance' now have to defend a man who callously insults the disabled."[15] Many people seemed to wonder how a president who could be so sensitive to matters of race in America could be so insensitive to matters of disability. This inconsistency led commenters to conclude that President Obama must be a "fraud."

Yet should we draw the conclusion that a single insensitive or biased remark cancels out a speaker's trustworthiness or credibility on social issues generally? If we adopt the principle of conditional trust, then the third condition requires that we maintain our trust in the speaker in just this kind of situation. We should understand that just because a person has one set of social issues on her or his radar does not mean that those issues are on that radar all the time. President Obama's sensitivity to race does not automatically entail his sensitivity to disability. Or at least it did not in that moment. Even social issues that we may pay special attention to can disappear from our radar or can remain disconnected from other related issues. Unfortunately, too often we organize social properties into simple and unrelated groups such as "all Women" or "all African Americans" or "all gays and lesbians." Rather than seeing the intersections and complexities of these properties in the lives of actual people, we abstract them from real life to analyze them. By doing so, we fail to consider the ways that social properties relate to each other. If our focus is on race, then we imagine *all* the people of that race. If it is on gender, then we lump *all* the people of that gender together. But in reality, race, gender, and other social categories operate in complex intersectional ways and relate to each other in similarly complex ways. Discrimination, bias, and stereotyping all are expressed in different ways and target groups differently even while there are underlying commonalities. All African Americans, for instance, do not experience discrimination in exactly the same ways. African American Christians share some experiences of race discrimination with African American Muslims but also differ with regard to religious privilege.

The point is that there are different ways that we experience social privilege, social bias, and discrimination, and they operate in complex ways. However, to talk about them we have to isolate them as discrete, individual categories, and in so doing we can forget that they are interconnected. Of course, bias and discrimination are inflicted on the basis of race (or class, gender, religion, disability, sexual orientation, etc.), but how they are experienced by the wide variety of people who are identified with that race is varied and complex. It is hard for us to think and talk in this intersectional and complex way, so we often reduce our language and our beliefs to simplified categories. We then focus on the one or two categories that matter most directly to us and lose sight of our connection to the others. The result is that like President Obama, we can say something profound about one social category while later saying something disparaging or insensitive about another. Does this mean that we, and the president, have a clear negative attitude toward the group we insult? The principle of conditional trust maintains that unless there is a pattern of such remarks, the answer should be "no."

Given how little of our public discourse focuses on the intersectional nature of social properties, it is not surprising that we find it hard to think about a wide variety of social groups and how they are affected in related ways by bias and stereotyping. While President Obama offered a sophisticated analysis of race, his treatment of disability was not, at the moment of that interview, as sophisticated or as sensitive. Yet race bias has connections to disability bias in our country's history.[16] Black skin itself was treated as an abnormality, and African Americans were often described in early medical journals as lacking normal cerebral functioning.[17] Was the president ignorant of this history? Is this evidence of him being a fraud when it comes to social justice?

If we adhere to the third requirement of the principle of conditional trust, we recognize that people may sometimes say things that are inconsistent with their more firmly held beliefs and values. This can happen particularly with social issues because of the way we seem to compartmentalize and oversimplify social identities. Our attention to class issues may make us lose sight of gender, or our focus on religion may make us lose sight of race, yet all of these categories and the related biases and stereotypes associated with them share commonalities. They are rooted in fear, lack of information, lack of exposure, unjustified inferences, and faulty reasoning. Additionally, they arose out of social systems of inequality, privilege, and power, and these same systems work to perpetuate our ignorance of injustice and limit our connections to similarly oppressed groups.

Obama's insensitivity to disability in his remark to Leno is not sufficient evidence for judging the president to be a fraud when it comes to social justice. What we should learn from the remark is that even those who pay careful attention to one variety of social injustice may fail to pay attention to others. This is understandable, since so much of our public discourse treats social differences as unique and unrelated categories. After the president made the remark, White House spokesperson Bill Burton said, "The President made an offhand remark making fun of his own bowling that was in no way intended to disparage the Special Olympics. He thinks the Special Olympics is a wonderful program that gives an opportunity to shine to people with disabilities from around the world."[18]

Unfortunately, this somewhat bland and appeasing statement was a lost opportunity for Obama to add some nuance to public dialogues about social bias and stereotyping. That is, he could have reminded the country that we are all capable of resorting to biases and stereotypes when joking in an unreflective manner even when we are very attuned and sensitive to some specific ones: "I am often sensitive to race bias, but I admit that disability bias may not be as prominent on my radar. Consistent reflection and attention to bias is difficult to maintain given that we rarely have opportunities to consider their intersections. But I am committed to doing this important work, and this experience has proven to be a memorable learning opportunity." A statement like this by a president would remind Americans that no individual or group has the perfect vantage point from which they can see all the dimensions of social bias and stereotyping.

These problems run deep in both our conscious and unconscious beliefs. It takes work to be reflective, sensitive and attuned to how bias operates in our thinking and our judgments. When the stakes are so high, when one insensitive or misinterpreted comment means that you can be pegged a racist, a sexist, a homophobe, or insensitive to the disabled, it is not surprising that people are reluctant to speak freely and openly about social difference and social identity. The principle of conditional trust is an effort to lower the stakes and establish a certain amount of common ground and mutual compassion.

The Recognition of Mutual Vulnerability

The fifth and final skill required for intellectual empathy is the *recognition of mutual vulnerability*. To be clear, vulnerability as it relates to this skill is not meant as a position of weakness or defenselessness. Rather, vulnerability as a skill of intellectual empathy is a willingness to be open to self-correction and transformation. Vulnerability begins with an understanding of the bodily dimensions of reasoning and argumentation, particularly when it comes to matters of social difference. Admitting our social biases can *feel* physically uncomfortable. We may be embarrassed, afraid, or defiant. Hearing about biases that others have toward the social groups to which we belong can *feel* hurtful and even infuriating. Similarly, discovering that those who share our social characteristics also face some of the same things we do can *feel* comforting and even exhilarating. In these discussions our heart might race, our stomach might knot up, or our blood pressure might rise. Matters of social difference and social bias are not abstract issues that are disconnected from our experiences. We live with them, we embody them, and they identify us. It is not surprising that we react physically when they are misunderstood, criticized, or honored. And yet because we are so embedded in systems of social identity and difference, our willingness to engage in an analysis of their effects should be seen as a brave and worthwhile pursuit. Adopting an attitude of vulnerability means that we go into the conversation ready to be affected and willing to be transformed. While it may seem paradoxical, vulnerability and openness are not positions of weakness but are actually positions that require courage and strength.

One way that we can foster this courage and strength is by relaxing our defensive reactions when we engage in dialogues about social issues. When I say "relax," I don't mean to be diminishing the significance of our reactions or pretending that they are easy to change. Beliefs about social issues are complex, and an attitude of "Whatever, dude" is not going to help. Instead, I mean that we should relax into a dialogue about social issues in the way that we relax into a difficult physical feat. When we are about to take a high dive into deep water, set out on a long run, or attempt a difficult hook shot in basketball, relaxing our bodies and our minds into the experience will no doubt improve the outcome. Being rigid, uptight, and inflexible can lead to injury and errors. In the same way, we should intentionally try to relax our defensive reactions and loosen the tight hold we have on our self-image when plunging into a dialogue about social issues.

Humor can be an effective mechanism for bringing about this kind of intentional flexibility. I have in mind here the humor that allows us to laugh at ourselves and our imperfect grasp on social biases and stereotypes. Humor that is honest, critically engaging, and nonarrogant provides a way for us to remain open and connected with others. Comedian Dave Chappelle, for instance, has said,

> Things like racism are institutionalized and systemic. You might not know any bigots, and you feel like, "Well, I don't hate black people, so I'm not a racist," but you benefit from racism just by the merit of the color of your skin. There's opportunities that you have, you're privileged in ways that you may not even realize because you haven't been deprived in certain ways. *We need to talk about these things in order for things to change.*[19]

Comedians such as Chappelle, Margaret Cho, George Carlin, and others who cross social boundaries do so because of their willingness to laugh *with* (rather than *at*) their audience and because at the heart of their humor, they are unpacking all the complex components embedded in stereotypes and social systems of injustice rather than just reaffirming them.

In their extremely thoughtful analysis of humor and social differences, Patrick Grzanka and Justin Maher consider how the popular online blog, book series, Facebook page, and Twitter feed Stuff White People Like (SWPL) differs from the work of comics such as Chappelle and Cho.[20] SWPL, rather than challenging multiple forms of intersecting systems of injustice and stereotyping, works to categorize nonstigmatized aspects of white middle-class and wealthy identity such as food and vacation options. Examples include microbreweries, Frisbee sports, and Conan O'Brien. According to the feel-good diversity model discussed in chapter 2, SWPL treats whiteness as monolithic and unrelated to its intersections with class, gender, sexual orientation, and, most significantly, power. As Grzanka and Maher write, "the humor of Chapelle, Rock, Cho and others tends to (though not always) critique multiple systems of oppression and address multiple dimensions of difference. *SWPL,* on the other hand, aims its lens at one system of oppression: race. Such a one-dimensional approach to anti-racist work resonates with the long-standing criticisms of black feminists such as Collins who argues that the only people who can afford (figuratively and literally) to limit their analytic lens to one dimension of difference are those for whom the stakes of antiracist work are not so high."[21]

Lois Leveen, a writer who also teaches racial studies, literature, and American history, explains that jokes about social stereotypes, when they are told by the people subjected to the stereotype, can often make the stereotype and its believers seem much more laughable than the group stereotyped.[22] Leveen gives the example of Phil Nee, a Chinese American comedian who joked that "It is not easy being Chinese. My girlfriend left me last week for some other guy who looks exactly like me."[23] Nee's joke assumes that the stereotype "All Asians look alike" (remember the cognitive bias of the out-group homogeneity effect from chapter 4) is factually accurate and then carries the stereotype to its absurd extreme. The result is that the stereotype and its proponents become the real joke rather than the joke teller and the laughing audience. Nee's recognition of the stereotype also reveals his awareness of how he is perceived by some non-Asian people, and by joking he wrestles back control of his identity by revealing the stereotype's absurdity. When the people in the audience are able to laugh with him, they are also standing with him on common ground.

Of course, humor can also be used as a powerful weapon to reinforce oppression and discrimination. Some comedians, rather than exploring and challenging social stereotypes, promote them in arrogant and adversarial ways. This kind of humor contributes to the perpetuation of bias and stereotyping and normalizes them in ways that make it harder for us to honestly assess and eradicate their influence. Male comedians who flaunt their male privilege by reaffirming stereotypes about women in their performances are not challenging inequalities but celebrating them. Nonwhite and ethnic comedians who embody stereotypes of their own race in their performances are not resisting or rejecting the stereotypes but reinforcing them. Robin Means Coleman, a professor of communications and AfroAmerican and African studies argues that "Black sitcoms that emphasize self-deprecating humor, physical comedy, provocative and flashy clothing, and 'ghettocentric' characterizations, all contribute to a narrowly defined portrait of African American men and women."[24]

So, while humor can be used to create alliances and challenge stereotypes, it can also be used to divide and conquer. As intellectually empathic thinkers, we should create and seek out opportunities for humor that acknowledges our mutual vulnerability and respects our humanity. Dialogues and debates about social identity and social differences are not simply cerebral exercises abstracted from who we are. They are personal. For that reason, they engage us intellectually, emotionally, and physically.

But for the same reason, they can also give us some of the most significant opportunities for critical thinking. If we can accept that the fight-flight and victim-culprit dichotomies are not our only choices and if we can both trust and embrace our mutual vulnerability, we reduce those risks and increase the possibilities for reasonable, respectful, and in some cases humorous discourse.

So, with the principle of conditional trust and the recognition of mutual vulnerability added to our list, we have now established the five skills involved in intellectual empathy. They are:

1. Understanding the invisibility of privilege,
2. Knowing that social identity is intersectional,
3. Using the model of cooperative reasoning,
4. Applying the principle of conditional trust, and
5. Recognizing our mutual vulnerability.

With these in place let's next consider how we can effectively take intellectual empathy out into the world.

Questions for Review

1. What is one lesson we can learn from Uncle Moe?

2. What are the three conditions that need to be met when applying the principle of conditional trust in a dialogue about social identity and difference?

3. Why should we, as intellectually empathic critical thinkers, pay special attention to information and evidence related to social myths and stereotypes? Give one concrete example of how you could gain more of this kind of information.

4. Why is it important to remain in a dialogue with someone whom we judge to have made a stereotypical comment? How does doing this require using one or more of the five elements of intellectual empathy?

5. How does the recognition of our mutual vulnerability relate to the role that emotion plays in our thinking and reasoning about social identity and difference?

6. In what ways can humor help us to find common ground on issues of social identity and difference? In what ways can humor make it harder to find common ground? Use examples from the comedians and types of comedy referenced in this chapter.

Questions for Further Thinking and Writing

1. Think of a racist, sexist, stereotypical joke you know that assumes a reductive nonintersectional conception of social identity. Now consider how this stereotype could intersect with a stereotype about another group. Why is it important to see the connections between different forms of bias and discrimination?

2. Describe an experience where you (or a person with whom you were talking) established some common ground on an issue of social identity and difference. Describe the intellectual and emotional qualities of that experience.

3. Can you think of a time when you may have been sensitive to one aspect of social difference but failed to be sensitive to another (such as the example of President Obama and the Special Olympics)? What did it feel like to discover your blind spot? How did you address it in that context?

Additional Resources

The Southern Poverty Law Center's mission is to "Fight hate and bigotry and to seek social justice for the most vulnerable members of our society." The center's website, at http://www.splcenter.org/what-we-do, has a variety of resources related to stereotyping, social differences, and equal rights.

The YWCA (Young Women's Christian Association) has put together a terrific "Anti-Racist Toolkit," available at http://www.ywca.org/atf/cf/%7BE8D61FD8-7CED-4851-805D-C673BD5C88CD%7D/YWCAANTI-RACISMTOOLKIT.pdf.

You can find a variety of Dave Chappelle's stand-up routines and excerpts from his television comedy show on YouTube and on Comedy Central's website, http://www.cc.com/shows/chappelle-s-show. Some of the most notable for challenging racial stereotypes are "The Racial Draft," "Black People and Chicken," "The Niggar Family," and "Clayton Bigsby: The Black White Supremacist."

You can find some of the best examples of Margaret Cho's humor at YouTube, http://www.youtube.com/watch?v=yOZh_g13Oi8&list=PLA893292C2CB173D6&index=7.

Hari Kondabolu is a very funny Indian American comedian whose album *Waiting for 2042* references the date that whites will supposedly no longer be a statistical majority in the United States. His humor addresses the intersections of race, class, gender, religion, sexual orientation, and social power. You can find links to his performances and more at his official site, http://www.harikondabolu.om.

7 | Taking Intellectual Empathy Out into the World

Playfulness, World Traveling, Loving Perception

The kind of humor that challenges stereotypes and creates common ground between different groups of people has the qualities of "playfulness," "world traveling," and "loving perception" described by Latina feminist philosopher Maria Lugones.[1] We will look at each of these qualities in turn and then relate them to the work of intellectual empathy.

By "playfulness" Lugones does not mean a frivolous attitude or even a competitive desire to win but rather playfulness in the sense of a willingness to play the fool, to not "speak the language" fluently, to not assume that you know the rules but to let them emerge, and to be open to self-construction or reconstruction. This sense of "fool" does not imply a silly or stupid person who neglects common sense. Rather, a "fool" in Lugones's sense relates to the character of the wise fool that is so common across a wide variety of the world's cultures. Historian Vicki K. Janick in her book *Fools and Jesters in Literature, Art, and History* describes the wise fool as "one who perceives and acknowledges his own weaknesses and desires as well as the weaknesses and desires of others."[2] The fool represents a challenge to the pretense of order and control and thus disturbs our complacent acceptance of ordinary meaning.[3] In this way, "playfulness" or "playing the fool" in Lugones's sense is an effort to remain self-aware, self-examining, and attuned to the structures and attitudes that maintain social order. Being willing to play the fool means that we suspend our self-concept with the goal of exploring the roles that may be constraining us.

"Worlds" in Lugones's sense are not bound by borders and nations but instead by social identities and cultural norms. We each inhabit different worlds as we move between our families, our jobs, our friends, our religious traditions, and our social and political communities. "Worlds" in this sense are not imaginary; they are inhabited by flesh-and-blood people. Worlds have languages as well as norms and expectations. Languages can include first languages such as English but can also comprise different words, dialects, and meanings within the same language. If you are a native English speaker, the language you speak at home might differ in some significant ways from the English you speak at school or with your friends. Similarly, the norms and expectations for behavior can differ significantly as we move from our homes to our school and professional lives and then among our friends. This kind of movement is what Lugones describes as "world traveling." Think about a student who in one day can inhabit the world of her classroom, her family home, her job at a local child care center, and then in the evening get together with friends at a bar. Though she may speak English at school, her job, and out with friends, she still will use different words and phrases and have different expectations about her audience in each of these different contexts. If she speaks a language other than English at home, this will add a further level of complexity and meaning to her interactions. It may be easier for her to transition from the world of her classroom to her job and harder to transition from the world of her friends to her family home. And while she inhabits the world of her classroom, she does not cease to be someone from the world of her family home.

Lugnoes describes the experience of being at ease in a world, which means that we have achieved a certain level of competency and ability in that world. We know the language, we like the norms and expectations of that world, we feel humanly bonded in the sense of being cared for and caring for others in that world, and we share a history. Some of the worlds we inhabit are not worlds in which we may feel at ease. In others we may feel at ease to a greater or lesser degree. The point is that inhabiting a world is not a guarantee that you will feel or be made to feel at ease. Some worlds we were born into, some worlds we were invited into, and some worlds we are either forced to inhabit or are prevented from entering. We inhabit worlds both by choice and through no fault of our own. Our ability to travel within and among worlds will be affected by how at ease we feel within those worlds.

Finally, Lugones, inspired by philosopher Marilyn Frye's essay "In and Out of Harm's Way" (1983), develops a notion of "loving perception" that she contrasts with "arrogant perception."[4] To arrogantly perceive another person, to "ignore, ostracize, render invisible, stereotype, leave completely alone, or interpret as crazy,"[5] is to fail to identify with that person. When we arrogantly perceive others, we see only the ways they can provide something for us, how they can serve our interests. To perceive another person lovingly does not mean that we necessarily feel affectionate toward the person but rather that we take on a lens of compassion and mutuality to "see others through their eyes, to go into their worlds and understand what it is to be them and what it is to be ourselves through their eyes."[6] Loving perception is a desire to know and assess the social, historical, philosophical, and personal aspects of the lives of people who may not inhabit our worlds. It requires that we work to temporarily suspend our own will, our own interests, our own fears, and our own imaginations. In this way, loving perception provides a way to know thyself through a sincere effort to know the people who inhabit worlds different from one's own. Loving perception also provides us with a way to see our dependency on each other (remember our discussion in chapter 5 about the way that dependency has been treated as something bad or abnormal). Lugones reminds us that it is only through our relationships with other people that our language becomes meaningful and we are understood. Without this kind of mutual understanding, we are left unintelligible and isolated. Loving perception is a willingness to make meaning, to world travel so that we can understand each other.

Lugones contrasts her sense of playfulness and world traveling with what she refers to as an agonistic attitude, one that is self-important and world erasing. The nonplayful world traveler is a reluctant traveler who when faced with other worlds adopts a conquering attitude of self-righteousness. The nonplayful traveler never allows herself the experience of inhabiting a new world and will not permit herself to have her own beliefs and judgments called into question.

What is important for our purposes in Lugones's account of playfulness, world traveling, and loving perception is that it can function as a navigation tool for understanding people who occupy different worlds. Lugones argues that a difference in interpretation is often the result of significant social divisions between people. These divisions are shaped by social and political systems but are reinforced when we as individuals fail to identify and explore the experiences of those whom we judge to be different, naive, misguided, irrational, or morally suspect.

Lugones explains how power differentials often allow those who are privileged to ignore and thus not identify with the experiences of those who are disadvantaged. As a result, the facts of social disadvantage, including the kinds of conditions that create the beliefs and attitudes held by socially disadvantaged groups, is further obscured by the lack of awareness on the part of the socially privileged. The more socially privileged a group is, the more its beliefs, attitudes, and concerns are aired, analyzed, and met. The less socially privileged a group is, the less so. And because those with social privilege never have to consider how they are seen in the worlds of those with less privilege, they fail to understand their identity fully.

For instance, an American woman who is white and Christian and has to move from New Jersey to Nebraska because her company is relocating will most likely not be concerned with whether she will be welcomed by her neighbors or whether she will find a house of worship or even a suitable salon to get her hair done. These expectations would be very different if the woman was African American or Muslim. This is more than just a matter of saying "Well, goods and services are just geared toward the majority and not the minority!" While it is true that in a for-profit economy the target market is the majority, we still have an obligation to know, as critical thinkers, if there are important facts we are missing about the experiences and daily struggles facing our neighbors, coworkers, and fellow citizens. This is especially so in a for-profit economy because this data will not tend to make its way onto the radar of the majority, given that it has little commercial value. On the other hand, the experiences and daily struggles of the socially privileged and those in majority groups are usually well known, since they permeate through the culture.

For instance, the struggle that many employees of major retailers face between asking for the Christmas holiday off to spend with family versus opting to work so as not to risk a layoff is one that has garnered media attention and generated a national debate.[7] Most Americans, no matter what their faith, know when the Christmas holiday is and what the holiday entails. Americans are saturated with Christmas advertising, Christmas products, Christmas music, and Christmas events. Americans who are Jewish, Muslim, Buddhist, Jain, Sikh, or Hindu also have holidays and traditions that are meaningful to them and involve spending time with their families. Yet the actual holidays are almost unknown to Christian Americans along with the dilemmas their adherents face trying to balance work obligations with family and religious obligations. Non-Christians understand how they are seen in the arrogant perception of Christian Americans because they have experienced being ignored, stereotyped, ostracized, or described as crazy. Because Christian Americans are socially privileged, they have not had to consider how they are perceived in the worlds of Jews, Muslims, Buddhists, Jains, Sikhs, or Hindus.

W. E. B. Du Bois, an American sociologist and the first African American to earn a doctorate from Harvard, called this phenomenon "double consciousness."[8] That is, people within a society who occupy a minority status (or a social status that is oppressed or vilified) have to know the beliefs and values of the majority culture if they are going to navigate and survive. Members of the minority group must also know their own culture, including the aspects of it that nurture and give them a sense of identity and self-worth as well as the very negative biases and stereotypes held by the majority group(s). This can create a kind of cognitive dissonance wherein an individual who experiences the very positive and fulfilling aspects of the minority and majority cultures must also make that consistent with what those in the majority culture devalue or ignore in their minority experience. As Du Bois wrote, "One ever feels his twoness—an American, a Negro; two souls, two thoughts, two unreconciled strivings; two warring ideals in one dark body, whose dogged strength alone keeps it from being torn asunder."[9]

Du Bois's concept stems from the particularly cruel and unjust treatment of black Americans in our nation's history. Yet his notion of double consciousness has resonated with other Americans who have faced oppression and social disadvantages because of their gender, race, ethnicity, religion, and/or sexual orientation. One way that we might alleviate the dissonance of double consciousness is by adopting a loving perception and playfully world traveling, in Lugones's sense. What this would mean is that we explore the worlds of others, particularly groups whose experiences are not like our own, so that we might gain insight into their concerns and understand how we may be contributing to their struggles.

This is of course easier said than done. Many of us feel uncomfortable inserting ourselves into a social or cultural event that is out of the bounds of our history and identity. We feel uncomfortable because we fear looking foolish or standing out, not knowing the customs or the norms. We may also feel that we are being disrespectful by inserting ourselves into the practices of a group to which we are not members. These concerns are understandable, and this is why Lugones recommends that if we do world travel, we do so playfully and nonarrogantly, entering with a desire to learn and maybe be transformed. And though we might appear awkward or foolish at times, we will leave more experienced. This is not a guarantee that every group will welcome us, since some groups might find our presence disrespectful or unwelcome. This is a chance you take when you travel. Yet as many real world travelers will tell you, if you visit a country, a culture, or a community with an open heart, a desire to understand, and a willingness to sometimes be awkward and foolish, you will more often than not have the opportunity to learn. However, Lugones also reminds us that in some worlds we will clearly not be safe. This is because those who inhabit those worlds perceive us in such arrogant and nonloving ways that we risk far too much by being playful. It would be a mistake for, instance, for a young woman to enter a strip club and be playful, in Lugones's sense, in the hope of understanding that world.

So, how do world traveling, loving perception, and playfulness relate to intellectual empathy? Mutual vulnerability (see chapter 6) is an effort at learning to apply loving perception in our dialogues and debates about social issues. This does not mean that as intellectually empathic critical thinkers we have to feel affectionate toward everyone with whom we argue. Rather, as intellectually empathic critical thinkers we should cultivate a desire to know about other worlds, especially the worlds inhabited by those with whom we disagree and debate. Mutual vulnerability also entails that we keep in mind our own social identities and how people in different worlds perceive us. We should extend empathy to each other in this context because we are both affected by wider historical and social systems of inequality and oppositional and limited categories of identities while still being complex and feeling beings.

Two people, or even a group of people, engaged in a debate about social issues should be alert to the mistake of world erasing, meaning that those who occupy a position of privilege or social advantage should not arrogantly resist or deny the experiences of those with less privilege or social advantage. Exploring the experiences of someone from a different world and trying to see how that person and you are constructed within it can be risky. It is also risky to report on your world, particularly if you have been dismissed or ignored in the past. Mutual vulnerability is the recognition of these risks from the point of view of both the traveler and the local. Playfulness, in Lugones's sense, is the recommended strategy for the traveler. Loving perception is the recommended strategy for the inhabitant. Together a commitment to mutual vulnerability can create the kind of conditions for both to be effective critical thinkers.

What might world traveling look like, then, in Lugones's sense? Before answering that question, it is worth considering the kinds of things that are often celebrated as opportunities for world traveling or diversity but actually reaffirm existing inequalities and fail to challenge biases and stereotypes.

Diversity and World Traveling as a Feel-Good Politics

Sara Ahmed, mentioned in the introduction to this book, describes the way that many diversity initiatives are presented as things to be "celebrated, consumed, and eaten."[10] For instance, many educational and business institutions will promote diversity and world traveling through events such as fashion shows and food fairs. Since fashion and food are generally pleasant and innocuous ways to represent culture, diversity is reduced to a safe dip into and out of a culture by sampling some traditional costumes and dishes. One problem with this way of interpreting worlds and the related notions of multiculturalism and diversity is that it ignores worlds that are not tied to ethnicity and region. There is no traditional costume or food to represent LGBT people, the disabled, the elderly, or the poor and working class. Another problem is that groups who are more culturally dominant are mistakenly thought not to have a unique or specialized costume or cuisine, since their fashion and food options permeate everyone's worlds. Fast food, for example, which is ever present in American culture, is not usually considered to be an example of traditional food representative of a social group. It is, most people would say, for everyone. Yet fast food reflects the interests of the dominant American food economy whereby processed beef, potatoes, salt, and sugar are prioritized. These options work well for industries that were created and developed in the United States and continue to have significant influence over national and even global food production. Hamburgers, french fries, and soda have a history and a context and a story in the same way that corn and peppers do in Mexico and cauliflower and cumin do in India. The omnipresence of fast food makes it seem like it has no cultural ties, but if we include economic, environmental, political, and health concerns in our understanding of "cultural," it clearly does. By ignoring this fact, ethnic food becomes all the things that "those other people" eat. The dominant American culture, we should not forget, is also a series of particular choices based on resources, politics, and values. Finally, the fashion and food fair model puts the world traveler in the position of a consumer, one who is all too comfortable for most Americans. By tasting unfamiliar worlds and even socializing with the inhabitants, you still do so as a consumer who is paying for the experience and hence has a certain amount of power. The customer, we are told, is always right. There is very little responsibility or accountability that we bring to a situation when we are there just to sample the variety of options.

A world traveler, as we will understand it, is not someone who seeks out traveling solely for the purposes of self-fulfillment. Nor is it someone who enters a world solely to help and protect (from the traveler's point of view) the world's inhabitants while failing to acknowledge the history of hard work and responsibility that has gone into maintaining that world. Help in this sense is not based on evidence or experience but instead is based on the assumption that the traveler knows what is best for the people in that world. I am reminded of a time when I was working with a group of college students on a service project late in the fall semester. The students wanted to contribute in some positive way to the issue of homelessness in our area, and since the weather was getting colder, they came up with the idea of collecting mittens to donate to a local shelter. The students believed that all that was left to do, aside from advertising the mitten drive and collecting mittens, was to contact the shelter to find out the best time to arrive with the delivery. When I asked the group members if they had contacted the shelter first to find out if they even needed mittens, the answer was no. The students' assumption was that homeless shelters need everything, so why wouldn't they need mittens? However, once the call was made it turned out that in fact mittens and most every other type of warm clothing were currently in abundance in the shelter. What was actually needed was help with sorting clothing donations by size and season. By making contact with the shelter's director and then going there to work, the students in the group had to reexamine their assumption that they knew what was best. After working there for the day, the students also had the chance to see that things were well organized and were designed to specifically meet the needs of the current residents. The students had never considered that job training and healthy eating programs would be part of a homeless shelter's offerings.

Caryn McTighe Musil, senior scholar and director of the Civic Learning and Democracy Project at the Association of American Colleges and Universities, notes that short-duration projects whereby students work with their local communities can have the unintended effect of perceiving "the community as a resource to mine particularly for the benefit of the onlooker; while the student may gain new facts, the experience might simply reinforce stereotypes without widening the students' cultural lenses."[11] Being a traveler in our sense is not the same thing as seeking personal fulfillment, nor is it an opportunity to help by ignoring the authority and expertise of the world's inhabitants. It does mean that we are sensitive to the history of privilege and power so that when we seek to travel to a world, we remain aware of our privilege and how it has been used to erase the experiences of those with social disadvantages.

Similarly, playing the fool in Lugones's sense does not mean that we enter worlds without any protection, awareness, or information. Rather, we play the fool in the sense of being active learners, starting from a position of humility and an openness to new evidence. In the case of the mitten drive, a position of humility and openness to evidence could have led the students to seek out the authority of the shelter's director and residents as appropriate sources for information regarding the center's needs.

Virtuous Hearing and World Traveling

What kind of world traveling would support our efforts at intellectual empathy? As a start, one very basic way to begin world traveling is by becoming better listeners. This might seem like a very passive way to travel, but listening can be very active. In addition, listening the right way can be a component of moral action. Philosopher Miranda Fricker uses the phrase "virtuous hearing" to describe the habit of listening with a "reflexive critical awareness" to correct for "prejudice in our judgments of credibility."[12] Active virtuous listening would mean that we pay attention to the experiences of people with social identities and experiences different from our own while also considering the following kinds of questions:

- What biases and preconceptions might be affecting how I listen to this person (or group)?
- Am I rushing to the judgment that this person is not telling the truth, that the person is exaggerating her or his experiences or misunderstands those experiences?
- Do I feel defensive (and world erasing)?
- Is it hard for me to adopt a playful attitude of loving perception because I am tense, anxious, or uncomfortable?

Without even having to go very far, we can world travel by getting into the habit of virtuous listening. We can begin by seeking out opportunities to hear people talk (and write) about their experiences of race, class, gender, sexual orientation, religion, and dis/ability. Documentary films such as *The Color of Fear, A Girl Like Me, A Class Divided, Tough Guise, Class Dismissed,* and *Reel Bad Arabs,* among many others, give us the opportunity to see and hear how individuals and groups navigate the complexity of social identity within systems of privilege and power. Blogs and websites such as Racialicious, Feministe, Disability Intel, Mused Online, and Brown Girl Problems are just some examples of online communities organized around issues of social identity (and the additional resources at the end of each chapter list more). These forums can provide a way for interested readers who are not directly part of these communities to learn about issues relevant to members of the community. In addition, novels, plays, and performances that center on social identities other than our own provide us with narrative accounts of how it feels to be in a world from different perspectives. However, all too often when films and books focus on identities other than the most privileged, they are taken to be for "those other people" and not for the mainstream culture. As world travelers, we should resist the erasure of these worlds by actively seeking out art that promotes a range of social perspectives and provides us with data about the varieties of social experience. Again, we should not do this because it is the politically correct thing to do or because it allows us to experience exotic cultures; we should do this because it fosters critical thinking and mutual understanding.

Beyond narrative mediums such as documentaries, blogs, performances, and literature, our daily interactions with people at school, at work, and in our communities can be opportunities to develop virtuous listening and world traveling. Which voices do we pay attention to by default, and how could we actively shift our attention to different voices? What events, community meetings, and local gatherings do we ignore because we believe they are for "those other people" and hence not of any interest to us? Taking the risk of attending and participating in a gathering that centers on some aspect of social identity different from our own, and where people like us are not leading, can be an opportunity to begin world traveling.

Thus far I have described opportunities for world traveling where the world's inhabitants have made explicit that others are invited in. Documentary films, novels, and even advertised community meetings and local events are designed to be public and open to a wide audience. I start with these kinds of opportunities for world traveling because the organizers expect (and often hope for) a wide range of participants. This is different from an event that is designed to give members of a social group, particularly a group who experiences social disadvantages, the opportunity for solidarity, humor, support, and friendship. Sara Ahmed explains that as a faculty member of color in a predominately white university, she sometimes has to work hard to find a "break from whiteness." She recounts an experience at a large academic conference where a black caucus had been set up for academics of color to meet and discuss issues related to the conference theme. Ten people showed up, four of whom identified as white. Ahmed says that the meeting's organizer, for understandable reasons, did not want to insist that anyone leave. Yet Ahmed felt very uncomfortable. She had expected that time and that space to be a chance to talk to other academics of color. She writes, "It felt as if the one space we had been given—to take a break from whiteness— had been taken away."[13] Eventually one by one the white attendees left for different reasons, but what Ahmed learned from the occasion was "the political labor that it takes to have spaces of relief from whiteness."[14]

World travelers with social privilege need to be cognizant of the fact that just by being present in some circumstances, it can be world erasing for inhabitants who seek relief from privilege. As intellectually empathic world travelers, then, we want to be sure that we are entering worlds where our presence is expected. Being expected is not the same thing as being welcomed. We should not expect as travelers that our presence in a different world should be a cause for celebration by that world's inhabitants. For instance, just because you took the risk of attending a religious ceremony outside of your own faith tradition, this does not mean that you are now a hero to that religion's adherents. Similarly, a straight person who agrees to go to a gay bar for the first time with a friend who is gay or lesbian should not make the experience about how amazingly open-minded and tolerant oneself—the straight person—is. This is not to say that traveling to different worlds is easy or without risk of appearing foolish or out of place. Rather, it is to emphasize that the experience of world traveling should be about a respectful openness and humility where the world's inhabitants become central and not the fact that you are traveling.

Responsible Reporting When Travelers Arrive in Your World

Thus far we have been considering how world traveling and virtuous listening can help us to develop and apply the skills of intellectual empathy. Similarly, we should consider the ways that as inhabitants of worlds, we might develop and apply the skills of intellectual empathy when we encounter travelers. Assuming that these travelers are not wholly uninvited—that is, that we are not seeking relief from privilege as Ahmed described it—how should we respond as inhabitants? Well, we have established thus far that travelers do not necessarily have to be welcomed. This is a temptation that is often hard to resist if the traveler has social privilege relative to the world's inhabitants. The one man who attends a women's studies meeting can receive more attention and accolades than the women who are there regularly. In an effort to show our appreciation for the alliance, the socially disadvantaged can wind up recreating the very power differentials they hope to challenge by prioritizing the presence of the socially privileged. So, while we can recognize the potential risks that a traveler makes when coming into our world, it does not follow that it is our responsibility to necessarily make all travelers comfortable. This does not mean that we should make them uncomfortable! Instead, the traveler's comfort is not our responsibility and is not even a goal of intellectual empathy. Instead, if travelers are in our world practicing virtuous listening, it should be incumbent upon us to engage in the corollary skill of *responsible reporting*. What I mean by this is that in the presence of travelers to our world, as intellectually empathic critical thinkers, we should attend to the following questions:

- What biases do I have about this traveler's social identity?
- Do I assume that someone like this cannot be trusted? Do I assume that such people will never get it?

- Does their presence make me feel like I am on the offense?
- Do I assume I am not safe, not trusted, not respected?

Responsible reporting would mean that we consider these questions as well as the fact that we may be rushing to judgments about travelers without any relevant evidence. Remember that the fourth skill for intellectual empathy, the principle of conditional trust, requires us to assume not only that someone reporting on her or his own experiences is credible but also that those who hear our reports are trustworthy. Again, if we have evidence to the contrary, we are right to withdraw that trust.

There is a different kind of temptation that can arise when the traveler is socially disadvantaged relative to the world's inhabitants. On the one hand, socially advantaged inhabitants with good intentions may go out of their way to ignore the differences out of a desire to equalize the power dynamics for the traveler. Imagine, for instance, that I invite a student to attend an academic conference so she will gain professional experience and have the opportunity to network with other academics. In an effort to make her feel more like a peer, I ask her to join a group of faculty at a restaurant for dinner. By ignoring the power differentials that exist between us, even out of good intentions, I may inadvertently put the student in a very awkward position, particularly if the restaurant is significantly overpriced for a student budget. If she declines because she cannot afford it, she may fear that I will interpret this as a lack of professional interest. If she accepts, she may have to wrestle with the embarrassment of not being able to order a complete meal. My inability to recognize that there are power differentials between us and that I have an EZ Pass on some roads where she is blocked winds up reaffirming the very inequalities my invitation was designed to counter.

On the other hand, if socially privileged world inhabitants go out of their way to address the power differentials between themselves and travelers, that too can have unintended negative effects. For one thing, it is all too easy for the inhabitant to misread these differences through the lens of social stereotypes. So, in an effort to make the traveler comfortable, the inhabitant might try to anticipate what she or he may like on the basis of the traveler's social identity. Preparing a Mexican-themed luncheon for a Mexican American job candidate applying at a predominantly white business would be just one absurd example of this kind of mistake.[15]

More significantly, naming the power dynamics as a way to minimize their effects while ignoring their intersectional and context sensitive aspects serves to reify opposition and privilege. For instance, if a black woman shows up at a meeting where all the other attendees are white men and if the men in the group, in an effort to minimize the power differentials, say something like "Well, we just want you to know that we are all equal here, and though you are a woman and black we will work hard to see the merit and value of your contributions," we could imagine the woman's outraged reaction. To see this even more clearly, let's imagine that the woman is a physician attending a meeting of medical students organizing an event. The woman's race and gender intersect with her professional expertise and authority to make the oversimplified presumption of her "disadvantage" inaccurate. By presuming that race and gender alone are sufficient for assessing the power dynamics, the men wind up asserting their privilege and erasing hers.

So, what can we do with social privilege and disadvantage when we encounter travelers in our world? For one thing, we should work to assess the complexities of these dynamics so that we don't think in terms of one or two social categories but instead in terms of intersections. Second, we should put virtuous listening at the forefront of our interactions. What can we learn about travelers? What are their concerns? What experiences have they had in the past, and what led them to the worlds we inhabit? If we recognize that the social systems that shape people's identities are *related to* but not *identical with* the way people are, we can be open to knowing more about who they are and what matters to them specifically.

At the same time, we can also work toward changing those social systems. Seeking out opportunities to know more about how groups are working toward social justice, particularly social groups different from our own, is one path toward social action. We can use our social privilege to bring attention to the disadvantages faced by other social groups, provided we recognize the fact that they were working on change before we were ever on the scene and that our role is not as hero or savior. Instead, our privilege gives us the opportunity to stop traffic in the EZ Pass lane to bring attention to the long lines and the understandable frustration in "those other" lanes. This is something that is so hard to do if you don't have access to the EZ Pass lane. So, men who point other men to the inequalities faced by women, whites who point to other whites when it comes to the circumstances of people of color, and affluent people who point to the circumstances of the poor are all examples of how privilege can be used to interrupt the ignorance of privilege.

Most important, we can begin all of our efforts at understanding, analyzing, and transforming social identity by starting with empathy and compassion. We are all inheritors of a history of injustice and inequality, and we have all had to manage the aggression and opposition that comes with that history. As a result of that history, some of us have benefitted at the expense of the suffering and disadvantage of others. But even given this reality, it is still oversimplified to divide us all into either oppressors or the oppressed. We exist in a complex interplay between our own sense of self, social and structural pressures and representations, and the limits of our language. A willingness to see that we all face these constraints is a first step toward moving to some common ground. If we find that our class-mates, coworkers, and members of our community say they are committed to justice and fairness, then we should take them at their word. We should be willing to start the work of intellectual empathy together, recognizing that it is difficult, risky, challenging, and emotional. Through the work of creatively and intellectually imagining how circumstances look through other people's eyes, particularly people with different social identities, we can begin to open up new possibilities and challenge the oversimplified and oppositional dualities inherent in race, gender, sexual orientation, social class, religion, and dis/ability.

Questions for Review

1. Describe playfulness in Lugones's sense. How is it different from play in the sense of a competition?

2. Does loving perception require us to actually love the people with whom we debate and argue? How is loving perception different from arrogant perception?

3. Describe Du Bois's notion of double consciousness. Can you see a relationship between an intersectional account of identity and double consciousness?

4. What is the problem with encouraging diversity by organizing a food fair (or a fashion show)?

5. What is the point of the mitten project example? How did it (unintentionally) reify existing inequalities rather than address them? Can you think of another example from your own experience where this has happened?

6. What are the responsibilities of world travelers? What are your responsibilities when a traveler seeks to come into your world? What kinds of things make a world unsafe for travel?

Questions for Further Thinking and Writing

1. Describe an experience you have had when someone entered your world with a world-erasing attitude. What kinds of behaviors of theirs contributed to world erasing from your point of view? What could the person have done to inhabit your world more effectively?

2. Describe a time when you believe that you were not virtuously heard by someone who had more social power than you. What do you think made it hard for that person to listen virtuously?

3. Describe either a successful or unsuccessful experience world traveling. What made the experience work or not work? What might you do differently now that you have considered Lugones's account of world traveling?

Additional Resources

Feminist philosopher Linda Martin Alcoff's essay "The Problem of Speaking for Others" provides a very important contribution to the research on social justice, particularly as it relates to listening and reporting. You can find it (and other resources) on her web page, http://www.alcoff.com/content/speaothers.html.

A significant concern among people interested in social justice and world traveling is the problem of cultural appropriation. The online magazine *Everyday Feminism* has an article on the differences between cultural exchange and cultural appropriation, http://everydayfeminism.com/2013/09/cultural-exchange-and-cultural-appropriation/ with links to a variety of examples.

A recent phenomena that social justice theorists have been writing about is voluntourism whereby primarily white Western middle-class and wealthy young people volunteer to do service work in the developing world. There have been some very harsh criticisms of this kind of world traveling, because in some cases it may be reifying existing power and privilege differentials. For a debate about voluntourism, see http://www.theguardian.com/world/2013/feb/13/beware-voluntourists-doing-good.

A blog and Tumblr site called gurlgoestoafrica, at http://gurlgoestoafrica.tumblr.com, takes a critical look at Facebook and Instagram photos of white women (and sometimes men) posing with children in a variety of different African nations apparently there to do volunteer work. In exploring this site, ask yourself whether the blog and the accompanying photos are consistent with principles of intellectual empathy.

Conclusion: From Conversations to Coalitions

I began this book with the promise that intellectual empathy would help you to develop the skills to know yourself better, to know the situations and circumstances others face, and to work toward removing some of the obstacles in the way of thinking critically about social justice. To begin developing these skills, we looked at how our beliefs are formed in relation to social systems of power, identity, difference, and inequality. While many of our beliefs *feel* like they are our own and while we believe that we are totally in control of them, some are significantly determined by a past that we were not even a part of making. We inherit beliefs in the same way that we inherit a world where the language and social structures around us are all already in play.

This does not mean that we can't change either our beliefs or the social structures, but to do this effectively we have to first understand the role they play in our thinking and reasoning. We can't understand this by simply introspecting on our own. Understanding how social systems define us and confine us requires understanding how we are seen through each other's eyes. We can only do this if we have the requisite self-knowledge as well as accurate reports from other people, particularly people whose experiences are very different from our own. Yet everywhere, it seems, there are reasons not to engage in the kind of conversations that would give us that kind of information. Either we will be misunderstood, or we will be told that we can't understand, or we will be misidentified or misrepresented, or we will be hurt, insulted, or infuriated. There does not seem to be much sense in engaging in these conversations if they continually cause pain and frustration.

I have tried to show in this book that the pain and frustration that gets in the way of these conversations is not just a by-product of being human. Instead, it is an essential feature of the social inequality that we have inherited and that sets limits on our beliefs, our language, and our interactions with each other. While we may have an investment in addressing social injustice, this does not mean that the institutions and social systems we are part of share that investment. Though institutions are made up of people, the history and the rules and laws that keep an institution stable still shape the behavior of the people involved. So, we have to work inwardly and outwardly when we are trying to evaluate the positive and negative aspects of our social identities.

Intellectual empathy is a part of the work of social justice. It is not the same thing as organizing a protest, calling attention to a particular unjust practice, or creating new and alternative social identities. Rather, it is meant to provide a way to talk across difference so that people can accomplish those other more activist goals more effectively and collaboratively. There are too many forces working against these important conversations. Like the three students I described in the preface of this book, we are left making important observations and giving important reports behind closed doors, away from people who might misunderstand or misrepresent us. Given that we are all capable of misunderstanding and misrepresenting someone in some way, let's start from the position of this humble recognition and resist the pressures keeping us apart.

Intellectual empathy provides a way to reduce some of the risks of these conversations without sacrificing meaningful content. Breaking open the dichotomies that have constrained our thoughts, our feelings, and our language, we can both speak and listen to the complexity of people's experiences. We value the emotional and affective elements of our social experience, and we understand how they work in conjunction with our beliefs to shape our thinking and reasoning. As intellectually empathic critical thinkers, we know that we are flesh-and-blood people with histories, relationships, challenges, and successes. We love, work, think, laugh, cry, and argue with people. With people, we also make meaning.

I hope that you are able to use the skills of intellectual empathy to begin building unlikely coalitions. What I mean by an "unlikely coalition" is a purposeful connection to a social group that may not share primary aspects of your identity. One of my favorite examples of an unlikely coalition is a program that was developed in my state where hunters provide food for community shelters around the state. I learned about this program from a hunter who previously had no interest in homelessness or food insecurity. He did, however, have an interest in not letting venison go to waste and was led to the program through a friend. Initially the hunter merely donated any extra meat from his hunts. However, the program got him interested in where the meat was going, and he wound up visiting a shelter in Detroit. There he met some of the shelter's residents along with several of the volunteers and administrators. One of the volunteers was a vegetarian who had ethical issues with hunting. The two seemed an unlikely pair. However, both wound up seeing that they shared a critical point of intersection: distributing available food sources in a way to meet the needs of the most vulnerable members of the community. These two people did not share many of the same social identities or values, but they shared enough to solve a problem that was meaningful to them both. In the process, they also came to better understand something they either ignored or stereotyped. In this way, unlikely coalitions can transform individuals and communities. We do not have to have a lot in common to do a lot together. Intellectual empathy will hopefully provide a way for you to find these points of intersection and build upon them to make positive changes in the work that you do.

Glossary

ad hominem argument. From Latin for "to the man." A logical fallacy whereby the arguer attempts to discredit an opponent on personal grounds rather than on the merit of the reasons the opponent has given. Ad hominem arguments come in a variety of forms.

adversarial method. A method of debate in which general claims, counterexamples, and deductive reasoning are prioritized over truth seeking and consensus building. The adversary method often aims at winning an argument rather than discovering new and relevant information. The adversary method favors traditionally male privileged characteristics such as aggression and competition while disparaging those same qualities in women and in men of color.

argument, logical sense. A series of statements that includes at least one premise (reason) and one conclusion (a point of view). Arguments are evaluated on the basis of the premise's acceptability (believability), relevance (of the content of the premise to the content of the conclusion), and how well the premise grounds or gives support for the truth or the likelihood of the conclusion.

binaries. Concept pairs that are presented in opposition to each other. For example, mind/body, reason/emotion, male/female. The theory of binary opposition stems from the work of Ferdinand de Saussare and the theory of structuralism in linguistics.

blame filter. A tendency for someone who faces social marginalization to blame whole groups of privileged people for her or his particular marginalization without considering the actual complexity of the groups, including intersectional aspects of group identity. For example, women blaming "all men" or "most men" for sexism or gender bias without considering how race, class, ethnicity, or sexual orientation play a role in male privilege. (For a corollary tendency of those with social privilege, see **guilt filter**.)

burden of proof. Describes the responsibility for an arguer to provide further evidence. Ordinarily in logic and critical thinking we begin with a presumption in favor, meaning that we take the evidence presented to us as acceptable unless we have evidence to the contrary. If we do in fact have such evidence, then the burden of proof is now on our partner to provide further supporting evidence. It is important to remember that without contrary evidence, we should always start from the position that others are giving us acceptable premises.

cognitive bias(es). Habits of thinking and reasoning that may make it easier to take in and organize information but may nevertheless get in the way of adequately assessing evidence and considering alternative points of view. Cognitive biases often serve to preserve our existing web of belief rather than making it more flexible and open to new sources of information.

cognitive dissonance. The uncomfortable (even stressful) experience of holding two different beliefs that are contradictory or inconsistent. In terms of intellectual empathy, it is important to be sensitive to the fact that people may have a very hard time initially accepting a belief about their social identity relative to social power (that they are privileged or face structural oppression) if it is inconsistent with firmly held beliefs about their personal identity.

cognitive schema(ta). A way of organizing information related to concepts so that the concepts are not only defined but are also infused with our experiences, values, emotional history, and expectations. Cognitive schemata play a role in how we act and react to the data within our environment.

cognitive unconscious. Refers to the processing of information via our perceptual faculties, memories, thoughts, beliefs, and language without our conscious awareness. The cognitive unconscious plays an important role in understanding the effects of **implicit bias**.

color blindness. The view that we should all look past social identities such as race, ethnicity, religion, gender, sexual orientation, and disability with the goal of coming to know people as individuals rather than as members of social groups. While the idea of color blindness might in principle be a good thing, it ignores the history of institutional racism, sexism, and other social biases as well as the ways that history has shaped our individual cognitive systems of belief and information processing. Color blindness is often touted by the socially privileged because it maintains current inequities by ignoring the effects of our unjust and discriminatory past.

concept. An individual unit of thought and language that has a set of associated features. Concept formation allows us to take in a variety of seemingly different inputs and form a general idea. The word "cup," for instance, includes a variety of different objects that all share a set of general features.

conditional trust, principle of. The principle of conditional trust is a starting assumption of intellectually empathic reasoning. Traditional logic assumes a principle of charity in argumentation whereby we assume that our debate partners are capable of basic logic and consistency. In other words, if we somehow interpret them to be irrational or inconsistent, the burden is on us to figure out what went wrong in our interpretation. Along similar lines, the intellectually empathic thinker begins with the assumption that others are trustworthy and credible. If we start by assuming that someone is less than trustworthy or credible, the burden is on us to figure out what went wrong in our interpretation. The principle of conditional trust is a means for countering the effects of epistemic injustice.

confirmation bias. A common cognitive bias whereby we seek out and pay attention to evidence that confirms our existing beliefs and ignore or discount evidence that disconfirms our existing beliefs. Confirmation bias is related to our tendency to be conservative with regard to significant changes in our belief systems.

cooperative reasoning. An alternative to the adversarial method of argumentation whereby arguers seek out points of commonality and agreement and work together to reach the most justified conclusion. Cooperative reasoning does not pit arguers against each other as opponents but rather as partners seeking truth. This does not mean that they always agree or that they are simply nice but rather that they understand the value of dialogue and respect the effort made by their partner.

diversity. Refers to efforts to create more socially diverse communities, including race differences, sex and gender differences, socioeconomic class, ethnicity, religion, sexual orientation, and dis/ability.

diversity fatigue. Particular to the project of intellectual empathy, diversity fatigue refers to the negative response that either socially privileged or socially disadvantaged individuals may have to diversity efforts. Diversity fatigue is often the result of a failure to incorporate a more intersectional analysis of social identity as well as a more mutually responsible environment to think and reason about social differences.

double consciousness. A term introduced by W. E. B. Du Bois to refer to the split identity that African Americans have had to struggle with because of racist oppression. Du Bois describes his experience of being both black and an American and how he is proud of both identities even while he must manage their moral incongruities. Du Bois teaches us that double consciousness also means that those who face social disadvantages must know both the values and experiences of the oppressors while still valuing their own experiences and history.

ease. In the sense of being "at ease in a world" whereby an individual feels familiar and comfortable and knows the language, customs, and expectations within a social group. We can have ease in more than one social group.

empirical. Claims that are acceptable or believable relative to experimental (and sensory) justification rather than value judgments or logical argumentation.

epistemic injustice. The failure of people in positions of privilege to ascribe credibility to those who are socially disadvantaged or oppressed. Epistemic injustice can take two forms: testimonial and hermeneutic.

EZ Pass. Based on the actual idea of a highway, EZ Pass, that allows its holders to gain easy access in and out of stopping points, this is a metaphorical EZ Pass that makes it very easy for those with privilege to travel on the "road" to rights and opportunities while those with social disadvantages are slowed down and helped up.

fallacies, logical. Commonly occurring argument patterns that are often psychologically persuasive but upon further analysis are actually logically unjustified or irrelevant. Fallacies are context sensitive, meaning that the same pattern is not fallacious in every context.

fight or flight. A response that many people have to the experience of having to discuss issues of social difference, including privilege and power, with people who do not share the same social identities. The fight response is often adversarial and competitive, with the goal of winning or even shaming one's opponent. The flight response is to keep silent or actively avoid the issue. Intellectual empathy is a way to create more and more cooperative and rational responses.

guilt filter. Like the related blame filter, the guilt filter is a tendency for those who have identified their social privilege to feel guilty and responsible for those whose identity may include social disadvantage or a history of oppression. The problem with the guilt filter, as with the blame filter, is that it fails to account for the complex and intersectional aspects of social identity. In addition, the guilt filter can mask a rescue tendency that those with social privilege may adopt toward those with social disadvantage, thereby reaffirming social injustices. The white person who fails to take into account the expertise of a black professional, for instance, and instead seeks to provide help or assistance while recognizing her or his own lack expertise may be operating with a guilt filter.

implicit association test (IAT). A measurement developed in social psychology to assess a person's automatic associations with social identity concepts.

implicit bias. A positive or negative association regarding a social identity that exists within our web of belief but does not register within our conscious awareness. Implicit bias is particularly significant for those who consciously believe that they do not harbor any biased or discriminatory attitudes, because such a belief can impede the work of accessing and reflecting upon one's unconscious attitudes.

inclusion. A more recent version of diversity, inclusion describes efforts not simply to add more and different people to organizations and institutions but instead to actively work toward creating a climate whereby diverse people and points of view are welcomed and respected. The downside to inclusion is that it can sidestep matters of social power, inequity, and historical injustice to present a happy diversity model whereby a variety of people and perspectives are viewed as adding color, flavor, and profitability.

intersectionality. A term first introduced by Kimberle Crenshaw to identify the ways that systems of privilege, oppression, and domination work together to forge our complex social identities. Intersectionality as a theoretical tool developed directly out of the work of black feminist scholars, most notably Crenshaw and Patricia Hill Collins, who drew upon the experiences of black women to show how their social identity was not the same as women's experience (since it was centered on white women's experience) or the black experience (since it was centered on black men's experience). Intersectionality provides significant insight into the complex ways that our privilege and oppression are mutually constituted.

LGBTI. Refers to people who identify as lesbian, gay, bisexual, transgender, or intersex.

loving perception. A term used by Maria Lugones, drawing upon the work of Marilyn Frye, to describe an openness and willingness to know others by starting from the assumption that we are each connected and not separate. Loving perception involves identifying with others so as to heal social divisions and injustices. Lugones contrasts loving perception with arrogant perception, which involves actively ignoring, ostracizing, and stereotyping others while seeing oneself as separate and unrelated.

mutual vulnerability. Another starting assumption for intellectual empathy, mutual vulnerability requires that we recognize that all those who engage in arguments about social issues (including those who are privileged with regard to the issue in question and those who are disadvantaged) face risks by arguing and debating the issues. These risks range from being labeled a racist, sexist, homophobe, etc., to not being taken seriously or being reharmed socially and psychologically when recounting experiences of social injustice. Mutual vulnerability seeks to minimize these risks by seeing all participants in the discussion as inheritors of an unjust social system as well as imperfect, trying to learn, capable of mistakes, and open to reflection and correction.

online disinhibition effect. The phenomenon of people altering their persona, character traits, and even values when communicating with others online. These are personas that we may try on because there is so little accountability to others online and because we can imagine and vilify our audience without having to respond to actual interpersonal evidence.

positive distinctiveness. A foundational concept in social identity theory, positive distinctiveness refers to an individual's inherent motivation to have a positive sense of self and social group identity.

presumption in favor. The alternative presumption to burden of proof, presumption in favor is the starting point for discussion and argument whereby we presume the acceptability of claims that are presented unless we have evidence to the contrary.

privilege. A position of social advantage based on aspects of our social identity that have nothing to do with merit or hard work but instead involve unearned social benefits based on a history of social injustice.

privilege, ignorance of. The unwillingness of those with privilege to recognize and examine the systems of benefits and disadvantages based on social inequities.

privilege, invisibility of. The challenge of identifying social privilege when one is a recipient because of the way it is treated as "normal" or "just the way things are." For example, the difficulty that a Christian may face in seeing that the nation's participation in Christmas inordinately benefits Christians and marginalizes all those who are not Christian as well as those who celebrate other religious holidays.

responsible reporting. A willingness on the part of those who are socially marginalized to accept that their stories will be heard fairly and with respect even by those with social privilege. Responsible reporting should only be adopted when all discussion participants are committed to reasoning with intellectual empathy.

social identity. Those aspects of our self-identity that relate to our membership in social groups. Social identity is not strictly defined by an individual but instead comes about through the interactions that an individual has within a social system. Some aspects of our social identity correspond with the way we see ourselves, but others have to do with the way we are seen by others.

Socratic method. First introduced in Plato's dialogues through the character of Socrates, the Socratic method is an effort to seek the most reasonable conclusion to an issue by starting from a position of informed ignorance (meaning that one does not know what conclusion to reach but does know the relevant related issues) and then questioning those who have already drawn a conclusion. The Socratic method relies on assessing consistency, coherence, and noncontradiction in the question-and-answer dialogue.

two-spirit people. In some Native American traditions, "two spirits" refers to a category of cross-gender roles (a male-female or a female-male) that existed prior to colonization by the Europeans. Two-spirit people were valued for their care work, their contributions to tribal health, and their leadership. Today there are important efforts to reclaim the history of two-spirit roles within some Native American communities.

victim-culprit dichotomy. The limited roles that seem to be the only available options when discussing and arguing issues of social difference. Those who are socially disadvantaged are assumed to occupy the victim role, and those who are socially privileged are assumed to occupy the culprit role. However, each of these roles may feel alien to those to whom they are ascribed. One can recognize one's social disadvantage without identifying as a victim, just as one can be socially privileged without feeling like a culprit. These roles can contribute to **diversity fatigue**.

virtuous listening. A term borrowed from Miranda Fricker that refers to the responsibility of those with social privilege to listen respectfully and without prejudgment to those who report their experiences of social marginalization and oppression. Virtuous listening means not assuming that it is all in the other person's head, not interrupting to offer an alternative explanation that preserves social privilege, and not having to have the last word. Virtuous listening is a simultaneously active and reflective process.

web of belief. A term coined by W. V. O. Quine to refer to the interconnected system of beliefs within an individual's psychology. Within the work of intellectual empathy, the web of belief includes concepts, schemata, and emotional and visceral associations as well as values, hopes, and expectations.

world traveling. A term used by Maria Lugones that refers to the experience of moving between social groups and social systems of privilege and power. Each day as we move between home, school, work, our houses of worship, shops, restaurants, cultural events, and social gatherings, we enter and leave worlds with their own languages, norms, customs, and expectations. Lugones encourages us to be open to experiences in new worlds and not to be world erasing.

Notes

PREFACE

1. For some background on these factors and their current effects, see Richard Rothstein and Mark Santow, "A Different Kind of Choice: Educational Inequality and the Continuing Significance of Racial Segregation," Economic Policy Institute Education Report, August 22, 2012, http://www.epi.org/publication /educational-inequality-racial-segregation-significance/.

2. Ibid.

3. Sidney Fine, "Michigan and Housing Discrimination, 1949–1968," *Michigan Historical Review* 23, no. 2 (Fall 1997): 96–97, http://www.law.msu.edu/clinics /rhc/MI_Housing_Disc.pdf. The quotation is that of the Michigan attorney general, interpreting the powers of the new commission.

4. Rothstein and Santow, "A Different Kind of Choice," 19.

5. Georg Szalai, "Lowe's Pulls Ads from TLC Show 'All-American Muslim,'" *Hollywood Reporter,* December 9, 2011, http://www.hollywoodreporter.com/news /lowes-pulls-ads-tlc-show-271983.

6. Michael McAuliff, "Boston Bombing Suspects' Identity Sparks Fear of Backlash for American Muslims, Sikhs," Huffington Post, April 19, 2013, http://www .huffingtonpost.com/2013/04/19/muslims-boston-bombing_n_3118859.html.

7. "Economy at a Glance: Detroit-Livonia-Dearborn, MI," Bureau of Labor Statistics, 2012, http://www.bls.gov/eag/eag.mi_detroit_md.htm.

8. Ibid.

9. Marissa Schultz, "Food Stamp Cuts Hit Home in Michigan," *Detroit News,* October 31, 2013.

10. David Jesse, "Metro Detroit Students Relieved over Compromise Plan on Loan Rates," *Detroit Free Press,* July 18, 2013, http://www.freep.com/article/20130718 /NEWS06/307180129/.

INTRODUCTION

1. Bill Bishop, *The Big Sort: Why the Clustering of Like-Minded America Is Tearing Us Apart* (Boston: Houghton Mifflin, 2008).

2. Sara Ahmed, *On Being Included: Racism and Diversity in University Life* (Durham, NC: Duke University Press, 2012), 46.

3. Gregory Mantsios, "Media Magic: Making Class Invisible," in *Race, Class, and Gender in the United States: An Integrated Study,* 4th ed., edited by Paula Rothenberg (New York: St. Martin's, 1998), 451.

4. Ibid., 389.

5. See, for instance, Marc J. Hetherington and Jonathan D. Weiler, *Authoritarianism and Polarization in American Politics* (Cambridge: Cambridge University Press, 2009).

6. E. L. Uhlmann and G. L. Cohen, "'I Think It, Therefore It's True': Effects of Self-Perceived Objectivity on Hiring Discrimination," *Organizational Behavior and Human Decision Processes* 104 (2007): 207–23.

7. L. D. Bobo and C. Z. Charles, "Race in the American Mind: From the Moynihan Report to the Obama Candidacy," *Annals of the American Academy of Political and Social Science* 621 (2009): 243–49.

8. N. Dasgupta and A. G. Greenwald, "On the Malleability of Automatic Attitudes: Combatting Automatic Prejudices with Images of Admired and Disliked Individuals," *Journal of Personality and Social Psychology* 81, no. 5 (2001): 800–14.

9. S. Duncan and L. F. Barrett, "Affect Is a Form of Cognition: A Neurobiological Analysis," *Cognition and Emotion* 21, no. 6 (September 2007): 1184–1211.

10. J. Storbeck and G. L. Clore, "On the Interdependence of Cognition and Emotion," *Cognition and Emotion* 21, no. 6 (September 2007): 1213–38.

11. Gordon Gallup and Steven Platek, "Cognitive Empathy Presupposes Self-Awareness," *Behavioral and Brain Sciences* 25, no. 1 (2002): 36–37.

12. Clink Witchalls, "Why a Lack of Empathy Is the Root of All Evil," *The Independent,* April 5, 2011, http://www.independent.co.uk/life-style/health-and-families/features/why-a-lack-of-empathy-is-the-root-of-all-evil-6279239.html.

13. S. Trawalter, K. M. Hoffman, and A. Waytz, "Racial Bias in Perceptions of Others' Pain," *PLoS ONE* 7, no. 11 (2012): e48546, doi:10.1371/journal.pone.0048546; Daniel Goleman, "Rich People Just Care Less," *New York Times Opinionator,* October 5, 2013, http://opinionator.blogs.nytimes.com/2013/10/05/rich-people-just-care-less/?_r=0.

14. For an interesting account of this distinction, see Ralph White, "Empathizing with Hussein," *Political Psychology* 12, no. 2 (1991): 291–308.

15. For one of the first accounts along these lines, see Paul Thibodaux, *Political Correctness: The Cloning of the American Mind* (n.p.: Vital Issues, 1992).

16. Marilyn Frye, *The Politics of Reality* (Trumansburg, NY: Crossing Press, 1983).

CHAPTER 1

1. Jane O'Grady, "Willard Van Orman Quine: The Philosopher Whose Revolutionary Ideas Challenged the Way We Look at Ourselves and the Universe," *The Guardian,* December 30, 2000.

2. W. V. O. Quine, "Two Dogmas of Empiricism," *Philosophical Review* 60, no. 1 (January 1951): 20–43.

3. The term "mattering map" is used by philosopher and author Rebecca Goldstein in her very funny novel *The Mind-Body Problem* (New York: Penguin, 1983), 22.

4. E. V. Clark, *The Lexicon in Acquisition* (New York: Cambridge University Press, 1993); D. Ingram, *First Language Acquisition: Method, Description, and Explanation* (New York: Cambridge University Press, 1989).

5. S. Pinker, *The Language Instinct* (New York: Morrow, 1994).

6. Ingram, *First Language Acquisition.*

7. J. F. Kihlstrom, "The Cognitive Unconscious," *Science* 237 (1987): 1445–52.

8. Lea Winerman, "What We Know without Knowing," *Monitor on Psychology* 36, no. 30 (March 2005): 50, http://www.apa.org/monitor/mar05/knowing.aspx.

9. Anthony G. Greenwald and Mahzarin R. Banaji, "Implicit Social Cognition: Attitudes, Self-Esteem, and Stereotypes," *Psychological Review* 102, no. 1 (January 1995): 4–27.

10. See Monica Biernat and Melvin Manis, "Shifting Standards and Stereotype-Based Judgments," *Journal of Personality and Social Psychology* 66, no. 1 (1994): 5–20.

11. See Marianne Bertrand and Senhil Mullainathan, "Are Emily and Greg More Employable Than Lakisha and Jamal? Field Experiment on Labor Market Discrimination." *American Economic Review* 94, no. 4 (2004): 991–1013.

12. See Claudia Goldin and Cecilia Rouse, "Impartiality: The Impact of Blind Auditions on Female Musicians," *American Economic Review* 90, no. 4 (2000): 715–41.

13. See Alice Eagly and Steven J. Karau, "Role Congruity Theory of Prejudice Toward Female Leaders," *Psychology Review* 109, no. 3 (2002): 573–98; Cecilia Ridgeway, "Gender, Status, and Leadership," *Journal of Social Sciences* 57, no. 4 (2001): 637–55; Madeline Heilman et al., "Penalties for Success: Reactions to Women Who Succeed at Male Gender-Typed Tasks," *Journal of Applied Psychology* 89, no. 3 (2004): 416–27.

14. "FAQ on Implicit Bias," Stanford School of Medicine, http://med.stanford.edu/diversity/FAQ_REDE.html.

15. Stephanie Thornton, *Growing Minds: An Introduction to Children's Cognitive Development* (New York: Palgrave Macmillan, 2003).

16. E. Margolis and S. Laurence, *Concepts: Core Readings* (Cambridge, MA: MIT Press, 1999).

17. J. E. Young, *Cognitive Therapy for Personality Disorders: A Schema Focused Approach* (Sarasota, FL: Professional Research Exchange, 1990), 9.

18. F. Datillio, "Examining the Scope and Concept of Schema: Should We Look beyond Cognitive Structures?," *Psychological Topics* 19, no. 2 (2010): 224.

19. H. Tajfel, *Human Groups and Social Categories* (Cambridge: Cambridge University Press, 1981).

20. R. Cohen, "The Incredible Vagueness of Being British/English," *International Affairs* 76, no. 3 (2000): 576.

21. Rusi Jaspal, "Language and Social Identity: A Psychosocial Approach," *Psych Talk*, September, 17–20, 2009.

22. K. A. Ethier and K. Deaux, "Negotiating Social Identity in a Changing Context: Maintaining Identification and Responding to Threat," *Journal of Personality and Social Psychology* 67 (1994): 243–51 (reprinted in M. A. Hogg and D. Abrams, eds., *Intergroup Relations* [Philadelphia: Psychology Press, 2001]).

23. Noam Chomsky, *Aspects of the Theory of Syntax* (Cambridge, MA: MIT Press, 1965), 58.

24. Peggy McIntosh, "White Privilege and Male Privilege: A Personal Account of Coming to See Correspondence through Work in Women's Studies," Wellesley College Center for Research on Women, Working Paper 189 (Wellesley, MA: Wellesley College Center for Research on Women, 1988). Better known in excerpted form as Peggy McIntosh, "White Privilege: Unpacking the Invisible Knapsack," *Peace and Freedom* (July–August 1989): 9–10; reprinted in *Independent School* 49 (1990): 32.

CHAPTER 2

1. Michael S. Berliner and Gary Hull, "Diversity and Multiculturalism: The New Racism," The Ayn Rand Center for Individual Rights, http://ari.convio.net/site /News2?page=NewsArticle&id=5195&news_iv_ctrl=2467.

2. "Two-Spirit History," NorthEast Two-Spirit Society, http://www.ne2ss.org /history/ (originally published in *Two-Spirit Times,* June 25, 2013).

3. For a much more thorough and powerfully argued version of this point, see Eduardo Bonilla-Silva, *Racism without Racists: Color-Blind Racism and the Persistence of Racial Inequality in America.* Lanham, MD: Rowman & Littlefield, 2013.

4. Quoted in Susanne Baer, Janet Keim, and Lucy Nowottnick, "Intersectionality in Gender Training," Working Paper, Vienna, Quing Proyect, mimeo, 2009, p. 22.

5. Patricia Hill Collins, *Black Feminist Thought: Knowledge, Consciousness, and the Politics of Empowerment* (Boston: Unwin Hyman, 1990).

6. Kimberle Crenshaw, "DeMarginalizing the Intersection of Race and Sex: A Black Feminist Critique of Anti-Discrimination Doctrine, Feminist Theory, and Antiracist Politics," *University of Chicago Legal Forum* (1989): 139–67.

7. Ibid., 145.

8. bell hooks, "Racism and Feminism," in *Aint I a Woman: Black Women and Feminism* (Boston: South End Press, 1981).

9. Audre Lorde, *Homophobia and Education* (New York: Council on Interracial Books for Children, 1983), 9.

10. S. Swanson, S. Crow, D. Le Grange, J. Swendsen, and K. Merikangas, "Prevalence and Correlates of Eating Disorders in Adolescents," *Archives of General Psychiatry* 68, no. 7 (July 2011): 714–23, http://archpsyc.jamanetwork.com/article .aspx?articleid=1107211.

11. N. De Braganza and H. A. Hausenblas, "Media Exposure of the Ideal Physique on Women's Body Dissatisfaction and Mood: The Moderating Effects of Ethnicity," *Journal of Black Studies,* no. 40 (2010): 700–16.

12. Joan Acker, "Inequality Regimes: Gender, Class, and Race in Organizations," *Gender & Society* 20 (2006): 441–64; Heather Antecol, Anneke Jong, and Michael D. Steinberger, "The Sexual Orientation Wage Gap: The Role of Occupational Sorting and Human Capital," *Industrial and Labor Relations Review* 61, no. 4 (July 2008): 518–43.

13. "The Simple Truth: About the Gender Pay Gap," AAUW Report, 2013 Edition, http://www.aauw.org/files/2013/03/The-Simple-Truth-Fall-2013.pdf.

14. U.S. Bureau of Labor Statistics, "Earnings and Employment by Occupation, Race, Ethnicity, and Sex, 2010," The Editor's Desk, September 14, 2011, http://www .bls.gov/opub/ted/2011/ted_20110914.htm.

15. Gallup-Healthways Well-Being Index, January 1–September 28, 2010. http://www.gallup.com/poll/145427/gallup-top-wellbeing-discoveries-2010.aspx.

16. Federal Bureau of Investigation, "Hate Crime Statistics 2011," December 10, 2012, http://www.fbi.gov/news/stories/2012/december/annual-hate-crimes-report -released/annual-hate-crimes-report-released?utm_campaign=email-Immediate &utm_medium=email&utm_source=civil-rights-stories&utm_content=160285.

17. For a good exploration of moral anger, see Elizabeth Spelman, "Anger and Insubordination," in *Women, Knowledge, and Reality: Explorations in Feminist Philosophy,* edited by Ann Garry and Marilyn Pearsell, 263–73 (Boston: Unwin Hyman, 1989).

18. Heather D. Boonstra, "Insurance Coverage of Abortion: Beyond the Exceptions for Life Endangerment, Rape, and Incest," *Guttmacher Policy Review* 16, no. 6 (summer 2013), http://www.guttmacher.org/pubs/gpr/16/3/gpr160302.html.

19. bell hooks, *Killing Rage: Ending Racism* (New York: Holt, 1995), 261.

CHAPTER 3

1. Sarah Sobieraj and Jeffrey Berry, "From Incivility to Outrage: Political Discourse in Blogs, Talk Radio, and News Programs," *Political Communication* 28, no. 1 (2001): 19–41.

2. Christine Pearson and Christine Porath, *The Cost of Bad Behavior: How Incivility Is Damaging Your Business and What to Do about It* (New York: Penguin, 2009).

3. Alison Jagger, "Love and Knowledge: Emotion in Feminist Epistemology," *Inquiry: An Interdisciplinary Journal of Philosophy* 32, no. 2 (1989): 151–76.

4. T. Govier, *A Practical Study of Argument,* 7th ed. (Belmont, CA: Wadsworth).

5. Walter J. Ong, *Fighting for Life: Contest, Sexuality, and Consciousness* (Ithaca, NY: Cornell University Press, 1981).

6. Ibid., 118–19.

7. Olaf Pedersen, *The First Universities* (Cambridge: Cambridge University Press, 1997).

8. David Noble, *A World without Women: The Christian Clerical Culture of Western Science* (New York: Knopf, 1992), 4.

9. Kate Lowe, "The Stereotyping of Black Africans in Renaissance Europe," in *Black Africans in Renaissance Europe,* edited by T. F. Earle and K. J. P. Lowe (Cambridge: Cambridge University Press, Cambridge, 2005), 47 .

10. Janice Moulton, "A Paradigm of Philosophy: The Adversary Method," in *Discovering Reality,* edited by S. Harding and M. B. Hintikka, 149–64 (Dordrecht, Netherland: Reidel, 1983); David F. Noble, *A World without Women: The Christian Clerical Culture of Western Science* (New York: Oxford University Press, 1992); Janice Moulton, "Agonism in Academic Discourse," *Journal of Pragmatics* 34 (2002): 1651–69.

11. George Lakoff and Mark Johnson, *Metaphors We Live By* (Chicago: University of Chicago Press, 1980).

12. Moulton, "A Paradigm of Philosophy," 151.

13. Ibid., 150–62.

14. For an interesting discussion of this topic, see Andrew J. Hoffman, "Climate Science as Culture War," *Stanford Social Innovation Review* (Fall 2012), http://www.ssireview.org/articles/entry/climate_science_as_culture_war.

15. Catherine Hundleby, "The Authority of the Fallacies Approach to Argumentation," *Informal Logic* 30, no. 3 (2010): 279–308.

16. Ibid., 295.

17. Suzanne LaBarre, "Why We're Shutting Off Our Comments," *Popular Science,* September 24, 2013, http://www.popsci.com/science/article/2013-09/why-were-shutting-our-comments?dom=PSC&loc=recent&lnk=1&con=why-were-shutting-off-our-comments-.

18. Dominique Brossard and Dietram A. Scheufele, "This Story Stinks," *New York Times,* March 2, 2013, http://www.nytimes.com/2013/03/03/opinion/sunday/this-story-stinks.html?_r=0.

19. Richard Lardinois, "YouTube Announces a New Commenting System Powered by Google+," TechCrunch, September 24, 2013, http://techcrunch.com/2013/09/24/youtube-announces-a-new-google-powered-commenting-system/.

20. John Suler, "The On-line Disinhibition Effect," *CyberPsychology and Behavior* 7 (2004): 321–26. The book-length version of Suler's work on this topic, titled *The Psychology of Cyberspace,* is available at http://users.rider.edu/~suler/psycyber/download.html.

21. For instance, even if sites ban commenters because of inappropriate language, the commenter can reenter the discussion by creating a new pseudonym and a new e-mail address.

22. Suler, "The On-line Disinhibition Effect," 325.

23. Angela Watercutter, "Feminist Take on Games Draws Crude Ridicule, Massive Support," Wired, June 14, 2012, http://www.wired.com/underwire/2012/06/anita-sarkeesian-feminist-games/.

24. Molly McHugh, "Kickstarter Campaign Leads to Cyber-Bullying," Digital Trends Online Magazine, June 11, 2012, http://www.digitaltrends.com/social-media/kickstarter-campaign-cyber-bullies/.

25. Mikki H. Phan et al., "Examining the Role of Gender in Video Game Usage, Preference, and Behavior," *Proceedings of the Human Factors and Ergonomics Society Annual Meeting* 56, no. 1 (2012): 1496–500.

26. S. Hwang and G. T. Cameron, "Public's Expectation about an Organization's Stance in Crisis Communication Based on Perceived Leadership and Perceived Severity of Threats," *Public Relations Review,* 34(1) (2008): 70–73.

27. Lasana T. Harris and Susan T. Fiske, "Dehumanizing the Lowest of the Low Neuroimaging Responses to Extreme Out-Groups," *Psychological Science* 17, no. 10 (2006): 852.

28. Margaret M. Zamudio and Francisco Rios, "From Traditional to Liberal Racism: Living Racism in the Everyday," *Sociological Perspectives* 49, no. 4 (2006): 483–502.

29. Paul C. Gorski, "Cognitive Dissonance as a Strategy in Social Justice Teaching," *Multicultural Education* 17, no. 1 (2009): 54–57.

30. Michael Gilbert, *Coalescent Argumentation* (New York: Routledge, 1997), 49.

CHAPTER 4

1. Aristotle, *On Sophistical Refutations: On Coming-to-Be and Passing-Away,* translated by E. S. Forster and D. J. Furley (London: Hieneman, 1955).

2. A. Tversky and D. Kahneman, "Judgement under Uncertainty: Heuristics and Biases," *Sciences* 185 (1974): 1124–31.

3. B. F. Malle, J. Knobe, and S. Nelson, "Actor-Observer Asymmetries in Explanations of Behavior: New Answers to an Old Question," *Journal of Personality and Social Psychology* 93 (2007): 491–514.

4. John Blake, "The Return of the Welfare Queen," CNN, January 23, 2012, http://www.cnn.com/2012/01/23/politics/weflare-queen/.

5. Marilyn Brewer, "The Psychology of Prejudice: Ingroup Love and Outgroup Hate?," *Journal of Social Issues* 55, no. 3 (Fall 1999): 429–44.

6. Elizabeth Kaufman, "The NRA Wants More Guns in Schools: Can It Prevent Another Sandy Hook?," Time Magazine Online, December 20, 2012, http://nation.time.com/2012/12/20/how-to-prevent-more-sandy-hooks-arm-the-school-staff/#comments. (Note that the commenters' usernames have been changed.)

7. Paul Taylor and D'Vera Cohn, "A Milestone En Route to a Majority Minority Nation," Pew Research Social and Demographic Trends, November 7, 2012, http://www.pewsocialtrends.org/2012/11/07/a-milestone-en-route-to-a-majority-minority-nation/.

8. John Blake, "Are Whites Racially Oppressed?," CNN, March 4, 2011, http://www.cnn.com/2010/US/12/21/white.persecution/index.html.

9. Ibid., comments section.

10. L. Guliano, D. Levine, and J. Leonard, "Manager Race and the Race of New Hires," *Journal of Labor Economics* 27, no. 4 (October 2009): 589–683.

11. Heidi Shierholz, "Unemployment in February Remains Elevated across the Board," The Economic Policy Institute, March 7, 2004, http://www.epi.org/blog/unemployment-february-remains-elevated-board/.

12. Jordan Weissman, "How to Think about Affirmative Action Like an Economist," *Atlantic Magazine,* October 10, 2012.

13. Brent Hickman, "Pre-College Human Capital Investment and Affirmative Action: A Structural Analysis Policy of U.S. College Admissions," Working Paper, June 2013, http://home.uchicago.edu/~hickmanbr/uploads/AA_Empirical_paper.pdf.

14. R. Fryer and G. Loury, "Affirmative Action and Its Mythology," *Journal of Economic Perspectives* 19, no. 3 (2005): 147–62.

15. Blake, "Are Whites Racially Oppressed?"

16. Mark Kantrowitz, "The Distribution of Grants and Scholarships by Race," Student Aid Policy Analysis, September 2, 2011, http://www.finaid.org/scholarships/20110902racescholarships.pdf.

17. L. Berger and J. Waldfogel, "Maternity Leave and the Employment of New Mothers in the United States," *Journal of Population Economics* 17, no. 2 (2004): 331–49.

18. Monica McDermott, *Working-Class White: The Making and Unmaking of Race Relations* (Berkeley: University of California Press, 2006).

19. R. Vallone, L. Ross, and M. Lepper, "The Hostile Media Phenomenon: Biased Perception and Perceptions of Media Bias in Coverage of the Beirut Massacre," *Journal of Personality and Social Psychology* 49, no. 3 (1985): 577–85.

CHAPTER 5

1. Christopher Tindale, *Fallacies and Argument Appraisal* (Cambridge: Cambridge University Press, 2007), xiv.

2. My thanks in particular to Catherine Hundleby for suggesting this kind of exercise, particularly in relation to Christopher Tindale's work.

3. Miranda Fricker, *Epistemic Injustice* (Oxford: Oxford University Press, 2007), 1.

4. Ibid., 44.

5. D. Lisak, L. Gardinier, S. Nicksa, and A. Cole, "False Allegations of Sexual Assault: An Analysis of Ten Years of Reported Cases," *Violence against Women* 16, no. 22 (December 2010): 1318–34.

6. Miranda Fricker, "Forum on Miranda Fricker's Epistemic Injustice: Power and the Ethics of Knowing," *Theoria* 61 (2008): 70.

7. Jean Batalova and Aaron Terrazas, "Frequently Requested Statistics on Immigration in the United States," Migration Policy Institute, December 2010, http://www.migrationpolicy.org/article/frequently-requested-statistics-immigrants-and-immigration-united-states-1.

8. Ed Payne, "Transgender First-Grader Wins the Right to Use Girls' Restroom," CNN, June 24, 2013, http://www.cnn.com/2013/06/24/us/colorado-transgender-girl-school/.

9. Janeen Capizola, "School Says Transgender Boy's Rights Trump Girl's Right to Privacy in the Bathroom," BizPac Review, October 13, 2013, http://www.bizpacreview.com/2013/10/14/school-says-transgender-boys-rights-trump-girls-privacy-in-bathroom-85249.

10. "Excerpt from Santorum Interview," *USA Today,* April 22, 2003, http://usatoday30.usatoday.com/news/washington/2003-04-22-santorum-gays_x.htm.

11. "Richard Lamm on Multicultural," Original 2005 speech and revised version, Snopes, http://www.snopes.com/politics/soapbox/lamm.asp.

12. My thanks to Alison Bailey for making this point and providing the examples.

13. *The World Factbook 2013–14* (Washington, DC: Central Intelligence Agency, 2013), https://www.cia.gov/library/publications/the-world-factbook/index.html.

14. J. Loftus, "America's Liberalization in Attitudes toward Homosexuality, 1973 to 1998," *American Sociological Review* 66, no. 5 (2001): 762–82; J. Treas, "How Cohorts, Education, and Ideology Shaped a New Revolution on American Attitudes toward Nonmarital Sex, 1972–1998," *Sociological Perspectives* 45, no. 3 (2002): 267–83; G. R. Hicks and T. Lee, "Public Attitudes toward Gays and Lesbians: Trends and Predictors," *Journal of Homosexuality* 51, no. 2 (2006): 57–77.

15. *Diagnostic and Statistical Manual of Mental Disorders,* 1st ed. (Washington, DC: American Psychiatric Association, 1952).

16. "La. Sen. Karen Carter Peterson Not Apologizing for Racial Comments about Obamacare in the La. Legislature (Video)," *KPEL,* May 30, 2013, http://kpel965

.com/la-sen-karen-carter-peterson-not-apologizing-for-racial-comments-about
-obamacare-in-the-la-legislature-video/.

17. Robert Michael and Philip Rosen, *Dictionary of Antisemitism from the Earliest Times to the Present* (Lanham, MD: Scarecrow, 1997), 267.

18. This expression is attributed to the French Enlightenment writer and philosopher Voltaire and is quoted by the nineteenth-century German philosopher Georg Wilhelm Friedrich Hegel.

CHAPTER 6

1. Linda Kerber, "Separate Spheres, Female Worlds, Woman's Place: The Rhetoric of Women's History," *Journal of American History* 75, no. 1 (1988): 9–39.

2. For one of the best accounts of this history, see Genevieve Lloyd, *Man of Reason: "Male" and "Female" in Western Philosophy* (Minneapolis: University of Minnesota Press, 1993).

3. Mabel Berezin, "Emotions and the Economy," in *Handbook of Economic Sociology*, 2nd ed., edited by Neil J. Smelser and Richard Swedberg, eds. (New York and Princeton, NJ: Russell Sage Foundation and Princeton University Press, 2005), 109.

4. For an important treatment of this topic, see Alison Jagger, "Love and Knowledge: Emotion in Feminist Epistemology," *Inquiry: An Interdisciplinary Journal of Philosophy* 32, no. 2 (1989): 151–76.

5. I mean to include in family relationships our family of origin as well as family we have chosen.

6. Drew Silver, "World's Muslim Population More Widespread Than You Might Think," FactTank: Pew Research Center, June 7, 2013, http://www.pewresearch.org/fact-tank/2013/06/07/worlds-muslim-population-more-widespread-than-you-might-think/.

7. "The Global Religious Landscape: Muslims," Pew Research Religion & Public Life Project, December 18, 2012, http://www.pewforum.org/2012/12/18/global-religious-landscape-muslim/.

8. "Why Don't Women Have More Rights in Muslim Countries?," On Faith, August 27, 2010, http://www.faithstreet.com/onfaith/2010/08/27/why-dont-women-have-more-rights-in-muslim-countries/223.

9. United Jewish Communities, *The National Jewish Population Survey 2000–01: Strength, Challenge and Diversity in the Jewish Population,* Jewish Federations, September 2003, http://www.jewishfederations.org/local_includes/downloads/4606.pdf.

10. Laura Keister, "Religion and Wealth: The Role of Religious Affiliation and Participation in Early Adult Asset Accumulation," *Social Forces* 82, no. 1 (2003): 175–207.

11. Paul Johnson, *A History of the Jews* (New York: Harper Perennial, 1988), 169–230.

12. Mortimer Ostow, *Myth and Madness: The Psychodynamics of Anti-Semitism* (New Brunswick, NJ: Transaction Publishers, 1995), 95–150.

13. "Transcript: President Barack Obama on 'The Tonight Show with Jay Leno,'" *New York Times,* March 19, 2009, http://www.nytimes.com/2009/03/20/us/politics /20obama.text.html?pagewanted=all&_r=0.

14. Charles Murray, "Have I Missed the Competition?," National Review Online, March 18, 2008, http://www.nationalreview.com/corner/160521/have-i-missed -competition/charles-murray.

15. Michael James, "President Obama Jokes about Being a Bad Bowler: It's Like the Special Olympics," ABC News Online, March 19, 2009, http://abcnews.go.com /blogs/politics/2009/03/president-ob-15-3/.

16. Theresa Glennon, "Race, Education, and the Construction of a Disabled Class," *Wisconsin Law Review* 1237 (1995): 1237–475.

17. Douglas Baynton, "Disability and the Justification of Inequality in American History," in *The New Disability History: American Perspectives,* edited by Paul K. Longmore and Lauri Umansky (New York: New York University Press, 2001).

18. Stephen Silverman, "Obama Apologizes for Special Olympics Comment," People Online, March 20, 2009, http://www.people.com/people/article/0,,20266949 ,00.html.

19. D. Chappelle, "Dave Chappelle," *Inside the Actor's Studio,* Season 12, Episode 10, BRAVO, originally aired February 12, 2006, available at http://www.imdb.com /title/tt0850928/videogallery?ref_=tt_pv_vi_sm (my emphasis).

20. Patrick R. Grzanka and Justin Maher, "Different, Like Everyone Else: Stuff White People Like and the Marketplace of Diversity," *Symbolic Interaction* 35, no. 3 (2012): 368–93.

21. Ibid., 384.

22. Lois Leveen, "Only When I Laugh: Textual Dynamics of Ethnic Humor," *Melus* 21, no. 4 (Winter 1996): 29–55.

23. Ibid., 43.

24. R. R. Means Coleman, *African American Viewers and the Black Situation Comedy: Situating Racial Humor* (New York: Garland, 2000), 130.

CHAPTER 7

1. Maria Lugones, "Playfulness, World Traveling, and Loving Perception," *Hypatia* 2, no. 2 (Summer 1987): 3–19.

2. Vicki K. Janick, *Fools and Jesters in Literature, Art, and History* (Bridgeport, CT: Greenwood, 1998), 3.

3. Ibid., 20.

4. Marilyn Frye, "In and Out of Harm's Way," in *The Politics of Reality: Essays in Feminist Theory,* edited by Marilyn Frye, 66–72 (Trumansberg NY: Crossing Press, 1983).

5. Lugones, "Playfulness, World Traveling, and Loving Perception," 7.

6. Ibid., 8.

7. Aaron Guerro, "The Holiday Hustle: How Stressed-Out Retail Workers Find Balance," *USA Today,* December 12, 2013, http://money.usnews.com/money/careers /articles/2012/12/14/the-holiday-hustle-how-stressed-out-retail-workers-find -balance.

8. William Edward Burghardt DuBois, *Souls of Black Folk* (Hayes Barton, 1965).

9. Ibid., 6.

10. Sara Ahmed, *On Being Included: Racism and Diversity in Institutional Life* (Durham, NC: Duke University Press, 2012), 69.

11. C. Musil, "Educating for Citizenship," *Peer Review* 5, no. 3 (Spring 2003): 6.

12. Fricker, *Epistemic Injustice* (Oxford: Oxford University Press, 2007), 91.

13. Ahmed, *On Being Included,* 36.

14. Ibid., 37.

15. For fans of the television comedy series *The Office,* this seems like just the kind of mistake that manager Michael Scott (played by Steve Carell) would make.

Index

ability. *See* disability and ability
abusive language, 28, 93, 95, 126
acceptability of argument premise, 82
accountability, 10, 89–91, 178
actor-observer bias, 108–9
ad hominem-abusive attack, 126
ad hominem arguments, 88–89, 93, 95, 125–27
ad hominem circumstantial, 126–28
adolescence, 29, 39, 44, 66
Adversary Paradigm, 87
aesthetic beliefs, 27
affirmative action, 113–17
"Affirmative Action and Its Mythology" (Fryer and Loury), 114
Affordable Care Act, 145
African Americans, 118, 175–76; bias against, 31; humor, 166–67; self-determination, 75–76; social disadvantages, 53
African American women, 60–63, 70–71; double oppression, 62–63
African nations, volunteers in, 188
Africans, stereotypes about, 85
age, as social identity, 99–100, 135
aggression: in arguments, 83–88; in online comment forums, 81, 88–95
agonistic attitude, 174
Ahmed, Sara, 4, 92, 177, 181, 182
Alcoff, Linda Martin, "The Problem of Speaking for Others," 188
American Psychiatric Association, 142
"A More Perfect Union" speech (Obama), 162
anger, 101; in arguments, 80–81; guilt-anger dichotomy, 10, 70–73, 87, 92,

158; as rational response to injustice, 71–73, 83. *See also* aggression; hostility
Arab Americans, 1, 98–100
"Argumentation Theory" (Gilbert), 105
Argument Culture, The (Tannen), 105
arguments: in academia, 84–85; acceptability of premise, 82; adversarial history of, 81–88; bodily dimensions of, 165; cooperative model, 95–102; criteria for a good argument, 82–83, 88–89; defined, 80; grounds for truth of conclusion, 82; relevance as criteria, 82; war as metaphor, 86, 145. *See also* ad hominem arguments
Aristotle, 106
arrogant perception, 173, 175

Banajin, Mahzarin, 31–32
Baron-Cohen, Simon, 13
beliefs: aesthetic, 27; assessment of, 26; cognitive unconscious, 30–31; core, 24–27, 30, 107, 142; defensiveness about, 138; and emotion, 43; empirical, 27–28; expressed in online forums, 91; formation of, 23–26, 189; impact on others, 17; inconsistency and, 163–64; individual habits and, 106–8; intermediary, 26–27, 29; moral, 27–28; peripheral, 24–27, 30, 107; as revealed by behaviors and reactions, 30; revision of, 24–26, 35, 101, 107, 130, 189; web of belief, 23–29, 35, 98